SPITFIRE WINGMAN

FROM TENNESSEE

my love affair with flight

Colonel James R. Haun, USAF

1911 - 2001

Stormwatch Press

Cover painting by William Hallmark
www.williamhallmarkart.com

Stormwatch Press
2504 Sherman Court
Nashville, TN 37214-1316
(615) 491-4631
www.coljimhaun.name

 ISBN-13: 978-0-9790002-0-1
ISBN-10: 0-9790002-0-3

Originally self-published in 1994 as:

WHO SAYS THERE ARE NO OLD BOLD PILOTS?!

by permission of The Nashville Tennessean - *Gerald Holly photo, 1975*

Contents

U.S. Army Air Corps photo

Acknowledgements

For their friendship to Col. Haun and family, for encouragement -- in some cases through financial assistance -- but for each individual's priceless historical, photographic, or technical input,

we sincerely thank:

William Kershner

John E. Florence

Mrs. Mary F. Lee

Mrs. Patsy Foote

Cal Taylor

Ernest Igou

Gail Halvorsen

David H. Eberhardt

William S. Tunner, MD

Major General Hoyt S. Vandenberg, Jr.

Jim and Peggy Haun
November 2006

Spitfire Wingman

Foreword

Have you ever met a star in life's Movie?

Recalling a Man of Stature

by eldest son, Jim Jr.

STATURE: 1: natural height (as of a person) in an upright position.

2: quality or status gained by growth, development, or achievement.

So says Webster. How about,

3: an innate gift of noble character?

In any case, in both life and use, this word is tricky. Mighty Goliath had stature #1, but the lad who laid him low with a well-chosen gully stone embodied statures 2 and 3.

My Dad, whose air adventures you are about to join, had only a high school diploma. He never claimed to be a hero. Despite his barrel chest and intimidating biceps, he wasn't a full inch over six feet. He played a seemingly minor role through the midst of 'big doings' on the global stage. Once, while discussing people who might significantly impact the world, he said, "I'm not that big." Except with a playful grin, he never sounded his own trumpet. Even in the short preface that follows he modestly denies any notable effect on his chosen field of aviation.

Yet without exaggeration I can say that I was blessed to have as 'Daddy' a man of true – and truly unusual – ***stature***. Nor am I alone in what sounds here like a son's prejudice. Many who knew him sensed an unassumed 'greatness' in his jaunty stride and ready wit. My Mom always said, "I hitched my wagon to a star." When Dad wasn't there to hear them, I've heard old friends and fellow officers unconsciously honor him as "Big Jim." Typically, one of them addressed him recently in writing as "The best pilot I ever knew."

I would go so far as to say that most people live their entire lives never having personally known another human possessing a thimble-full of this elusive quality. Generals, congressmen, prime ministers, presidents and kings sometimes lack it. Often mere actors portraying historical characters capture more of this indefinable 'impressiveness' than those we assume they model. Certainly Washington, Lincoln, Churchill, JFK, and Reagan 'had it' – but exactly what 'it' is can be hard to pin down. At least we can say such men stand out from the crowd for 'soul qualities' beyond simple intelligence or 'cleverness'. I believe it springs from an unassailable ***integrity***, welded to self-control, that tends to make these individuals the same alone as in public. Short on guile, their word is their bond. Old-fashioned as it sounds, these are people who, despite superficial flaws, act in reference to a steady ***moral*** gyroscope. On a deep level, they know better than to mock words like ***truth*** or ***justice***.

It can be scary to live close to one of these, often war-tested, males – who can pin you to the wall with a look. You might not always like them but you can't not respect them. (In my Dad's case, mix one part each Errol Flynn, John Wayne, and Yul Brynner.). Gifted with tremendous will, he had a determination that could ignore pain. I never heard him whimper. Nor did the Colonel ever abandon that steely sense of right and wrong regarding essentials. Once, when I was twenty and

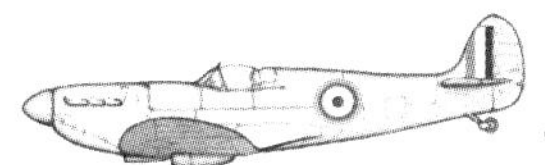

failed to show up for my part-time job flipping hamburgers, when Dad heard about it, his rebuke included the amazing demand that the next time I couldn't be there I was to call him *so he could take my place!* On the other hand, in those days he also told me flat out that if I was ever guilty of a capital crime he would 'pull the switch' himself. I never doubted either commitment!

But neither was he 'moralistic' – some snooty paragon of virtue. His boundaries were wide enough to allow a disarmingly free style. For example, rather than set up my rebel nature for a future hankering toward alcohol as 'forbidden fruit', he always invited me, at age nine or so, to take a sip of his VO and water – held behind his back as if no one would see. (If that was reverse psychology, it worked; that vice never attracted me!) Although this Command Pilot preferred to be thought of as 'the strong silent type', that often gruff exterior was more a military uniform worn over the deeper man – the gentle and good-humored character you are about to meet in his writing. Likewise, whatever the momentary role, in social relations he displayed a genius for the 'common touch'. Instinctively knowing that our inhabiting a body – while giving potential for tragedy – also yields comic scenarios, his sense of humor gravitated toward 'less polite' absurdities of our physical makeup. He understood first hand, for instance, that our digestive tracts produce a flammable gas. (Unfortunately or not, his book shows admirable restraint in this area.)

His day-to-day speech, too, was uniquely colorful. Some favorite phrases, like "a cloud of dust and a blaze of glory" appear in his story. But citing others: Men tended to be either 'characters' or 'jokers', while women were 'frails'. "Oh very well" signified stoic acceptance of harsh fate. A beautiful day for flying was always, "Severe clear." He addressed preachers as "Doc." If he saw 'some joker' driving recklessly, he'd invariably say, "Go, fool – hell's not half full!" Or if he noticed a person who was, let's say, 'esthetically challenged', he'd be sure to say, "Look at the head on that!" (Not that he was ever overtly cruel to anyone; this was the same man who hated to see a wounded quail suffer needlessly. – Without apparent emotion, he'd simply pop off their heads.) And a sizzling steak was sure to be proffered with, "Grab it and growl."

So apart from essentials, his ethics were common-sense practical. As you will learn throughout his tale, he wasn't above playing the system as it presented itself – as when he utilized a C-133 on a legitimate mission to move his little Henry-J auto from California to his next duty station in Minnesota. Or recall his wartime 'runabout', the stripped-down Thunderbolt dashing between London and Brussels. Or during the Berlin Airlift, his admiration for his sidekick Sid Parks' creative 'requisitioning' of military supplies. But he never 'played politics' in the sense of pandering to others, whether above or below his rank – not even in navigating the ego-infested waters around the Presidential air fleet at Washington National. In fact, aside from his being three-quarters bona fide maverick, I have no doubt he didn't make General largely because when Duty to Country conflicted with potentially disastrous decisions by superior officers, he simply couldn't in good conscience keep his mouth shut. In a letter written in 1997 to his model, General Robert M. Lee, whom he complements there as "the most admired and respected of all Generals I had ever known," the Colonel says, "I realize I said some rather unkind things about some people in my book. I won't apologize for one word. I merely reported what I SAW AND HEARD."

In short, his priorities were finely tuned.

Two quick personal memories and I'll let him speak for himself.

I didn't know this remarkable father until he returned from WW II when I was five. One of my first glimpses into his character came during the time we were getting acquainted in Memphis when he took me with him downtown to get some hardware. I think I stayed in the car, which was parallel parked close to the curb between two other vehicles. Having returned with his purchase, my

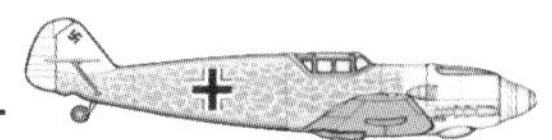

Spitfire-jockey old man was wheeling into the street when our car barely nicked the left rear fender of the one parked ahead of us. Dad immediately stopped, pulled back into the space just left, grabbed paper and pencil from the glove box, and began scribbling. I could hardly believe it. He was writing down our name, phone number, and what happened! To me, even at that age, this seemed like asking for trouble. Then no sooner had he walked around to leave the note on the windshield, than the car's owner, wearing a sports jacket, showed up, walking curiously towards us down the sidewalk. I watched intently as the two talked, then as they together took a quick look at the scratch on the fender – finally this perfect stranger starts pumping my Dad's hand for all he's worth! I'll never forget the man's words, which he kept repeating: *"I have met a gentleman! I have finally met a gentleman!"*

I'm writing this at age 64. Embarrassing to confess, in 1968 I was 28 and all too obviously one of what Dad in his book calls the 'Woodstock alumni'. A victim of higher education, I had fallen for the silliness that 'sex, drugs, and rock and roll' could usher in a future of peace and joy. Naturally I wanted to help the Old Man understand what a beautiful, profound revolution was underway. I mean, here he was still into Budweiser by daylight and vodka by evening, while I had been enlightened to a 'better, more spiritual way'. So on one of my visits from the Left Coast I boldly gave him four marijuana 'joints' with encouragement to – when he got around to it – "See what all the fuss is about." Other than maybe a sardonic grunt, he didn't comment, but I watched him toss my offering in the top dresser drawer next to his handkerchiefs. My life choices in those years were, rightfully, a great disappointment to him. Anyway, about five years and a couple of divorces later, I happened to be visiting my parents' home and for some reason checked that top dresser drawer. There lay the same four joints, apparently untouched. I recall his saying at the time that he never wanted to "not be in command of Old Jim."

As you will quickly learn from this autobiography, the Colonel was first of all a man of action. He flew, swam, sailed, hunted and fished all over the globe. He read and admired Hemingway as a kindred soul – without succumbing to that writer's fatalistic worldview. (Though Dad took a dim view of humanity in general, he loved individuals as he discovered them.) A gun collector and marksman who could make skeet disappear with the best, he for years loaded his own ammunition and even molded lead bullets for his muzzleloader by melting lead pipe in a skillet on the stove. Every Fourth of July he would rouse the neighbors with black powder 'sheebangs' from that same 32-caliber flintlock squirrel rifle. He could make a harmonica weep, and he sometimes strummed a four-string guitar to sing lyrics of dubious origin – like: *"She was poor but she was honest – the victim of a rich man's whim."*

He married one woman and loved her for 63 years until death parted them. In the early '70s he stopped giving to the United Methodist denomination when he learned they were sending money to Communists in Latin America. He caught marlin off Florida, constructed a hard wood writing desk, built a biplane from just plans in his garage, played golf, voted Republican, didn't swear (often), didn't squander money, didn't care for cats, and took his mongrel dog Bud flying.

Here's his story:

Preface

"Hero, Third Class"

It is a fortunate man whose life's work is also his hobby and his consuming interest. I was privileged to start flying in 1929 in airplanes of, or very similar to, those of World War One vintage. Those old 'seat-of-the-pants' airplanes were flown solely by feel and attitude, which experience allowed me to fly many of the later types of vastly different performance without the luxury of a prior check-out, and certainly increased my life-span. Conversely, when I think of all my contemporaries who have long since 'bought the farm' for one reason or another, I must conclude that I either have had an excessive amount of pure luck, or else have a most vigilant Guardian Angel.

I have contributed nothing to the development of aviation, unless the teaching of large numbers of people to fly can be so construed. I certainly acquired a large number of real friends in the process, which has made the trip down this road most rewarding.

When folks ask me what I did in the war, I tell them I was a Hero, Third Class. You can make Third by just being there and having the hell scared out of you a few times. I guess that covers about everybody that comes under fire!

You may notice the excessive use of the personal pronoun 'I'. The reason is that the only things I can write about are things I have experienced.

My deepest thanks to my son Jimmy and his wife Peggy for their many weary hours spent in editing this first, and definitely my last, literary effort.

James R. Haun, USAF retired
Nashville, Tennessee 1994

1927 Waco GXE

Ken Sumney photo by permission of OX5 Aviation Pioneers

[A year later Col. Haun wrote the following to the **OX5 Aviation Pioneers News***]*
Gentlemen,

This little book started out to be a record of some of my experiences so my grandchildren might know something of me and my times. As I sat here at the word processor it became so much fun that the thing just grew. I had a number printed locally for distribution to my friends in the flying community. It was so well received I made bold to submit it to several publishers, and received some very nice rejection slips from them.

If you would like to use a story or two in the OX5 News*, be my guest. Everything here is factual to the best of my memory.*

This month my Second Class physical was renewed and I soloed two students. Not bad for an old fellow pushing eighty-four. The two walking canes fit nicely in the back of my little Cessna 150.

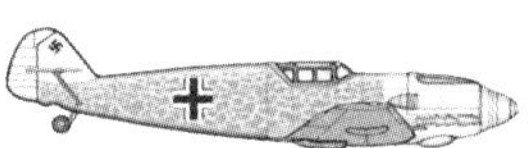

Haun family photos

"Let's go fly."

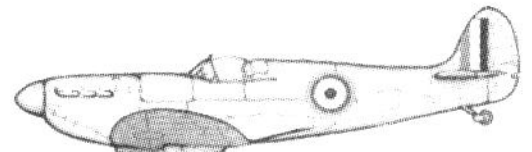

"I was born at an early age."

The Thousand-foot Song

The Colonel's son Jimmy recalls: "In 1957, having finished my flying lesson over the honey-bucket-fuming paddies of occupied Japan, Dad and I were returning to Showa Air Station at 1800 feet in the 65-horse Aeronca Champ. Without warning the old man, in a rare moment of irrepressible joy, suddenly stands the weary fabric-feathered bird on her right wing and lustily begins ***to sing*** **--** meantime proceeding to execute that amazing series of aerobatic cascades known as 'falling leaves' -- all the while fairly bellowing the 1940 Ella Fitzgerald ditty: ***'My Mommy told me... if I was goody... that she would buy me... a wubba dolly...'*** Leveling smoothly at the end of this exhilerating ballet, he reached past my shoulder to indicate the altimeter. There it sat, like locked, smack on 800 feet...our normal going-home altitude..."

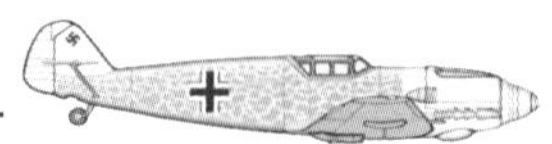

chapter one

THE EARLY YEARS

1911 – 1929: "PILLAR TO POST"

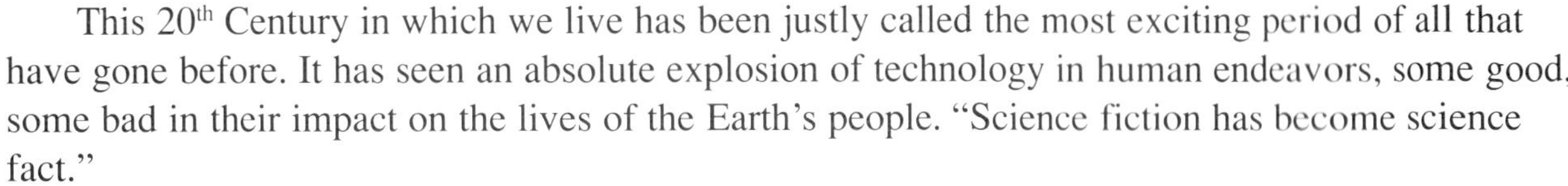

This 20th Century in which we live has been justly called the most exciting period of all that have gone before. It has seen an absolute explosion of technology in human endeavors, some good, some bad in their impact on the lives of the Earth's people. "Science fiction has become science fact."

It has been my good fortune to have lived through most of these times, so perhaps I will be excused for wanting to pass on to my descendants some of what I have seen and experienced. Call it a little bit of history.

Like the fellow said, I was born at an early age – in Memphis on the 21st day of September 1911 – a long time ago! I was what was called a 'Blue Baby', weighing three pounds. Dr. Meeker kept me alive all night by blowing in my mouth to keep me breathing. I am glad he had a strong set of lungs. Think what I would have missed!

My father, Wilson Yandell Haun, and my mother, Evelyn Carroll, were married at Henderson, Tennessee in 1910. I have an old newspaper clipping reporting on the event. Mother's parents did not attend. You see, Grandfather Haun was from East Tennessee, which was predominately Union during the Civil War, while the Carrolls were red-hot Rebels. Mother's uncle, John Carroll, had been a Captain in General Forrest's command. None of this was ever discussed with me, but I early picked up on the residue of hatred from that terrible war.

I had two younger sisters, Evelyn and Julia. Dad was a lawyer, a Republican, and a man of scrupulous honor and integrity. Once during the depth of the Depression, when he didn't have two nickels to rub together, I heard him tell a prospective client, "No, I won't take your case because you are in the wrong." Imagine that today!

I remember very little about my early years except one thing that had a lasting effect on my future. I was in the first grade of school in 1917 during the First World War. One day an airplane was heard circling around town and the entire school was let out to see this strange thing. Remember, the first airplane flew only eight years before I was born.

That first airplane I saw was from the new Army training field north of Memphis at Millington. I kept bugging Dad until he agreed to drive Mother and me in his Model T Ford that weekend to see it. What a thrill that was! Dozens of Jennies taking off, landing, and circling around making the most beautiful sounds I had ever heard. One Jenny took off right over our heads and the pilot waved to us. Mother waved back, which I thought quite unladylike, as she hadn't been properly introduced to him. That day my fate was sealed for all time.

My Mother died five days before my ninth birthday. She had been given gas to have her teeth pulled and developed pneumonia. Her death destroyed my Dad. For the rest of his life he remained a quiet, lonely, withdrawn man. There were so many things I would have liked to talk to him about, but never did. His letters to me while I was overseas during the war gave me most of what I know about him.

After Mother's death, we three children were sent to live with her kin. I went to Henderson to my grandparents while Evelyn and Julia went to Mother's sisters, Edna and Exie.

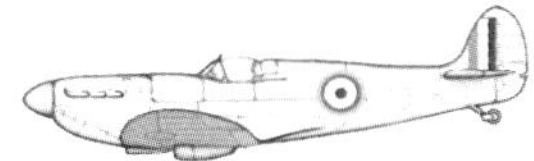

My Grandfather Carroll was a country doctor with high standing in the community. He drove a buggy pulled by two fine bay horses. Many times I went on his appointed rounds with him visiting his patients. Whenever we saw patients, whatever their problem, I was always allowed to give them one spoon of Cocoa Quinine.

All roads in those days were gravel or dirt, making it an either dusty or muddy drive. There were few if any bridges, so crossing creeks meant fording or taking ferries across any sizeable stream or river. There were few automobiles on the roads, so the horses became quite agitated at the sight and sound of these new contraptions. One day on a very dusty road, a man came roaring along in his Model T, appropriately clad in a white cloak, or duster, cap and goggles. As he passed us the horses reared up and broke into a run. Grandad fell out of the buggy but managed to hold onto the reins and finally got the horses under control. When we got back to the house and discovered that the driver of the car was my father, a rather chilly atmosphere developed. I believe Dad stayed the night but left early next morning, as the trip to Memphis took a full day.

A railroad ran past the rear of Grandad's property and made a perfect area for me and my young friend Harry Combs to learn the fine art of jumping on and off a slow moving freight. The train slowed down again at the small town of Pinson where we would get off and wait for the next one home. My Uncle Tom worked for that railroad and just happened to be aboard one day and caught us. We were hauled aboard the caboose for a lecture about young boys who had no arms or legs from being run over by trains, so we decided to look for other means to occupy our spare time. However, the skills learned were to come in quite handy in later years.

Grandad had some doctor books up in his attic which I diligently studied until I knew almost everything about the human body, its various parts and their functions. For a while I considered becoming a doctor, but the memory of those airplanes and those lovely sounds won hands down. One day Grandad came home with all his whiskers shaved off, so I hardly recognized him. He had developed a skin cancer under his left eye that was to kill him within the year.

I spent another year at Jackson with Aunt Edna and Uncle Charlie and then returned to Memphis. Dad's two sisters, Fanny and Kitty, had moved in with him and brought three of their schoolteacher friends with them; so there were five old maid schoolteachers upstairs while Dad and I lived downstairs. Dad had retreated into his own private world, so you might say I was raised by that bunch of old gals – that is, what raising I got. We lived in what has been called 'Genteel Poverty'; the Depression came early to our house.

Haun family photo

I was a pretty good student, especially in History and Geography. There were no organized sports, but we had our own neighborhood ball team (I was the catcher). We also had a Boy Scout troop, which I loved, where I became an Eagle Scout. I also became an avid reader, especially of History, and still am.

After graduating from grade school I went to South Side High…that was about three miles away and no buses, so I ran, or rather loped, to school. There was one boy in school who had a car, but none of us paid him much mind. The ROTC program was quite popular; we had an Infantry Company. We carried the Model .03 Springfield rifle, firing pin removed, and wore the regulation WW I winter uniform. That gave us warm clothes all winter.

South Side usually won the inter-city drill contests; I was a sergeant. I did fairly well with all of my grades with the exception of Latin. I took Latin four years, and finally passed Latin-1 the last year. Dad said I'd never amount to anything.

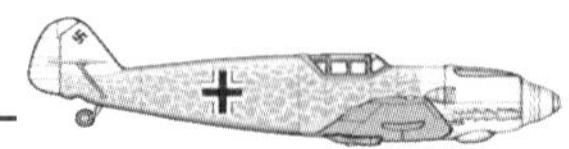

I forgot to mention the summer I spent with Aunt Exie and Uncle Allen in Nashville. Uncle Allen was a Church of Christ preacher and spent most of his time holding revival meetings around Middle Tennessee. He had built a little camp down on the Buffalo River. He and I spent a lot of time down there hunting, fishing, and holding revival meetings. My voice hadn't changed yet and I had a fine set of pipes, so I usually led the singing, complete with gestures…I also ate a LOT of fried chicken. We Hauns were Methodists and had all been 'sprinkled' as children, which gave Uncle Allen much anguish over the state of my soul. One day we were fishing on the Buffalo. Uncle Allen pushed the boat over on a sand bar and told me to get out, that he was going to baptize me…which he did, very thoroughly. I remember my main preoccupation at the moment was watching a muskrat climbing up on a log. I don't know if it did my soul any good or not, perhaps time will tell.

image cropped from CMTC photo

ROTC students were encouraged to go to the summer camps of the CMTC (Civilian Military Training Corps), all expenses paid. I went one year to Ft. Oglethorpe, Georgia, near Chattanooga. Imagine my surprise when it turned out to be a Cavalry post. We lived in tents and had plenty of wholesome food. Our mounts were tired, dispirited nags. I had my saddle come off once at the jumps and I took a header. The Corporal hauled me off to the barn for special instructions on how to properly saddle a horse and knocked me around a bit to impress the lesson on my memory; all quite proper in those days.

On the rifle range I shot 'sharpshooter' with the .03 Springfield, but had trouble with the .45 Colt Automatic. I never did like that weapon. As to our other activities, I wore the soles out of my issue shoes in one month.

One Sunday I caught a bus over to Chattanooga's airport where, I had heard, they would take you for a nice long airplane ride for two dollars, so I decided to try it. The pilot had a beautiful new Travelair, all shiny and smelling of polish, oil and exhaust gases. It was a wonderful sensation. We flew all over town, the river, and close to Lookout Mountain. That was the beginning of a lifelong love affair.

That same summer I got a job riding a bicycle for Western Union as a messenger boy. I covered Memphis like the dew, day and night. Western Union boys were not allowed to have seats on their bikes as they were supposed to be up and pumping all the time, and we could mount on the run, like cowboys. At night I liked to get a stack of telegrams for way out in town. I'd hang on to the back of an express streetcar for a rapid and effortless journey. I developed a corn about six inches long on my butt from sitting on the bar. It was a good job for a healthy young kid. I went everywhere people lived or worked, and sometimes I made as much as fifteen bucks a week, which was a lot of money in the Depression.

Every week at payday I bought a meal ticket for two dollars and fifty cents from a restaurant close to the office. This gave me five good meals a week. I have a vivid memory of the first time I

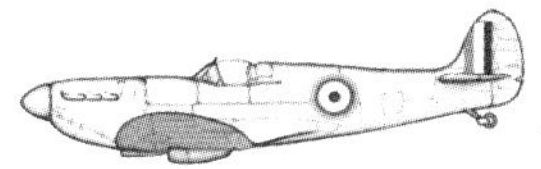

tasted a little half head of lettuce with French dressing. Fantastic, and it came with the meal! I believe that is still my favorite dish.

I bought an old Harley Davidson motorcycle and got it running fairly well. Thus mounted I spent most of my spare time out at the old Bry's (pronounced *breeze)* airport, just hanging out, as they call it today. I met a fellow named Jake who owned a Waco 10; he had recently soloed, and had about ten hours. Jake liked to fly out to the old abandoned field at Millington for landing practice. He offered to take me along if I would buy the gas, which cost fifteen cents a gallon at that time. I could afford that so I jumped at the chance. The Waco had dual controls in the front seat, so I could, by keeping two fingers lightly on the stick, follow its movements during takeoff, circling and landing, and get the feeling of the airplane as it slowed down, settled – and when the bottom dropped out for a three point landing in the grass. Of course, I had been practicing approaches and landings on the chalk rail at school for years; now I got to *feel* it, and from that day on I never had the slightest trouble with landings.

"That was the beginning of a lifelong love affair."

Haun family photos

Command-Aire

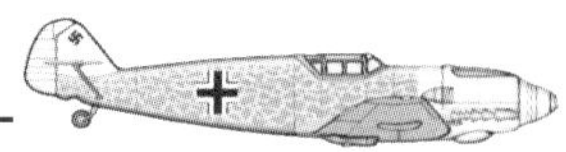

chapter two

LEARNING TO FLY

1930: "MEMPHIS BOY WONDER"

I bought a wrecked Waco 9 from a fellow named Henry Hertz for $400, at $25 a month. Later I learned I could have bought one already flying for that much! I didn't want Dad to know about my project, so I moved to a friend's barn. Of course I fancied myself quite capable of rebuilding an airplane, having spent so much time hanging around the airport watching. I did a fair job of it over the next year; it certainly wouldn't have won any prize at an air show, but it flew. There was no FAA in those days or any requirement for inspection of aircraft or licensing of pilots. It was every man for himself; the accidents and deaths only made the local papers.

Perhaps I should describe the airplanes of that day. They bore very little resemblance to the monsters of today, carrying hundreds of passengers at speeds sometimes exceeding the speed of sound and with range to span the oceans. Those early birds were frail little things made of wood and fabric and held together with wires.

my Waco 9

Haun family photo

My Waco was quite an improvement over its predecessors in that it had shorter, thicker wings, giving it more lift and a little more speed. It had a welded steel fuselage for strength; the wings were all wood construction. The entire airplane was covered with high grade cotton cloth which, when painted with a special 'dope', shrank to drum tightness that was airtight and waterproof. It was an open cockpit biplane carrying two passengers in the front cockpit and the pilot in the rear. It had no brakes but depended on the tailskid digging into the grass to stop it.

The OX-5 engine was manufactured in large numbers to power WW I trainers like the Jenny. After the war they were sold as salvage and powered most of the new production aircraft. There were far better engines being made, but they were too expensive for general use. The OX was fairly dependable if it got all of the tender loving care it demanded, which called for an hour at least before each flight.

The OX was an eight cylinder, water cooled, single ignition, all-aluminum jewel weighing about 450 pounds, and would deliver 90 horsepower at 1400 rpm. The valve rocker arms were cast aluminum and pivoted on a steel pin without a bushing, requiring frequent replacement. The fuel came by gravity from the gas tank to the carburetor with no way to filter or trap any water or trash. It had two high-speed jets. If a drop of water got in one jet, you immediately lost four cylinders. Two drops and things got real quiet. To guard against this we poured the gas through a chamois

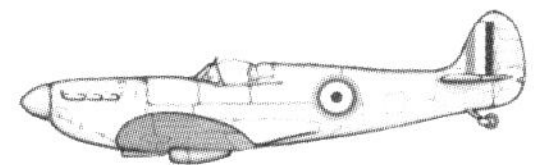

skin fixed over the funnel. I had a number of forced landings but there was always a nice pasture within gliding distance. In fact I have never damaged an airplane due to engine failure. Now as to a wild, hairbrained kid acting a fool, that's a different story.

The Waco was finally finished and hauled out to Bry's Field for assembly. A friend test-hopped it and said it flew O.K. A fellow called Bugger Red agreed to give me flight instruction for a quart of moonshine whiskey per hour, at 50 cents a quart. He soloed me after three hours. The next day after my solo, I was standing around with my helmet and goggles on, trying to look like a pilot. A young couple showed up, asking if anyone could take them for a ride. I told them, "Sure, it'll cost you two bucks." They paid up and I took them for a nice ride in the Waco. With the two dollars I bought ten gallons of gas, and I was in business.

But I had bad luck with my Waco shortly thereafter. It happened this way. A local dance band calling themselves 'The Ten Tennesseans' were scheduled to play for a dance at Osceola, Arkansas one weekend. Three of us decided to fly over in my Waco and attend. Of the three, Malcolm qualified as the old, experienced pilot, with at least 50 or 60 hours, so he would do the flying.

There was no airport at Osceola, but there was nice flat farmland with lots of pastures and hay fields, so that presented no problem. At that time it was permissible to land just about anywhere and be welcomed. On arrival we circled the town to announce ourselves and attract some attention. We found a very good hayfield just outside town alongside the highway next to a schoolhouse and landed there. A number of cars gathered so we had no trouble getting a ride to town. I had a wonderful time at the dance just standing around watching those beautiful girls all dressed up in their finery. I had never been to a dance before, as up to that time I had been too busy working or hanging out at the airport to waste my time on such trivial things. The Arkansas version of moonshine was being passed around quite freely, and the more I imbibed the more I became convinced this Romance Business deserved further scrutiny.

Around two a.m. the party had started to slow down so someone suggested that we adjourn to the airport and do a little flying. Believe it or not I bought the idea! Quite a crowd headed out, intent on waking up this peacefully sleeping little town. We succeeded. Malcolm climbed into the pilot's cockpit while I stood by to crank. The engine was a bit slow to start and the extra exertion swinging the prop made my already queasy stomach rebel. By the time I had finished upchucking, Malcolm had taken off, as we say, "in a cloud of dust and a blaze of glory." All I saw were the flickering exhaust flames as he disappeared into the dark. While he was away buzzing around town we got the cars lined up to light his landing area. When he came back he circled a couple of times and then started his approach. We couldn't see him but could hear the whistle of the wind in the wires, then BANG, followed by the sounds of an airplane getting crumpled up. That little privy out behind the schoolhouse had snagged the right wheel and pitched him in on the left wings. It was a sad looking mess.

We pulled Malcolm out in one piece. He had a nasty cut on the bridge of his nose but otherwise wasn't hurt. We drove into town to find a doctor. We found one who had had his sleep disturbed a short while before and was not in a good mood. He didn't use any novocaine but proceeded to sew Malcolm up with a very big needle and what looked like shoemaker's thread. We caught a bus back to Memphis.

The next day we borrowed a flatbed truck and drove back to pick up the remains. When we arrived at the field the airplane was not there. We found it over behind the schoolhouse where it had been dragged by a team of mules, causing considerably more damage. There was a man sitting on top of it who said he was the superintendent of the city schools. He greeted us:

"This airplane belong to you boys?"

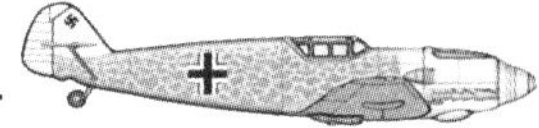

"No sir, we just came to pick it up for a feller."

"Well you can't have it 'til you pay for my privy. That will cost you five dollars."

Between us we were able to scrape up five dollars and pay the man; then we loaded up the truck and went home, or rather to the barn. It took me another year to rebuild the poor thing. Malcolm didn't offer any help.

While I was saving up enough money to repair my Waco I was out at the airport every chance I had. Ed Ackerly had an ancient Standard that had seen service during WW I as a trainer. It closely resembled the Jenny but I was told that it didn't fly quite as well, though it had the same OX-5 engine. If you have seen *Waldo Pepper*, he flew a Standard in that movie, except he had a Hisso engine, which had about twice the horsepower of the OX and could leap tall buildings. You certainly couldn't do that with the OX model. The fabric was so old and rotted you could easily put a finger through it. Ed couldn't fly, but he let me fly it some. I would have climbed aboard a barn door if someone said it would fly! That thing had built-in headwinds all over it, with a double bay of struts and so many wing-brace wires that, like the feller said, "If you turned a bird loose between the wings and it got away, it ain't rigged right." Its instrument panel was devoid of anything but the ignition switch.

Haun family photo

the Standard

The approved procedure for checking the engine before flight was very simple. With chocks in front of the wheels you started the engine; after it had warmed up a bit, you opened the throttle wide open, shoved the stick full forward, and if she tried to raise the tail off the ground she was fit to fly!

I was out chasing a slow moving freight train one day when I noticed a definite flutter in the outer part of the left lower wing, so I reluctantly decided to terminate the flight. The trick to landing it was to come in rather high and point the nose down at the spot you wanted to land on before you cut the power. It had the gliding angle of a streamlined brick. When you flared, she landed right there and rolled maybe fifty feet. We found the main spar in the wing broken, probably having been damaged in a ground loop, a common occurrence. Ed decided to completely rebuild the airplane, which I thought a good idea. More about that later.

By now with eight or nine hours under my belt I was accepted as a full-fledged pilot, at least by me. Henry Hertz, the man I bought the Waco from, called to see if I would go with him to Little Rock, Arkansas to pick up an Eaglerock he had bought. Naturally I accepted and we went over on the bus one weekend.

It was tied down at the Little Rock airport and evidently had been there a long time with weeds grown up enough to almost hide it. We needed to turn it around but found that we couldn't lift the tail. Trouble was its wings were completely filled with rainwater. With our pocketknives we went around punching holes in the trailing-edge fabric and let it drain for an hour. We checked the engine over good and started it up. It developed normal power. It didn't have a compass but we had a clear day and a road map.

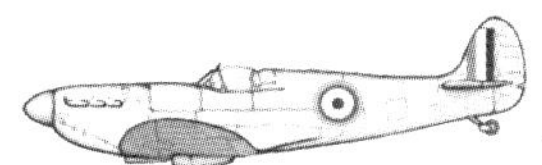

The trip home, following Highway 70, was uneventful until we arrived over Bry's Field. I had never seen or even heard about this particular model. It had been built near Denver where the air is thin and an airplane needs either more wing or more power to get off the ground. This model had an extra long lower wing for that purpose. Well, I made my approach much like I would in the Waco. The thing floated and floated until the field was all used up so I had to give it power and go around for another try. Not having an air speed indicator, I had to judge my airspeed by the whistle of the wind in the wires. I had seen pilots slip and fish-tail to lose speed and height, so I decided to see if I could do that. Something worked so that I got it down in one piece. Henry got another pilot to give me some landing instructions until I was pronounced fit to carry passengers.

I finally got my Waco rebuilt and took it out to Bry's Field. Ed had also finished the rebuild job on his Standard. He'd done some extensive modification that changed its appearance quite a bit. He had shortened the fuselage about three feet, clipped the upper wing to the same length as the lower, and completely recovered it and put on a nice paint job…it really looked good, if rather novel. Ed met me at the gate, as I rode in on my Harley, and proudly showed off his handiwork. After I had expressed my admiration, which he modestly acknowledged, he said, "Well, she is ready to fly, and you are the only person I'll let fly it." Well, by now I had some twenty hours and was hot…and having had my ego stroked, said "Sure, let's crank her up."

I later found out he had asked everyone else, but had no takers.

The first time around the field, she was very right-wing heavy, requiring almost full left aileron. Incidentally, the control stick was three feet long. A hole eight inches in diameter was cut in the fuselage on both sides to allow the stick to be shoved further out if you needed more aileron control. The original had the same holes. After a lot of re-rigging, loosening and tightening various brace wires, I took it around again – this time she's exceptionally left-wing heavy. We were standing around scratching our heads about what to do next when a stranger walked up and announced that he could rig it right. He had on riding britches and boots, with a hairline-waxed moustache, and a copy of *Warbirds* in his hip pocket. He said he had just returned to the States after flying for the rebels in a South American revolution. Well, he certainly looked the part, so Ed told him to go ahead. He supervised while the rest of us changed struts around, added a little angle of incidence here and there, and checked all the wire tension until he declared it would now fly straight up. I suggested he show us, but he declined, stating that he had important business in town, and he departed.

Everybody was standing there looking at me; they didn't exactly dare me, but it was evident that my nerve was being tested, and what young feller can take that? So I swallowed a small cannonball and climbed in. I didn't buckle the seat belt in case I had to get out in a hurry.

This was a bright Sunday afternoon. A nearby black community had turned out for a baseball game at the north end of the field. Home plate was right where I had to go to have the full length of the field for takeoff. Everybody moved to let me get in position. Now the north end of the field was perhaps ten feet higher than the south end with a gentle dropoff half-way where I would be airborne. As I passed over this dropoff I suddenly had several feet of altitude. She started to roll to the left. I used full aileron and rudder trying to stop the roll, but to no effect. The left wing hit first, followed by various other parts. When the nose hit, I started out, as I was not buckled in. My head went right through the windshield, which was isinglass, and had a long crack down the middle, allowing me to go through it very easily, but it grabbed me around the neck. When she came to rest upside down I was hanging by my neck, hands and knees. By gripping tightly with my knees, I was able to break off the windshield, and fell out on my head. I crawled out and saw a little bit of smoke from the hot oil on the exhaust, but no fire. I stood up, looked around, and observed the whole

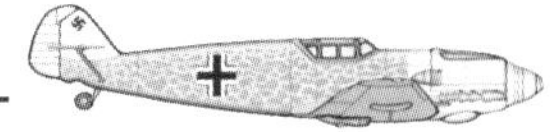

ballgame descending on me with a rush. All I could see was white teeth and eyes. It probably scared me, so I jerked off my helmet and goggles and stuffed them in my back pocket, thus hiding my identity. Cars from the hangar started arriving, but I slipped through the crowd and headed for the hangar.

It was common knowledge in those days that if you had an airplane wreck, you must climb right back in another plane or you would never fly again. I had just put new piston rings in my Waco and it was tied down with the engine idling, running in those new rings. I untied her, jumped in and took off over the crowd. I was circling overhead looking at the mess I had made when an ambulance roared up. They pulled out a stretcher and began a diligent search for my remains. Ed never had much to do with me after that.

There is a sequel to this story. Several years later I was hawking rides at the new Municipal Airport. Spying a likely looking couple, I approached them with the standard, "Get a million dollar thrill for a dollar bill! Young lady, can't you talk your boyfriend into taking you for an airplane ride?"

He came right back with, "Hell No, she can't; anybody who would get into one of those things is a damn fool. I used to be an ambulance driver…"

So help me, that's the gospel truth.

The years 1932-33 were probably the very depth of the Depression. The unemployment rate was about twenty percent or more and those who did have work made only enough to keep body and soul together. Men were selling apples on Main Street downtown. Young black boys sometimes came through the neighborhood selling rabbits they had killed with sling shots or sticks. Twenty-five cents for a nice fat rabbit. Cotton sold for less than five cents a pound, when it could be sold – and boll weevils hadn't ruined it. I remember when a union tried to organize the Ford Assembly Plant in Memphis. They had no success at all. Ford was paying five dollars a day and had long lines of applicants waiting at the gates.

Evelyn and Julia had come home after The Aunts moved into their own apartment. I don't recall that we ever actually missed a meal, but we ate a lot of peanut butter! We were as poor as church mice, but so was everyone else, so we just rode with the punch. I don't think we really realized just how poor we were. It's all relative. I bought a nice suit for fifteen dollars and the store threw in a single shot Stevens 12 gauge shotgun with the deal. You could buy that same gun at any hardware for three bucks.

Dad had an old car, a Chandler, stored in what had formerly been the hen house. It was much cheaper to ride the streetcars, which would take you anywhere in town for five cents, including transfers. There was no need for other transportation as delivery service was provided by almost all businesses. There was the milkman, the iceman, the laundry man, the grocery boy and the doctor; you name it. They all used either horse drawn vehicles or the famous Model T Ford. My alarm clock was the clip-clop of the milkman's horse and the clink of the bottles as he brought them to the front porch. The cash was in the empty bottles. Meanwhile, I had come up in the world and was now employed by a Bottlers Supply house as the shipping clerk, the mail clerk, the stockroom clerk, the truck driver and the janitor, with a half day off on Saturday.

My old Harley had given up the ghost and the Waco was tied down in a small field near the edge of town. The field had tall trees all around it except for a gap wide enough to take off through. A nice little creek ran by it where we got water for the radiator. I always drained it during cold weather. We named our little airstrip 'Hog Waller Airport'. There wasn't much flying going on.

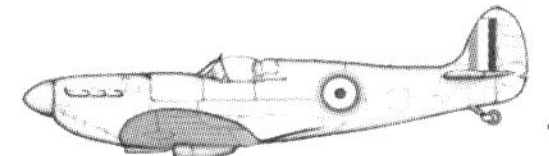

City of Joliet

Col. Haun memorabilia

Form 719

Nº 117374 DEPARTMENT OF COMMERCE CERTIFICATE OF DISCHARGE BUREAU OF NAVIGATION SHIPPING SERVICE

Ship's name: City of Joliet Official number: 219745

Port of registry: Houston Texas Net tons: 3804

Description of voyage: Foreign

Seaman's birthplace: Tenn. Age: 22

Character: V.G. Ability: V.G. Seamanship: V.G.

Capacity: Utility

Date of entry: 10/2/33 Date of discharge: 11/27/33

Place of discharge: Beaumont

Seaman's name: James Haun

I CERTIFY that the particulars herein stated are correct, and that the above-named seaman was discharged accordingly.

Dated at Beaumont

this 27 *day of* Nov. 1933

Master.

Seaman.

Given to the above-named seaman in my presence, this 27 *day of* Nov. 1933

U. S. Shipping Commissioner.

U. S. GOVERNMENT PRINTING OFFICE: 1931 11—529

Top: **Steam freighter *City of Joliet* dockside, Corpus Christi, Texas, 1930**

Lower: **Twenty-two year old Haun completes first sea-venture, November 1933**

chapter three

SEAFARING

1933: "OBSERVING A LEADER OF MEN"

A friend of mine named Doug Partee told me about his recent adventures on a freighter out of New Orleans, going to Europe. He said a local cotton broker that he had worked for had a deal with the steamship line to allow one or two of his employees to go along on these trips as workaways. This meant they were extra help on the crew but were not taking anyone's job. The pay was one dollar a month and you had to get to New Orleans the best way you could. He had been gone two months and got to see quite a bit of Europe.

At age 22, the wanderlust bug had bit me quite hard, and I thought I'd see if I could pull the same deal, as I had worked for that very company a short time before. I dropped by the office and they were able to give me all the necessary papers required by the steamship company. The bottlers supply business is quite seasonal, and winter was coming on. My boss agreed to give me a two-month leave of absence if I could provide a suitable replacement. That was no trouble at all.

That night at home, I told my Dad: "I'm going to Europe."

"When are you going?" he asked.

"Tonight."

"How are you going to get to New Orleans?"

"I'll go out to Yale Yards and hop a freight train."

I was packing a small bag and decided to take Grandad's old 38 Colt Revolver. Dad asked, "Why are you taking that?"

"Well, I thought I might need it."

"Are you capable of killing a person?"

"Maybe – if I had to."

"Then maybe you had better file off the front sight; that way it won't hurt so bad when he takes it away from you and rams it up your ass."

I left the gun at home.

Dad got out the old Chandler and drove me clear to the Yale Yards, south of town. His parting words were, "If you get in trouble, don't call me," and drove away into the dark. I've often wondered if I would have had guts enough to do for my sons what he did for me that night.

I knew Illinois Central Railroad was the main line to New Orleans. I went down to the far end of the yard to wait for a southbound freight. A short freight was pulling out, but there was no IC on the engine or the cars, so I let it pass. There were two men standing on the back of the caboose. I yelled, "Does this train go to New Orleans?" They yelled back, "Kid, get the hell out of this yard!" So I walked down a little farther and after a while a long train came and I saw that the engine and all of the cars said 'Illinois Central', so I picked an empty one with the doors open, and climbed aboard.

That was a cold miserable ride. The car must have had several wheels with flat spots from the way it bounced. We stopped at some little town before dawn and two more bums huddled on the floor. Early in the morning we stopped at a little town named McComb, Mississippi. We sat there all day, only getting bumped a couple of times. I was getting mighty hungry and thirsty and wishing I had enough sense to have brought a sandwich along. I could not get out in the broad daylight as I

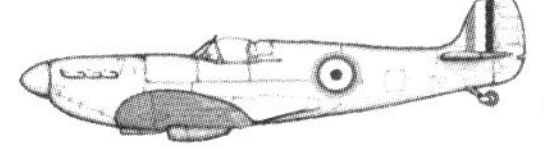

knew the yard dicks would be around. I did peek out and found what had happened. We had been shunted off onto a siding and just left there. There wasn't anything to do but sit there and wait for dark. When we decided it was dark enough, we had waited too long. We heard a car-knocker coming, banging on the doors with a stick the size of a baseball bat. He shined his flashlight on us and yelled for us bums to come out; which command we smartly obeyed. He looked me over several times.

"Kid, I know you. This is the third time I've chased you out of this yard. Now it's the chain gang for you!" I had seen movies about chain gangs so I wasn't a bit happy about that prospect. I rather think he really wanted me to get away, as at the next car he stuck his head way in and I was gone! I dived under the car and rolled across to the other side and hid behind the wheels until he quit looking, then crawled across two more tracks. Only then did I stand up and tiptoe quietly away.

The next freight I caught must have been an express as it only stopped once before getting to New Orleans. I was standing on a tank car in plain view. When it stopped, there in front of me was a yard dick shaking his head in disbelief. I climbed down and showed him my letters from the steamship company and promised faithfully never to get on another freight. I have kept that promise.

Closer to town I took a streetcar to the dock area. I found a flea-bitten little hotel, or rather, flop house. They let me in for twenty-five cents, cash in advance. I was badly in need of a bath and was so hungry I was right weak, but I cleaned up before going out to eat. Across the street was a place that sold what was called a 'Po' Boy' sandwich. This was a long loaf of french bread sliced down the middle and stuffed with various kinds of meats and cheese. I saved half of it for the next meal, which turned out to be breakfast as I slept right through till morning.

My instructions were to report to a certain doctor for a physical exam. His office was upstairs over what must have been an employment agency that was packed full of sailors 'on the beach' looking for berths. It was obviously not a healthy place for workaways to be. Seven of us were sent up to the Doc together. He asked if we had any kind of disease, and being answered in the negative he stamped our papers and gave us a bit of advice:

"Boys, downstairs there's a bunch of sailors hunting jobs. They think you are taking jobs from them. Now you go down those back stairs and when you hit the ground, run like hell." I did exactly that and didn't stop until I found the *City of Joliet* tied to the dock. I don't know what became of the other six.

The *City of Joliet* was a ten thousand ton Liberty Ship built during WW I. There were hundreds built and later put in 'moth balls'. I've seen great fleets of them moored around the coasts. This ship had one oil-fired steam engine, and one propeller. She had a crew of thirty; half of whom appeared to be officers, at least by the caps they wore. I was assigned a bunk in a tiny little cubbyhole in the very stern and right beside the donkey engine that turned the rudder. When the steersman on the bridge moved the wheel the thing set up an awful clanking that took a while to get used to.

I got in trouble the very first night. The sailors ate in shifts in a tiny mess room that had a long table down the middle with fixed benches, like a picnic table, that could seat about ten. I was seated back in one corner and no food seemed to find its way down to me. I asked the guy at the far end of the table to pass the beans.

"You're working for nothing; you don't expect to eat, do you?" He was a mean looking dude, built much like a barrel. I figured he was muscle-bound and needed straightening out, or I was going to get awful hungry. Now for some reason I was under the impression that I was a real tough guy, so over the table I went. Biggest mistake I ever made.

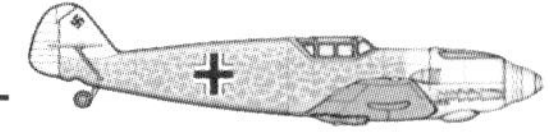

The fight must have been over mighty quickly, as I don't remember a thing about it. The next I knew a sailor was shaking me awake with the news that the Captain wanted to see me on the bridge. I must have been out all night as it was now morning. When I arrived, the Captain looked me over and didn't seem much impressed with what he saw.

"What's this about you picking a fight with my sailors?"

"Jeez, Captain, I've got to eat!"

He thought about that for a while, lit his pipe a couple of times and came up with his decision.

"You help the cook in the galley and don't get out on deck at night. We've lost boys like that."

The cook was a scrawny little cockney not long from Merry Old England. I had trouble with his accent at first, but he had such a limited vocabulary I caught on pretty quick. This was to help me later on in life.

My main job was to deliver the food to the officers' table and pick up the dirty dishes. They always had several courses requiring many dishes, bowls, cups and glasses. Then I had to wash the whole lot. The wash sink was as deep as it was wide and you filled it only half full of water. This was because as the ship rolled the water would slowly rise up to nearly the rim on one side, stop, and then slowly make its way up the other side. That night the Gulf picked up a swell and I got real queasy watching the orange grease in that water. I began to be a little sick, and before long I was really in a bad way. After a few necessary stops, I finally finished the dishes, but I was in bad shape. The cook took pity on me and gave me a packet of little white pills. He warned me not to take too many at a time, as they would swell up in my stomach. The next morning I stepped on deck into a beautiful day; the ship was still rolling but I felt wonderful. I asked Cookie what was that medicine he gave me that made me feel so good...he said 'tapioca'.

A voyage on a freighter could be most monotonous and boring unless you are kept busy, and I was certainly kept very busy. Besides all the dishes that had to be washed three times a day, there was the brass. I polished brass door knobs, brass door hinges, brass spittoons, brass everywhere. That job was never finished. By the time I finished one companionway, the last one had turned green again, and Cookie always had something for me to do. When I could sneak off, I loved to go below and watch the big steam engine pumping away. I believe it had four cylinders, standing upright, and turning slow, maybe about seventy RPM. What I would call the connecting rods fitted directly to the propeller shaft that was at least a foot in diameter. The shaft ran in a tunnel clear to the stern and was mounted on stands holding the bearings. When the ship pitched in swells you could see the shaft bend and flex. The bearings had to be oiled at regular and frequent intervals, by hand.

A little, rather nondescript-looking fellow named Gus was an oiler. He went around with a battered long-necked can and squirted oil on the bearings and anything else that looked like it might need it. I acted like I didn't know anything at all about machinery and asked a lot of questions. That trick usually works, so in short time we were great buddies. We got to talking about that night I got clobbered in the mess room.

He said, "You know, you can't fight worth a damn, swinging like a windmill. Tell you what. You be out on the aft deck at nine in the morning. I don't like that guy anyway and I'll show you how easy it is to whip a guy that size. I'll walk up to him and ask him for a light. When he puts his hand in his pocket I'll pop him in both eyes. Then he can't see and I'll work him over." That suited me just fine and next morning I was out on deck. Sure enough, that little guy proceeded to do exactly what he said he'd do. Walking by me afterwards he grinned and said, "See how easy it is?"

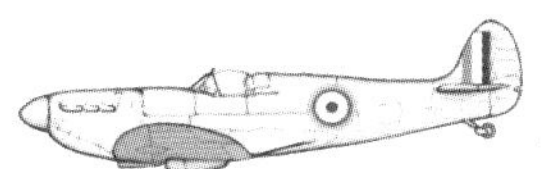

After rounding Florida we stayed in the Gulf Stream going north. The water here is a light blue, sometimes almost green. I enjoyed watching the flying fish jump out of the water in front of the prow and skim along about a foot high. It looks like they actually flap the fins they use to fly, and as fast as the wings on a hummingbird. Some of them can go quite a distance.

We kept plowing at a steady ten knots for about two weeks. The ocean turned a darker shade of blue as we turned to a more easterly heading and left the Gulf Stream. The wind turned cold and increased in strength. Life lines were rigged along the length of the open decks and the portholes were battened down tight. It took two more days for the storm to build to its full intensity. The waves built up into giant rollers with tops whipped into white foam by the wind. We were sailing parallel to the seas, which made the ship heave to a rather steep angle. As we rolled toward an oncoming wave, I could have sworn it was going right down the funnel! Of course the wave picked us up and rolled us toward the other side. At first I was a bit anxious about this whole operation until I looked up at the bridge. The Captain was standing out on the wing, obviously undisturbed, smoking his pipe (bowl turned upside down to keep the rain out). He looked like he was actually enjoying it. I decided that if he wasn't afraid, why should I be? I have used that same ploy many times since with nervous crew members or student pilots. Old Jim with his nerves of steel! It works.

But by the time we entered the English Channel we had crisp, crystal clear weather. The first ship I saw was a stunningly beautiful full-rigged three-master with more sail set than I thought any ship could carry. She passed fairly close on our port side. There must have been at least a hundred men swarming the rigging. Evidently a training ship from some navy, she was a solid gleaming white. Traffic soon increased with ships of all types and sizes, some on parallel, others on crossing courses. I wondered what would happen if the visibility suddenly closed down. That was before radar had been invented. The white cliffs of Dover stood in plain view, and I thought the gently rolling countryside of England unusually lovely.

Our first port was Le Havre. We were to be there three days and I didn't have any duties while in port. I wanted to get off and see some of France, but I didn't have much money. Gus came up with an idea how we could improve our finances. From the slop chest you could buy cartons of cigarettes at a ridiculously low price. I bought an armful that could be turned into gold if we could get the stuff past customs. It was easy. We were tied up against the wharf and within thirty feet of the open doors of a long warehouse. Gus went down the gangway where he was searched and passed through. I took the loot to the very back end of the deck, that just happened to be by the open door of the warehouse where Gus waited. My passing arm was in good shape and the cartons sailed one by one into the waiting arms of my buddy. Then we headed to a local gin mill that Gus knew. Pure Gold!

The next day I bought a round trip ticket to Paris. The trains were quite different from ours at home. The cars were divided into compartments with doors that opened directly onto the platforms on both sides. No waiting in line, just open a side door and hop in. But the train's whistle sounded like the whistle on a peanut vendor's wagon, a shrill high C.

I walked all over the city, from the Eiffel Tower to Notre Dame Cathedral and whatever. For lunch I finally stopped at a place that was obviously making and selling sandwiches that resembled our Po' Boys. After surviving the wrath of the old biddy at my inability to either speak or understand French, and having produced the necessary coins, I got one of the things. It wasn't at all tasty and was very tough. Come to find out it was horsemeat. The French have various customs that us country boys are not used to. For instance the public 'mens' room' is a little shield attached to a building wall with a side door. A guy walks in and his head, shoulders and lower legs show. His

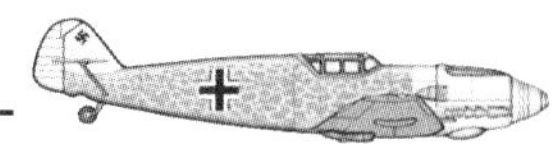

girlfriend may be standing there talking to him over the top of the shield. I don't think that would play in Peoria. Everybody was dressed in dark clothes, rather somber, and I didn't see a smile or hear a laugh while I was in France. The town of Paris is beautiful at night when it's lit up, but the police would not let me walk across any Seine River bridge at night, and there were lots of bridges. Perhaps folks were jumping in too often. I didn't find a hotel that looked like I could afford, but I did find an asphalt-paving machine with some heat still in it parked close to a stone wall. I stood between it and the wall all night where it was nice and warm. At the crack of dawn I was at the train station and slept all the way back to Le Havre.

Our next port was Antwerp. I had a few francs left, so I went to Brussels. I wasn't much impressed, so I got right back on the train and returned to the ship. Next stop was Rotterdam.

The country around Rotterdam is perfectly flat and would be under water were it not for the dikes. There are numerous ship channels on the approach, and rather heavy traffic. It's a strange sight to look a few hundred yards away and see big ships sailing sedately along through pastures and farms. The Dutch are ever trying to reclaim more land from the sea, with windmills constantly pumping away at the job. Rotterdam was different from anything I had ever seen, like a child's picture book. The people were remarkably friendly, big, nice-looking with very rosy cheeks – and yes, they wore wooden shoes that made a lot of racket. Flowers were growing everywhere, mostly tulips, and the whole town was spotlessly clean. In the residential section the houses were built close together to save the precious land. The women had an early morning ritual. They were out early wearing snow-white caps and aprons, in wooden shoes, scrubbing their front porches or steps with soap and water. The Germans bombed the place flat when they invaded.

I went out with some of the sailors that night. Instead of a taxi we boarded a launch that took us across the harbor to a beer joint. I had been somewhat acquainted with Tennessee moonshine that would scald the gullet and fog up the brain in a hurry. This Dutch beer came in tall frosty mugs and went down smooth as silk, and it tasted good. I figured I could handle this stuff just fine. I continued under this impression until it was time to head back and I tried to stand up. Legs wouldn't work – all floppy. Gus and the boys practically carried me to the launch. I remember the ride across the harbor. The wind had picked up and the waves had risen so the cold spray on my face did me worlds of good.

We had discharged our entire cargo of cotton and sulfur, but without a return load the ship rode very high in the water. The upper part of the propeller blades was not even submerged, which caused some vibration when thus under-weight. So the Captain had the rear cargo hold flooded with seawater, which helped some, but that remedy poked the bow or front end up almost out of the water. I sure hoped we wouldn't hit rough weather on the way home. The Captain must have thought about the same thing, because he had the forward compartment filled and we came home with a cargo of seawater!

We came down south near the Azores Islands and had good weather all the way. Rounding the tip of Florida, the Captain must have decided to take a short cut, as we got into some dangerously shallow water and had to pick our way very, very slowly through. I could plainly see the coral and seaweed of the bottom, but we didn't hit anything.

Instead of New Orleans we landed at Beaumont, Texas. The entire crew was paid off and I got my two dollars. Dad had sent me a money order for five bucks. Four of us paid some fellow two bucks apiece to drive us to New Orleans. I bought a ticket on the Illinois Central and rode the cushions home.

James Haun and Eleanor Welch

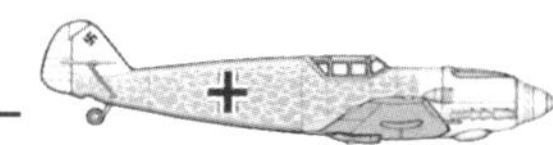

chapter four

MARRIAGE DURING THE DEPRESSION

1935: "MISS ELEANOR TAKES A FLYER"

When FDR was elected President things began to happen. He sent a lot of new bills to Congress intended to put people to work and most of them were passed. There was the CCC, the WPA, the NRA, and the RFC. The CCC was formed on almost military lines, with camps all over the country, usually including an Army officer in charge. Equipped with axes, saws, shovels, and pick axes they attacked the thousands of outdoor jobs that needed doing, such as replanting trees on worn-out land.

The WPA was given the money and manpower necessary to build bridges, dams, roads and public buildings. Today you will find a bronze plaque on many of the older structures with the date the WPA constructed it, and usually the name of the local congressman of that time.

The RFC loaned money to various businesses to help them get started again. Most of the rural areas of the South that had never had electricity were put on line, mainly from the generators in the dams on the Tennessee River.

The NRA was short lived as it was contested by the business community, and the Supreme Court knocked it down. They did get a minimum wage of twenty five cents an hour accepted, which was more than a lot of people were getting. This didn't affect me as I was already getting seventeen dollars and fifty cents a week at the Bottlers Supply House. All these projects cost a lot of money and Uncle Sam didn't have it, so he had to borrow it. Congress passed a bill upping the national debt limit by several billion dollars. The Treasury Department ordered the same amount of treasury bonds printed and sold to whoever would buy them and, presto, Uncle was in the chips again. This cute little trick has been pulled over and over again until now Uncle is some four trillion dollars in debt.

Speaking of uncles, my Uncle John died and left me four hundred dollars. Of course the first thing I did was go looking for some wheels. I found a perfect jewel, a very low time 1929 model Ford convertible, with a rumble seat. It was painted light green, with silver side mounts, and gorgeous yellow wheels. There were side curtains for bad weather and a hand operated windshield wiper on the driver's side. All for only one hundred and twenty-five dollars, cash! I named her 'Sally'. I drove that car for about five years and it never gave me a minute's trouble. Now with wheels, Romance reared its lovely head.

I had grown quite fond of a girl from church named Eleanor Welch. We had been to the same church socials, picnics, and Halloween parties. For one dollar we could ride the streetcar to town to see a movie, have a Coke, and catch a ride home. If we sat in the balcony, we could also have some popcorn. Not exactly a torrid romance for sure, but quite the norm for that day.

Eleanor went to the State College for two years, which put her somewhat higher on the social ladder than me, as I had been out there for only one day. What I saw on the curriculum had nothing whatsoever to do with flying. On the other hand, I had an airplane and could fly it, and I knew exactly what I was going to be and do. Dad was somewhat put out with me. With the arrival of 'Sally', Eleanor – poor girl – had to spend her Sundays out at the airport watching me perform. You might say she became an airport widow before she became a bride.

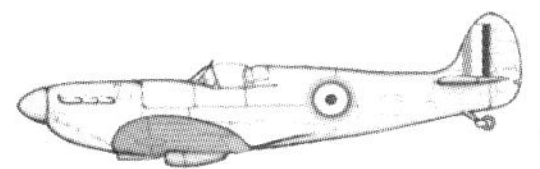

The CAB, forerunner of the FAA, started making rules and regulations concerning the airworthiness of aircraft and the pilots who flew them. All new production aircraft had to meet certain safety specifications in manufacture before they could be certified and licensed, and only licensed pilots could fly them. My old Waco, which was in sad shape from sitting out in the open at Hog Waller, could not be licensed. So I made a deal with Charlie Fast for enough time in his new Travelair to get my license, providing I could deliver the Waco to him at Armstrong Field, north of Memphis.

Eleanor and I drove out to Hog Waller; she would then drive to Armstrong to meet me. She climbed into the rear cockpit to handle the switch and throttle while I propped the engine. She returned to the car to watch me take off. As I climbed out through the gap in the trees, out of the corner of my eye I saw something fly by. When clear of the trees I looked up and saw the sky through a hole in the upper left wing about the size of a newspaper where the old rotten fabric was blowing off. I just had to deliver that bird to Charlie, so I continued north, flying as slow as possible, with more but smaller pieces leaving the wings. That was a long twenty miles. I approached the field straight in with full power, sinking steadily. The old bird crossed the fence with a few feet to spare. A friend of mine took a snapshot of the remains, which I have seen, but he wouldn't give to me. Said he had to keep it to back up his tales.

Charlie rebuilt the ship and sold it to a fellow named Frakes, a stunt pilot who worked air shows. His big act was to fly an airplane into a specially prepared barn that would then explode with fire and smoke, much to the horror and delight of the bloodthirsty spectators. That's where my old Waco ended – 'in a cloud of dust and a blaze of glory'.

There were three types of pilot licenses: first the Private, which required a minimum of ten hours solo. Next was the Limited Commercial, requiring fifty hours and allowing the pilot to carry paying passengers within the local area. Finally came the prestigious Transport License. This was the top, requiring two hundred hours, and setting you apart from other mere mortals and demanding a far-away look in your eyes when addressed on most any subject pertaining to flying.

I had never done any spins, which would be required for any flight test. Frankly I was rather frightened at the thought, having listened to so many horror stories about this dread maneuver. I had to work up courage to do this thing, so, one day I walked up to a group of hangar-flying pilots and blurted out, "Hey Ernie, how about teaching me to spin?" Now I couldn't back out. Ernie was in the middle of some tall tale, but when he had finished we went out and crawled into Charlie's Travelair. I climbed to about three thousand and leveled off. Ernie patted himself on top of his helmet, which when translated means, "I've got it." He spun two turns to the right while I followed him through the controls. We had lost about a thousand feet, so I climbed back to three. This time Ernie held both arms up with a thumb pointed at me. So…power off, pull the nose up high, stick all the way back and full right rudder. It worked! I loved it, as much for the thrill of the maneuver as the fact that I had been able to work up nerve enough to try it. I kept working on spins until I was comfortable with them and could consistently recover on the exact heading I wanted. One day I climbed to seven thousand feet to see how many turns I could get on the way down. After about eight or nine turns the nose tried to come up, meaning it was trying to go flat. It took full opposite control and a couple more turns to recover. That was the last time I ever spun more than three turns.

I went to the doctor who was the only designated 'flight surgeon' in town for my flying physical. The exam was concerned primarily with eyesight and depth perception. I passed OK, and while there in the office I managed to memorize the eye chart and thereafter never had any trouble until much later when they replaced the old chart with a thing you stick your head into and try to tell if the gaps in some little circles are up, down or crossways. Silly!

The Flight Inspector for our area was a man named George Wiggs stationed in Atlanta. He came to Memphis about once a month to give flight and written tests to prospective pilots. He also checked on work being done on any aircraft to determine compliance with pertinent directives, as well as holding court on any hapless pilot accused of such sins as buzzing, or combining alcohol and flight. He was tough as a boot. One day I saw him standing on the lower left wing of a biplane, jumping up and down until the spar broke. He got down with a satisfied grin on his face; "I knew there was something wrong with that wing." It wasn't smart to try to fool him.

I had planned on going for the top, or Transport License, but wiser heads advised me to go for Private first, then work my way up. The written exam consisted of ten questions such as *How high must you be to fly over a city, a football game, over farm land; what happens if you are caught buzzing your girlfriend's house*, etc. I passed that OK and we went out to fly. We made some turns around a barn, then several figure eights around two barns, and landed. Then he sent me up to do a two-turn spin to the right and land within two hundred feet of where he was standing. I did fine and he wrote out my Private License.

Form AC 20-8
11-1-37

UNITED STATES OF AMEFICA
DEPARTMENT OF COMMERCE
BUREAU OF AIR COMMERCE
WASHINGTON, D. C.

IDENTIFICATION CARD NO. 32870

This identification card issued on JULY 29 1938
to JAMES R HAUN
accompanies and is a part of Certificate of Competency bearing the same number.

The terms of this certificate include each and every provision of the currently effective Civil Air Regulations issued by the Secretary of Commerce pursuant to law.

Unless sooner suspended or revoked, this certificate shall be kept until taken up by a Bureau of Air Commerce Inspector.

By direction of the Secretary of Commerce

SIGNATURE OF HOLDER — CHIEF, REGISTRATION SECTION

Any alteration of this identification card is punishable by fine or imprisonment.

Col. Haun memorabilia

The next time he was in town, I went for my Limited Commercial. This written exam was a little more extensive – concerning mainly aircraft engines, their care, maintenance, and feeding. I did two-turn spins, both left and right. I now had my LC that permitted me to carry paying passengers within the local area. That is, I could hop passengers at the airport Sundays.

The written exam for Transport covered such things as cold fronts, warm fronts, dew point, fog formation, etc. The spin series called for three-turn spins, both left and right, with the recovery on the same heading as the entry, exactly. There was no hood work as nobody had any blind flying instruments or radio except possibly some of the early airlines with their Ford Trimotors and Condors.

George Wiggs was a WW I pilot and a Major in the Army Air Corps Reserve. Several years after I knew him, the Reserves started getting new, all metal low-wing airplanes with flaps. Prior to the introduction of flaps all pilots used the sideslip, forward slips, and fishtailing to lose excess height or speed on approaches to landing. George was approaching his home town field and made a steep, slipping turn to final with full flaps down. He spun in and was killed. I heard of a lot of the old timers being killed that way. As I think back over the years, I believe I can safely say that with every improvement in aviation, lives were lost. It is quite true that the sky is most unforgiving of mistakes.

Now I had a Transport License and nothing to fly. I needed a project. Sid Foster, a friend of mine, had been working on a little home-built airplane called a Heath Parasol using plans he bought from the Heath Company. Sid was the kind of fellow who always took forever to finish a job, so I offered to pitch in and help. He had all the components finished and all it really needed was assembling and covering. I had a shed in my back yard that would make a good place to work. This was before the days of 'Sally', so Eleanor borrowed her Dad's Essex. We tied the bare fuselage on top of the Essex and took it home. I put a scratch on the top of the car but Eleanor's Dad was a fine fellow and never mentioned it.

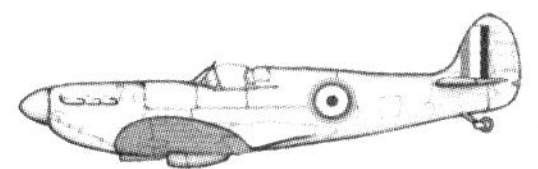

A large group of aviation bugs started gathering every night, so I had plenty of help. We got the landing gear on and the wheels mounted. These wheels were from a very small child's bicycle while the two-gallon gas tank mounted in front of the cockpit came from Sears. The engine was a four cylinder Henderson motorcycle motor that had been modified to take the three-foot long wooden propeller. There was no muffler but instead, four stub exhaust stacks, each about three inches long.

One quiet, peaceful night, sometime around midnight, we got it started. After letting it idle a while to check the oil pressure, we opened it up, wide open. Those short stacks really barked as she turned up 3300 RPM. Lights came on all over the neighborhood, windows popped open, and a shotgun was fired – evidently aimed high as no one was hurt. The neighbors took it all in good spirits, but there was no more engine running at night. We got it covered and doped in good time and moved it out to Armstrong on a truck.

I was the test pilot. On the first try it didn't seem to want to lift off, so I taxied back to the hangar. Thinking maybe we had a weight problem, I took off everything but my shorts, and for that or some other reason, this time it flew. Well actually, it just fluttered around on the edge of a stall! When I got back to the hangar, the guys had hidden my clothes and it took a while to recover them.

Haun family photo

My most enthusiastic helper was Charlie Wilkinson, a skinny scrawny little guy who weighed maybe a hundred pounds dripping wet. Charlie asked if he might taxi the bird around a bit; I couldn't see why not and told him to go ahead. I had given Charlie maybe an hour stick time in the Waco but that was all he had ever had. He ran up and down the runway a couple of times. On the third run he lifted the tail up a bit and the bird took wing. By the time he figured out what happened there wasn't enough room left to land, so Charlie goes off on his first and wholly unintended solo. He made three approaches to the runway and on the third when he was in just the right place, the engine ran out of gas. Believe it or not, he didn't even scratch the paint.

The Parasol had such poor performance we decided to modify it into a mid-wing wire-braced job like Heath's Baby Bullet racer. We would eliminate the drag of the wing struts as well as that of the pilot's body sticking up half-way out of the cockpit. The fuselage wasn't of the right size or shape, so we designed a new one. We drew the side view on the floor and made a jig with little blocks, just like you make wooden wing ribs. We used half-inch square spruce for the longerons and uprights, secured with plywood gussets, glue, and tiny nails. We made two identical sides and joined them in the same fashion. This makes a strong, sturdy frame and is still in use today in many ultra-lites. We put on the tail feathers and landing gear, with the engine sitting on its bearers and the whole thing resting on a sawhorse – with me in the cockpit. The guys moved the engine back and forth until the ship was perfectly balanced on the sawhorse. This located the center of gravity (CG). The center of lift (CL) of the wing, twenty-five percent of the chord, we located here across the upper longeron.

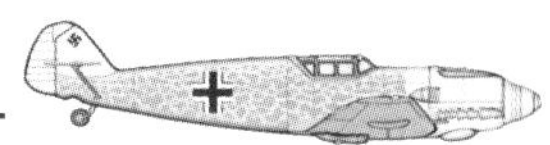

We made a couple of bad mistakes. To make it look racy we wrapped a sheet of aluminum around the cylinders (guaranteeing that it would run very hot) and a little cabane strut sticking up through the cowling to carry the landing wires. This strut should have been two or three times as high to support the load of the wings, especially on landing. It's a wonder the wings didn't come off in flight. We named our creation 'Doo-lolly' and took it out to the airport.

I was about to give it the first test hop when a little thunderstorm came up and we hung around in the hangar waiting it out. Having a captive audience I decided to regale them with an account of the first airplane I tried to build.

BOY FLIER BUILDS 'MOTORBIKE' PLANE 1933

Amateur Aviator First To Fly 'Parasol' Machine Here

By TONY MOORE

If some Sunday afternoon you are startled by a noise overhead resembling a couple of motorcycles and look up to find it a small plane with the pilot projecting from the fuselage like an Eskimo from his kayak, don't duck or run, because it probably will stay overhead.

The plane, a Keith Parasol, is the first of its kind and the smallest ship ever introduced into Memphis flying circles. It was constructed by Jim Haun, 20, local amateur plane builder and a graduate of South Side High School of the class of 1930.

The plane has a wingspread of 24 feet and the fuselage measures 16 feet from the nose to the tip of the tail. The power is furnished by a four-cylinder Henderson motorcycle motor. The plane has a maximum flying speed of 65 miles per hour and a motor turnover of 3200 revolutions per minute. Its total weight is a little over 200 pounds.

When in flight the plane can be shifted to either side by the wind resistance caused when sticking out your hand, according to the young builder. "If you enjoy your leisure hours in a rocking chair, you'll be right at home in the Keith Parasol," said young Haun, "for the plane can be made to nose up and down by shifting the body weight forward and back."

Young Haun secured the parts of the plane from the Keith Airplane Co., manufacturers, who sell the planes completely assembled or the parts accompanied by blueprints for assembly.

After many nights of labor at Armstrong Field Haun completed his job, and while adding the finishing touches announced that he would fly the product of his labors on the following Sunday.

Attendants at the field were all skeptical and voiced various opinions. Some pictured both plane and pilot scattered about the field, while others predicted that it would never leave the ground.

JIM HAUN

Sunday came and so did Jim, all set for his trial flight. After warming up the ship and listening to all the wisecracks of the audience, he taxied out to the runway.

The small, powerful motor roared as he opened the throttle and shot out across the field to gain flying speed. The crowd looked on expecting anything but what happened, when the tail of the ship lowered and she nosed into the air as smoothly as you could ask.

Young Haun flew about the field for a half hour and put the ship thru all the normal maneuvers of flight without the slightest mishap. When his quart of gasoline was about out he landed with the same ease he had taken off.

Since his initial flight, young Haun when not at work at the Memphis Bottlers' Supply Co. has spent most of his time with his new plane or rebuilding his old love, a Waco, which was cracked up by a friend a few months ago.

used by permission of ***The Commercial Appeal****, Memphis*

When I was about 12 or 13 I was building little model planes powered with rubber bands. You've all seen them. You wound the propeller until the rubber was as tight as you could get it, then tossed it up and it flew. Well, I figured I could make one large enough for me to get in and maybe it would fly. So I went to work. The finished product vaguely resembled an airplane, wings made with wood from egg crates and the propeller carved from a two-by-four. For power I cut up some old innertubes into strips that ran from the prop clear to the tail-post, right through the cockpit. There was a long broomstick for a throttle, meaning I could pull it forward to keep the prop from turning until I could get in. A neighbor had a long, steep driveway for a launch ramp. In position at the top, I cranked the prop until it was as tight as I could get it, and then locked the prop with my throttle. There was no seat so I had to get on my knees, straddling the tightly wound engine. When I pulled back on the throttle, the engine exploded with all its pent-up energy and I took the damnedest beating of my life. Dad said I'd probably sing soprano for years!

After the little squall had passed and the air was nice and smooth, I took 'Doo-lolly' up. Actually she flew hands off, and rather nicely. For some reason the engine always quit on short final. Probably carburetor float trouble. On the last flight I kept it up too long. The engine overheated so bad that it froze up. Fortunately I was directly over the field. I don't remember whatever became of 'Doo-lolly', which is just as well.

Eleanor and I had been going together for a couple of years and were very much in love. We wanted to get married, but there was the problem of money. In those days no man worthy of the name would consider matrimony until he had a steady job or trade, with the prospect of being able to support a wife and family. There was just no way an unmarried couple could openly live together. The mores of the time absolutely forbade such practice; the community simply would not

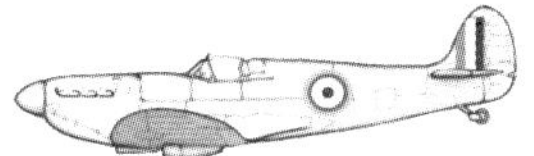

tolerate it. True, there was the occasional reluctant bridegroom who had to be, not too gently, nudged to the altar with the tip of the barrel of a shotgun, but that was never reported in the papers.

The country was slowly beginning to come out of the worst of the Depression as the economy began to respond to the many programs started by FDR. Business at the Bottlers Supply had picked up to that point that our bookkeeper, Miss Tester, was complaining of her heavy workload. I told her I knew a most capable young lady from our church who was a skilled typist with two years of college, who also knew a few words in Spanish. Miss Tester talked it over with the boss, Eddie Kohler, and Eleanor got the job. It paid twelve dollars a week, which, combined with my seventeen-fifty, came to a total of a hundred and fourteen dollars a month. That was about half what a railroad engineer made, so let's go for it!

My family disapproved strongly, considering it a recipe for poverty and tragedy. Of course the more they argued the more bull-headed and stubborn I became. Eleanor's Dad had a talk with me and suggested that perhaps we should postpone the wedding for a while. This of course made me more determined, so we went to the Court House for a license. I thought a license cost two dollars and I had two dollars, but I was informed that I needed five dollars. Well I knew my Dad didn't have any money so we called hers. I've always told folks that P. B. showed up with a shotgun but actually all he brought was the needed three bucks.

Our church was going through a bad time and splitting up into fragments. We had a new pastor who was a hell-fire and brimstone, screaming, holy-roller type that didn't set very well with most of us. So it was decided to have the wedding at Eleanor's house and import a different preacher. This was a small wedding with only family and close friends. The ladies decorated the front parlor very nicely. My aunt Fanny sang *Oh Promise Me,* my sister Evelyn was bridesmaid, and I had a guy from church named Frank Coward as best man. Why I didn't have one of my flying buddies instead, like Vaiden Phillips or Sid Foster, I'll never know. When the preacher came to the part about "With all my worldly goods I thee endow," I snickered.

I paid the preacher five bucks and had maybe ten left in my pocket. The ceremony completed, we ran out and jumped in Sally amid a shower of rice. I hadn't told anyone where we were going, to prevent the usual pranks. I wanted to see the Shiloh Battlefield, and Eleanor said she didn't care. We got to Selma, Tennessee before dark and had supper at the City Café on main street. We had the 'Blue Plate Special'. There was no hotel or motel in Selma but the waitress told us there was a nice lady that took in overnight guests. As we were leaving, I heard someone whisper, "Newlyweds."

The nice lady did have a nice room for us. We were up early for breakfast at the City Café, then drove out to the Shiloh battlegrounds. I saw the 'Bloody Pond' where Mother's Uncle John was wounded. I could have spent many more hours walking over those grounds, but we had to be at work in the morning. Nan had fixed us a room at Dad's house. We were on time for work Monday morning. On payday that first week we started our financial program with a shoebox with envelopes marked for each item in our budget, in which we placed the exact amount of money required. We've never had any serious money problems since that day.

"Sally"

chapter five

A LITTLE BARNSTORMING

1934 – '38: "A MILLION DOLLAR THRILL FOR A DOLLAR BILL"

Vaiden Phillips photo

The next weekend after our wedding we headed out to Armstrong. Where else? Vaiden Phillips had acquired a Curtis Junior that he would let me fly sometimes. It was more commonly called 'The Pusher' because the engine was mounted at the rear of the wing instead of in the nose, so it pushed the airplane instead of pulling it. All jet airplanes today are pushers. It was a fun aircraft, with its extra large wing that let it float around like a glider. The pilot sat in an open cockpit right in the nose with the passenger cockpit under the wing and just in front of the engine and prop. The engine was a three cylinder, air-cooled Zeakley of thirty-five horsepower. It had a bad reputation of occasionally blowing off a cylinder under full power. Vaiden had solved this problem with a strong cable wrapped around the three cylinders pulled very tight with a turnbuckle. The large windshield made it unnecessary to bother with helmet and goggles.

I bundled Eleanor into the back seat, Vaiden cranked me, and off we went. At the south end of the field there was a railroad line and some high wires. Standard for any airport. The little engine was popping away quite happily as I cleared the wires by at least a hundred feet. Suddenly BANG, and the little bird started vibrating violently. I figured the engine had blown a cylinder and was coming unraveled with my brand new bride sitting under it. I cut the switch and lowered the nose. I looked around to see if Eleanor was hurt and got a wide-eyed stare in return. The prop was stopped. There was a nice open field in front of me that appeared to have some crop growing in it. There was: It was ripe tomatoes and we made quite a mess landing. The trouble was easy to find. A long head-bolt had come out and taken about six inches of the prop tip off on its way down. We had to walk all the way back to the hangar. After that Eleanor seemed to lose all interest in flying. In fact she didn't get in another airplane for many years, until I was transferred to Japan and she could either fly or stay home.

About this time the new Municipal Airport was being opened up southeast of Memphis. It was a real smooth grass field roughly a mile square. There were three hangars and an administration building with a nice size lounge and a small snack bar. There were several offices upstairs and a little glassed-in perch for the airport manager on top. Charlie Fast decided to close Armstrong and move to one of the new hangars. Before he could complete the move he came down with pneumonia and died. Harry Wilson took over that hangar and started Mid South Airways, aided and abetted by the Faulkner brothers, Dean, John, and William, the famous author – the little jerk. That's where I hung out and had a few students on the weekends.

Haun family photo

About a week after our wedding we got quite a surprise at the office. Eddie Kohler decided he needed another salesman out in the territory and offered me the

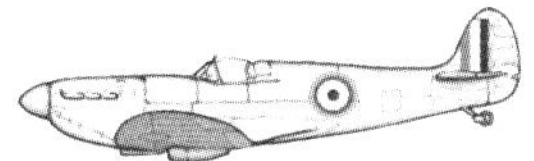

job. We called on all the soft drink plants in Arkansas, half of Mississippi, and half of Tennessee. The Coca Cola plants usually bought bottle caps by the carload, while the little bottlers sometimes bought in lots as little as a hundred gross. We also sold bottling machinery and cleaning powder.

I made one hundred fifty dollars a month plus expenses. At first I used my own car and got a dollar a day for its upkeep. What is there to tell about a job like that? You drive for hours, then go in some plant, tell or listen appreciatively to some old jokes, and if they need anything, write it up in your little book and drive some more. Some of the trips took four or five days, while the others maybe only two or three. When I wasn't traveling my time was my own, so I was out at the airport a lot.

I was down in southern Arkansas one day and saw a very small airplane sitting out in a field. Naturally I stopped and met the proud owner and builder. He had built it from plans he had bought. It was powered by a converted Model A Ford engine. The engine was converted by removing the flywheel and case and fitting a kit that had the prop shaft and thrust bearing. Properly done they made very dependable little powerplants and were used in several different types of small planes. I showed him my Transport License, which impressed him no end, and he asked if I would like to fly it. Is the Pope Catholic? It was a mid-wing job and flew very well, with the Ford engine as smooth as silk. Turned out that was the original test hop.

After a year or so, Eddie gave me a company car, a V8 Ford coupe that would really go, and I promptly totaled it over in Arkansas. Highway 70 ran from Memphis to Little Rock and was two-lane and paved, one of the few in Arkansas. All the rest were gravel. I was heading west on 70 and was going to turn south on the gravel road to Stuttgart. This is rice country and perfectly flat. Long before I got to the turnoff I could see a cloud of dust coming up the Stuttgart road. I figured he was going to Memphis with that load of baled hay, but as we both neared the junction that idiot decided to go to Little Rock. My locked brakes sent up a shower of gravel but to little avail. I hit the front wheel of the flatbed and partially unloaded it. I broke the steering wheel off and cracked both kneecaps. Man I hurt!

I just sat there in a cloud of dust and hay. The driver of the truck jumped out of his cab yelling, "Oh, my back, oh my back." I took a bus home. I thought surely Eddie would fire me, but he bought me another Ford instead. You see I had started teaching him to fly.

Vaiden decided to get rid of his Pusher so Joe Varossa and I bought it. Joe didn't take to flying real swift, but I finally got him soloed, but only one time. Once around the field he decided he had rather have me in the back in the future. I had a lot of fun with that little bird. I liked to chase buzzards. I had an automatic .22 rifle, and sitting right in the nose I could shoot around the windshield. A buzzard being approached from the rear will turn his head around and watch you over his shoulder until you get close. He then folds his wings and drops like a rock, much like the German fighter pilots. I found out there was a law against shooting buzzards.

A fellow over in Arkansas had an OX Commandair in good shape and wanted to trade for the Pusher, provided we delivered it. We had gotten tired of the Pusher so we decided to trade. We left home on a bright sunny day. While cruising along at about 2000 feet directly over the middle of the Mississippi River, the engine quit. With plenty of altitude there was no trouble reaching the Arkansas shore with time to pick a large cotton field with no crop growing in it. We landed down the rows. We couldn't find the trouble so decided to take the engine home and overhaul it. We went back next day and took it back with us.

We gave that little Zeakley engine a good overhaul with new bearings, rings, the works. It was a very hot summer day when we took it back and hung it. It cranked up nice, but I noticed there was no oil pressure indicated. Must be a faulty gauge or an air bubble in the line or something and it'll

come up in a minute, so lets go swimming. We actually did that! We swam for about half an hour in water so muddy you could almost walk on it and went back to the airplane. As we approached we could hear the poor thing squeaking and grunting, just barely turning over, about ready to freeze. Of course it was ruined, so we took it off again. When we tore it down we found the trouble. The oil hole in the thrust bearing was drilled off-center to fit the oil passage. We had put the bearing on backwards, thus covering up the passage and preventing any lubrication forward of that. So we rebuilt it again and it ran fine. The fellow brought his Commandair to Memphis and we traded on the spot. I believe he headed for St. Louis with the Pusher. I hope he got there.

I liked the Commandair. It was built as a trainer but mine had a front cockpit that seated two people. It was very strong and rugged and used automobile tires on the wheels. You could land it in really rough fields. I never went on any of the real barnstorming tours you read about, but several of us used to take two or three airplanes to some small town on the weekend and put on our little show and hop passengers. I always put on my death-defying loops, spins, and fantastic snap rolls. Here's a good place to tell you about 'Hard Rock'.

Haun family photo

We had a promoter named Al Gardner, a little hunchbacked fellow who went around organizing air shows for us. He talked the American Legion down at Corinth, Mississippi into sponsoring a show and printing up handbills; we would put on aerobatics and a parachute jump. We had a young black boy who would jump for a few bucks. After one jump he would pass the hat and if he got a couple of bucks he would roll the chute up and hold it in his arms. When he jumped again, he'd just throw the bundled chute up over his head. For some reason it always opened. I think Willie had a death wish. Anyway this day at Corinth, Willie didn't show. We were hauling passengers like mad, I had done my thing, and it was getting late in the day. The Legion boys kept asking when we would have the jump and it looked like we might be in for a rough time. Al came up to me with a tall, gangling, not so bright-looking fellow who said he would jump for us.

I asked what his name was and he replied, "Folks aroun' here calls me Hard Rock."

I said, "Well Hard Rock, have you ever jumped out of an airplane?"

"Naw, but Al said all I got to do is jump out and count to ten before I pull this ring."

I got to thinking about manslaughter charges and decided not to fly him. One of the other fellows did, though. Al and I just stood there watching as they climbed up to about two thousand and out came ol' Hard Rock. He fell and he fell and just before he disappeared behind the trees we saw a puff of white.

"Come on Al, let's go get him," I said, as Al put his flask back in his hip pocket. Well, you've seen those ponds farmers have to water their stock. As we walked up, there was Hard Rock standing in the pond with water almost up to his neck and the chute laying out on the bank. We grabbed the chute and dragged him out. Seems the chute had opened just in time to swing his feet down and the soft mud had cushioned his fall enough to where he wasn't really hurt. Al gave him a shot out of his flask, which brought him around nicely.

I asked him, "Hard Rock, why did you wait so long to pull the ring?"

He said, "Well, Al said to count to ten!"

Another time we were over at Forrest City, Arkansas. That day for some reason I was flying an Eaglerock biplane of a much later model than the first one back at Bry's Field. This one had a seven cylinder radial air-cooled engine of about two hundred horse power. Smoothest engine I had ever sat behind, but it had one bad habit. It had to be hand cranked, and if it kicked back, it always

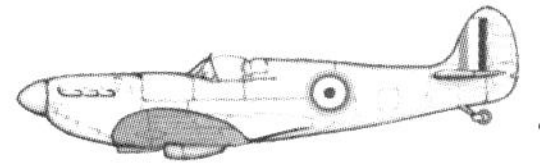

caught fire in the carburetor air intake. I had a guy named Jackson along to sell tickets, load the passengers, and swing the prop. If the thing kicked back, I would cut the switch and Jackson would jerk off his shirt and stuff it in the intake, which would put the fire out, a routine operation. Well, Jackson loaded in two passengers and went to the front. I couldn't see him but I could see the prop being pulled through a couple of times. "Contact." I turned the switch on and yelled, "Contact!" Instead of the engine starting, it kicked back so I knew we had a fire and cut the switch. I couldn't see Jackson so I unbuckled the belt and leaned out. There was ol' Jackson, lying on the ground with a most surprised look on his face and a big farmer standing over him, shaking his fist. "That will teach you to take your shirt off in front of my wife!" It happened!

We were always trying to dream up stunts to pull at these shows to sort of spice up the routine. One we pulled almost got us in trouble. That was over at Lepanto, Arkansas. I had a dummy built to ride in the back cockpit, not belted in. Jackson went over a nearby ridge and built a pile of brush with some gasoline and oil poured over it. I did my routine right over it and at the end pulled up in a slow loop and that let the dummy fall out; then I spun down and disappeared behind the ridge while Jackson tossed a match to the brush. That one really backfired. First, all of our prospective customers rushed to see the wreck, and one guy who happened to be kin to the local sheriff broke a leg jumping a fence. We were lucky to get out of that one with a whole skin. We never went back to Lepanto.

My Commandair was the last of the old OX powered airplanes around Memphis. Much better ones were being produced. The first little trainer was Mr. Taylor's Cub, whose company was soon bought out by Mr. Piper. Taylor designed the Taylorcraft, which was a better performer. Both aircraft were powered at first by a little four cylinder L-head, single ignition engine built by Continental. This was the engine that got commercial aviation off the ground. It developed only forty horsepower and burned about three gallons of gas an hour. The engine was later redesigned with larger cylinders and twin ignition. It developed sixty horsepower and would run indefinitely as long as you kept gas and oil in it. The first time I fired up one of these, I thought, "Man, we've got power now!" A lot of other companies built trainers using this engine, but the Cub and Taylorcraft were by far the most used by the schools. The Aeroncas, the Cessnas, the Ercoupes, etc., all came later. I was instructing in both types and much preferred the Cub. The Cub had a stick while the Taylorcraft used a wheel. I quickly learned that you could get a student soloed in about half the time with the stick control because with a wheel the student has a tendency to try to 'drive' the airplane, which messes up their landings no end. That still holds true today.

There were many other types making their appearance, such as the beautiful Lockheed that American Airways began using to carry the mail. This was a low wing, retractable gear, single engine ship built of molded or pressed wood. When one was due in we all gathered to watch. There were always bets as to whether he would get his landing gear down or not, as the idea of having your wheels on so loose that they could be raised or lowered was just a bit far-fetched. Well, one day he couldn't get his rollers down, try as he might. After trying for quite a while, he had to come on in with the gear up. He made a nice smooth landing but then the bird started coming all to pieces. The engine left first, followed by various other parts before the body broke in half. We saw the pilot crawling out, so nobody went out there. We knew he'd be awful embarrassed. He came walking up to the hangar with his parachute over one shoulder and a small sack of mail over the other. He was packing a pistol, as all mail pilots did in that day. He didn't speak to a soul, and from the look on his face nobody much wanted to speak to him either.

When FDR cancelled the airmail contracts, the Army took over the job. A flight of Curtis Hawk 'Pursuit' planes came to Memphis for that job. These airplanes had the Curtis Conqueror

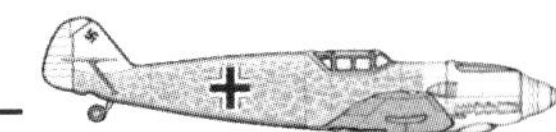

engines in them. This was a twelve cylinder liquid cooled job with two little stub exhaust stacks to each cylinder. Those engines would idle slower than any I had ever seen, with little puffs of smoke popping out of all twenty-four stacks. That six-hundred-horse engine was the forerunner of the WW II Allison, of twelve hundred horses. I did something for the old Sergeant running the line, and he told me to take my Commandair around behind the hangar as he had something for me. I did and he filled my tank with the high octane fuel they used and I burned some of it. The OX wasn't used to that rich a diet and I had to put in new rings.

A lot of Air Corps pilots were killed trying to fly in bad weather without any instrument training. The Army figured if you couldn't see in bad weather you couldn't fight so why bother with instrument flying. This feeling was still pretty much in vogue when I went on active duty in '40. I was the only pilot in the squadron that could make a range let down.

A friend of mine, Red Forman, ran a swimming pool where I hung out. He caught the flying bug and before I knew it had bought an airplane called a Mohawk Pinto. Maybe half a dozen had been built. It was a low wing two seater with a Genet five cylinder engine of around seventy five horsepower that was made in England, and the prop turned the wrong way. He asked me to teach him to fly it. He kept it out in the country on someone's farm with a field that was barely long enough for us to fly safely, as the bird didn't have very good climb performance. I gave him three or four hours and decided that it just wasn't safe for him to even think about flying it solo out of that field. I showed up one afternoon ready to risk all with another lesson, but the airplane was already flying. He came around once and I saw a girl with long black hair in the front cockpit. Red circled once more, gaining altitude, and then headed west. Being the type of guy who minds his own business, I left.

The next day I saw Red and suggested that he give that airplane a good trading. He agreed and we started looking for something that wasn't so likely to bring his flying career to a sudden stop. We found one over at Jackson he liked, and the owner wanted to trade. So all's well that ends well. Now Red had a nice Waco 10 and he could really learn to fly.

Well, I busted up another airplane, two in fact. I had reached that most dangerous time in a pilot's career when he becomes impressed with his dazzling skill, his complete mastery over his aircraft, and his invulnerability to 'the slings and arrows of outrageous fortune', aided and abetted by the plaudits of his adoring peers. In other words I had around five or six hundred hours of flying time logged.

My boss Eddie wanted to fly to Jackson to impress some friends, and there was a beautiful new Rearwin for rent by Southern Airways. The Rearwin was a tandem seated high-wing little bird with a seven cylinder Warner engine having a ring cowl wrapped around it that took away most of the forward visibility, except in level flight. On landings you had to come in with the nose kicked around to the right to enable you to see ahead until just before touchdown – when you kicked it straight again and landed.

At that time the town of Jackson had a little grass strip and one small hangar. As we circled the field we saw that it had been recently mowed and there was baled hay scattered about in a rather haphazard fashion. No sweat. I picked out a clear strip and really greased it on. We had a nice visit with his friends, and before we were quite ready to leave, Eddie suggested that the folks would like to see me go up and show them just what all that little bird could do. Nothing loathe, I put on my usual death-defying routine. Coming in for a landing I picked out the same clear path I had used before. With the left wing pointed at the spot and the nose kicked around to the right so I could see ahead, I side-slipped gracefully in. At the last second I kicked the nose around and the wheels kissed the grass in a perfect three point landing, followed instantly by a rending crash and a violent

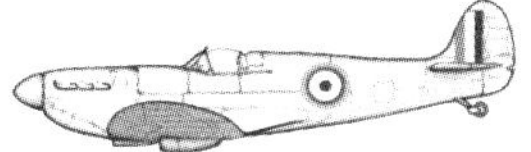

stop. Some idiot had moved a large stack of baled hay right in my way while I was up flying. For some time thereafter I was known as 'Haystack Haun'.

To set the stage for my next disaster, I need to give the circumstances. The Memphis Airport was building its first paved runway. This was about five thousand feet long and ran northeast-southwest. When it was completed American Airlines started running two trips a day through there using the new Douglas DC-3 aircraft. This was a tremendous, shiny bird that would carry twenty-one passengers plus the crew. It was hard to conceive of anything that big and heavy actually flying, but the two engines of a thousand horsepower each seemed to do the job nicely.

With the advent of airline operations it became necessary to devise some type of traffic control. There were no radios available for small aircraft at that time. The airport manager, being a brilliant civil engineer, came up with an excellent idea: On top of the administration building he installed a large rotating red beacon. When one of the airliners was due to arrive, this beacon was turned on and the field was closed to all other traffic until the airliner was safely parked. This arrangement was not entirely satisfactory, as the published schedules and actual arrival times sometimes varied a bit. Like an hour or so, while we waited to take off or circled around waiting to come in. Of course depending on where the sun was, sometimes the beacon could not be seen from the air, resulting in many harsh words and threats of punitive action. But we lived with it.

All of our little airplanes were tail-draggers, dependent on the tail-skid digging into the dirt to act as brakes, as very few actually had been built equipped with brakes. The airport manager, Albricht, came out with a directive that all takeoffs and landings must in the future be made on the paved runway because we were tearing his grass with our tail-skids, and making it look all ratty. Well, you simply cannot land on a hard surface runway with no brakes and a tail-skid. Like the feller said, "You can read the numbers on the tail going by the cockpit." I already had automobile wheels on my Commandair and devised some barely useable brakes and put a little fixed solid rubber roller on my tail-skid, while the Inspector decided to look the other way.

A fellow I had met had an early model Monocoupe powered with a little sixty-five horse Velie five-cylinder engine. (Monocoupe later made some fine, high performance airplanes, but this early model was very heavy, underpowered and an absolute dog.) There was no way to put brakes on it and Albricht had ordered him to move it off the field. The owner asked me if I would fly it out in the country to a farm north of town, and I made one of the worst decisions of my life. I said I would if we could get permission to fly it. Albricht reluctantly agreed, but with the understanding that I could not bring it back. At that time we all thought he had that much authority. So I agreed.

A friend of the owner was going with me to help me locate the field. Once airborne, I discovered my passenger had never been in an airplane so was no help whatsoever. After an hour or so I found the field, quite by accident. It was long and narrow with a ditch running lengthways down the middle and tall trees entirely around it. One side was blocked by a large haystack half way down, and in the other the proud owner had parked his car, effectually blocking that side. I buzzed him several times, but he just sat there on the fender smoking his pipe, with me getting madder by the minute. For some weird reason, hinted at earlier, I decided I'd land across the field, touching down just on the other side of the ditch and then ground loop it before coming to the trees. Me and Lindbergh!

I came in as slow as possible and thought I had it made, but my wheels hit the lip of the ditch and we bounced high. I instinctively gave it full throttle and headed for the trees. The little engine was doing its best when I pulled up to clear the trees, but there was one tree taller than the rest and the left wingtip hit a long limb, slewing the airplane around and killing what speed I had left. She hung there for a moment while I cut the switch and grabbed the two cross braces behind the

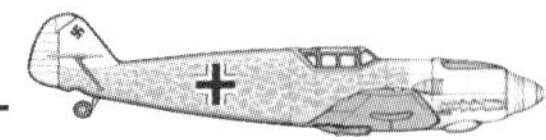

windshield. She spun a turn and a quarter from tree top high and hit vertically. The engine came back into the cockpit and forced my left leg through a longeron. The passenger seemed to be unconscious and bleeding from his head. The only door was on his side so I had to get him unbuckled, get the door open, and with my good leg kick him out. Then I crawled out. The cross brace I had been holding had broken and the stub had ripped a deep gash from above my right eye across to the left, nearly severing the left eyelid.

We were way out in the country but within minutes quite a crowd had gathered. Where they all came from I couldn't imagine. The passenger had a nosebleed but otherwise wasn't hurt. I asked to be taken to the Methodist Hospital in Memphis, as that's where I had my insurance. (Which cost me a dollar a month!) There, they asked me who my doctor was. I didn't have one, but they kept insisting that I must name one. I had a distant cousin, Sam Williamson, so I asked for him. They told me he was a female specialist, but he'd have to do. A good friend from the Airport named George Stokes, who flew for the *Commercial Appeal* and was also a photographer, came in while I was on the operating table. He kept running around the table clicking his camera.

Haun family photo

He said, "I'll bet I can get fifty bucks for this picture. I can almost see your brains!"

I was due to meet Eleanor at Britlings for supper, and asked George to meet her and tell her what had happened. The Doc in the meantime was sewing my head, using tiny little needles and black silk thread. I asked him to look at my left knee, as I was sure it was broken. He moved it around a bit and decided I was just loose jointed, and left.

The next morning that knee was swollen up twice its size and hurt something fierce. I asked for the doctor but was told that he had gone fishing and wouldn't be back for days. Another doc mak ing his rounds stuck his head in the door and asked how I was doing. I asked him to take a look at my leg, but he said he couldn't as he wasn't my doctor. I told him he was now, as I'd just f ired old Sam. They X-rayed the knee and found it broken in two places, necessitating immediate surgery.

After they had finished all the temporary repairs I was taken to a nice, private room way back in one corner of the building on the third floor. Eleanor and some of the guys from the Airport arrived. I didn't feel much like visiting, so they didn't stay long. Eleanor had a cot brought in and spent the night. She said I spent a rather restless night; they must have doped me up a bit. The next day being Sunday, there were quite a number of visitors. Bobby Edwards gave me a shot of Old Fearless from his flask, which was a bad thing because I started talking about the coming operation and, after another shot, decided that it would be nice to have the repair work done under a local anesthetic so I could watch it! There was some talk about overhead mirrors, etc. The Doc came in about this time and, just laughing, agreed. At least he didn't say No.

They wheeled me down to the operating room. The nurses had heard about me saying I wanted to watch and advised me that I didn't really, and this brought out my stubborn streak, so I insisted.

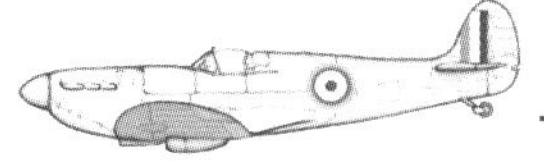

The Doc had arrived and was listening to all this, and called for a syringe of the local anesthetic and stuck it in the knee. There were three or four interns standing around to see the old master work.

He sliced the knee open and I grinned at the nurse holding a mask near my head. "See, it didn't hurt a bit."

Everybody gathered around while the Doc explained where the bones were broken and how they had already started to knit. The nurse at my head said, "Are you ready for this mask?"

"Naw, I don't need that thing."

Doc said, "Sweetheart, hand me the blunt chisel and mallet." The nurse placed the mask over my face, but I shoved it away just as Doc hit the first blow and the top of my head almost blew off. I refused the mask again as I figured that with every blow the job would be finished. Stupid, stupid, stupid. I don't know how long this continued, but it seemed forever. They finally finished and all the interns were loud in their praise of the Doc's skill. They sewed me up with a great big needle and kite string and hauled me off to bed. Oh, yes, and they put a cast on from my foot to my hip.

I stayed in the hospital for several more days, and every night I had a lot of company from the Airport gang. When it became apparent I wasn't about to die from my wounds, the nightly parties got a little rough. After visiting hours the off-duty nurses would let the guys in from the fire escape and let the good times roll. I had never smoked, but now that I was incapable of defending myself, they kept poking cigarettes in my mouth and pouring whiskey down my throat until, before I could get out of there, I had become addicted. A few years ago I kicked the whiskey habit, but my pipe still glows like a blast furnace.

The Doc had told me that I had lost all the fluid from the knee and that I would have a stiff leg the rest of my life. After the cast finally came off, I could not bend the knee. For the next year I worked on that knee every day, each day getting it to bend a little more, until finally it worked fairly well. It still gives me trouble, and when I get the urge to do something foolish, that thing will send a flash to the brain, reminding me what pure agony is really like. I won't say I haven't overstepped the bounds of conservative flying once in a while since, but I haven't accidentally scratched the paint on another airplane.

Well now, that's not exactly true, but I'll go into that later.

I got back to flying in about a month at the school. Eddie had the flying bug bad by now and wanted his own airplane. He learned of a Cessna for sale down in St. Petersburg, Florida. There was nothing to do but go see it, so three of us took a cabin Waco down there. I had never flown any of this new highpowered stuff so Hal Fry went along. The Cessna had a 145 Warner engine that pulled along quite fast for its day. Eddie bought it and he and Hal decided to fly it home while I was to take the Waco. I didn't have any trouble until I had to land at Gainesville for fuel. The Waco had a wheel instead of a stick, which caused me a few bad moments before getting it safely on the ground. When I arrived at Memphis the owner of the Waco was quite surprised to see me flying it instead of Hal. I understand he had quite a discussion with Hal about that later. Eddie and I flew the new bird around the country quite a bit and I thoroughly enjoyed it. I was getting plenty of flying so I sold the old Commandair; it was getting pretty long in the tooth. Never really missed it.

That winter there was a terrible flood in the Mississippi Valley. The levies over in Arkansas broke, so that totally flat country was flooded. People were trapped on housetops or any bit of ground that was above water. Joe Varossa's mother lived in a small town that was being flooded, so he and I decided to fly over there and see if we could get her out. We found that there was a long ridge nearby out of the water and rather crowded with people and livestock. There was a clear space big enough to land in, so in we went. Joe found his mother in the crowd and we offered to take her

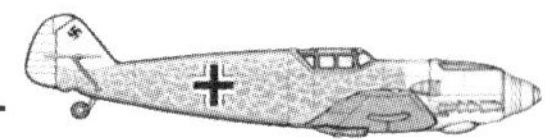

out. No way! She would swim out through floating ice before she would get in one of those air machines, so we flew home.

The next day or so calls went out for any pilot who could help search for stranded people. Red offered his Waco 10, which had a much better engine than mine. This was an open cockpit airplane with only tiny windshields to keep off the wintry blast. You can imagine how cold it was. Red and Vaiden were in the front cockpit and I flew from the back. We found some people and led the boats to them, then went looking for more. Red was having some sort of kidney trouble at that time and when he had to go, he really had to go! He was making frantic motions describing his problem. We were close to Blytheville, which had a little grass strip, so I headed for that. The field was covered with snow but I could see grass or weeds sticking up through it. Maybe the snow wasn't very deep so I made a tail high approach and just touched the wheels. I could feel them breaking through a skim of ice, which meant that the field was probably flooded under the snow. Full power and out of there! That didn't suit Red at all so he unbuckled and stood up in the front seat. Well I certainly didn't like that idea, sitting in an open cockpit behind him. The problem was solved when the icy blast hit him full force. With a sheepish look on his face, he sat down and I headed for Memphis pulling max cruise power. Red was to figure heavily in my future.

Sky Rod!

photo by permission of Andy Heins

1927 Waco 9 with 8-cylinder 90hp OX-5 engine

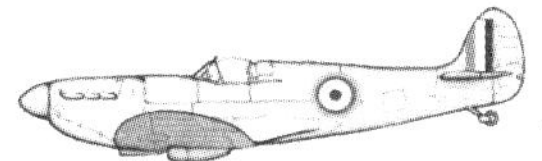

U.S. Army Air Corps photo

Haun family photo

Fred G. Hook, Jr.

chapter six

FRED HOOK

1936: "THE SPORTING TYPE"

About this time I met another character, Fred Hook, who would also be much involved in my later years. One day I saw a small crowd gathered around a uniformed policeman sitting on a bench holding his audience spellbound with some tall tale. I eased up close enough to see and hear. This was Hook; he was digging a hole in the tip of a pistol bullet with a pocket knife, making a highly illegal dumdum.

"And the next one I shoot won't stand trial."

Hook wanted to learn to fly and I took him on. I had him in the back seat of a Cub for his first lesson. We were cruising around south of the airport when there was a shockingly loud report in back of me. I turned around and saw a most unusual sight. Hook had his false upper teeth sticking out, his cap on backwards, and was shooting at a buzzard with his .45. I was suitably impressed and judging him to be the sporting type, pulled up and over in a loop, followed by a three turn spin. We became great buddies.

One day an Army trainer landed and out stepped George Stokes. He was all dressed up in an Army uniform. Red and I were standing there dumbfounded. George explained that he was a First Lieutenant in the Army Air Corps Reserve, and was on two weeks active duty, and no, they didn't charge him any rental on that big bird. In fact they actually paid him to fly it! Further, he just might be able to introduce us to the man who just might be interested in getting two such fine future warriors signed up. And so a long, slow process was started that changed both our lives completely.

Red's Waco 10 would cruise at every bit of 80 MPH, which wasn't near enough speed for Red, so he traded it in on a fine Clipped-wing Monocoupe powered by a 145 HP Warner engine. This was the same airplane Phoebe Omlie had used earlier to win several cross-country races. Her husband, Vernon Omlie, had flown Jennies in Mexico with the Pershing expedition against Pancho Villa. The couple had been barnstormers after WW I with Phoebe acting as wingwalker and parachute jumper. They operated a flying service at Memphis…a colorful pair.

That Monocoupe was a dream. It had a very fast rate of roll, making 8-point rolls easy. After I learned to handle it properly, I checked Red out in it and we took several interesting trips. The first was to Atlanta to meet with Major John B. Patrick. John B, as he was known far and wide, was the ranking Army Air Corps officer in the southeastern U.S. and as such controlled or oversaw the Reserve program. George Stokes had made an appointment for us to meet him and see if we could get into the Reserves. George must have made glowing recommendations regarding our sterling worth, as we were ushered into the August Presence without delay.

"Why do you boys want to get in the Army?"

"We want to fly those big airplanes."

"Hold up your right hands and repeat after me…Red, quit scratching yourself – you're taking the oath…" We repeated the oath, whereupon John B said, "I now pronounce you Privates in the Army Air Corps Reserve."

"Hell, Major, we don't want to be Privates, we want to fly those airplanes."

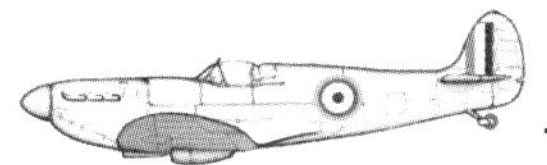

John B explained that we first had to complete an extension course called the 'Ten Series' covering various military matters, pass a physical exam, and have at least 400 hours flying experience of which at least 100 hours had to be in airplanes of 400 HP or more.

Naturally we had all that time. "The check is in the mail, Major… Sir."

He told us the courses would be posted to us and, as each subject was finished, we would mail it back. The corrected, or blue copies, would afterwards be returned to us. So, press on!

John B came out to see Red's airplane and commented most unfavorably on the weather. Sure enough, it was solid overcast and rather low, but nothing to bother two such intrepid airmen! So we left. As we buzzed on our way, the ceiling came lower and lower. We were following a railroad that happened to be going the same way we were, at 100 feet or so, when up ahead the tracks ran into a tunnel. I demonstrated my version of a Chandelle, which approaches but is not quite an Immelleman. We went back to the last town we had passed and spent the night. I believe it was Anniston, Alabama. Next morning the front had moved off and we proceeded on to Memphis in bright sun. We didn't bother to tell people that we were only Privates.

Shortly thereafter I began to receive the necessary literature covering various courses such as "Customs of the Service," "Interior Guard Duty," "Organization of the Army," etc., etc., etc. Red didn't bother to work any of this, but made a much better overall grade than I did by the simple expedient of having some girl copy all of my blue, or corrected copies. There were several others that did the same, including Hook. I can't regret that six months of hard work, as it helped give the Army a pool of ready-trained pilots when the War started. That bunch of ours did outstanding jobs. One of them was killed.

That summer Shell Oil Company, or maybe it was Gulf, sponsored a big air show at Miami. They offered free gasoline to any and all those who would fly in from anywhere in the States. I talked my boss and Eleanor into letting me go, and I went down with Red. I don't know how many went, but the airport at Miami was packed with airplanes of all kinds. When you landed you were led to a parking spot and given a claim check for your airplane so you could reclaim it when you were ready to depart. I suppose some people stole airplanes in those days, but I had never heard of it. We checked into a hotel and decided to see the sights. The weather was much too hot for our Memphis-type clothes, so the first thing we did was look for more appropriate garments. I ended up with a passionate blue thing, sort of like a jump suit, and Red bought a canary yellow one. I believe they call the material sharkskin, and indeed it was what Eleanor would call 'slinky'. We got dressed up in this garb and sallied forth. There was a likely looking bar that seemed well patronized, so we went in. The place was crowded with some of the weirdest looking guys you ever saw, all painted up and perfumed. There were no women in there. One cat came slithering up to me like he wanted to talk, but Red drug me out of there. Seems Red knew about those things, but it was all new to me.

After the air show was over, a bunch of us gathered in one of the hotel rooms for a little hangar flying. One guy told about flying over to Cuba; this got Red all fired up with the idea of hopping over there in the Monocoupe. I just plain told him I wasn't about to fly over all that water in a single-engine airplane. One of the other guys said he'd like to go and that if I would take his airplane back to Birmingham, he would go to Cuba with Red. I had to agree with that, so he gave me his claim check for a Cub.

Bright and early the next morning I was at the airport looking for a Cub that matched the number on my claim check, and eventually found it. While I was looking the little bird over, up walked a pretty young girl, who said, "I go with the airplane." While I'm standing there looking foolish, up walk two guys. Seems this couple had rented two airplanes and two instructors for the

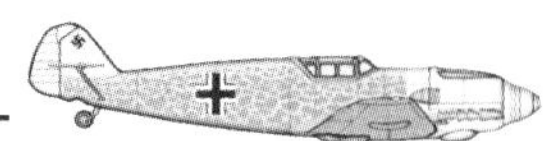

trip. As the girl's husband headed for the other aircraft, his parting admonition was: "Don't get lost." I crawled into the front seat of the Cub and noticed that the compass was reading north although the airplane was facing east. Also there wasn't 'map one' aboard. The husband took off in a Taylorcraft, which is somewhat faster than a Cub, plus a 15 or 20 knot wind was blowing from the north, the general direction I wanted to go. Well, in for a penny, in for a pound.

I took off and headed for the beach. All along the Atlantic there is what appears to be a continuous sand dune some ten or fifteen feet high down to where the actual beach starts. I figured I'd stay low behind that sand dune and over the beach to stay out of the strong headwind. Besides, having no compass, that was as good a place to be as any. Well that was a nice ride. We probably made some fishermen mad buzzing them at ten feet, but most of them waved back as we jumped over their fishing poles. We stopped at Vero Beach for gas and I got a road map. Nothing new about that, everybody flew by road maps. I was quite accustomed to flying without a compass; you used section lines, and in Florida the section lines are laid out straight and clear. At least over on the east coast. We stopped for gas again, I forget where, and continued on toward Gainesville. It had taken all day to get this far against the strong headwind. We landed at Gainesville just before dark and parked the bird for the night. The Taylorcraft landed and parked right beside us. The truth is sometimes stranger than fiction, or so they say.

Red picked me up the next day at Birmingham. While in Cuba he had bought a little monkey that didn't like to fly a bit. It was now well restrained with a makeshift strait jacket and all the mess had been cleaned up. We had an easy trip on home.

I continued training a few students on the weekends and flying Eddie around in his Cessna. Hook got his license and did some crop dusting for a company down in Mississippi named Finkley Bros. I stopped by their strip one day to visit with Hook, but he was out flying, so I had time to look around the operation. Over the front gate there was a sign that read "Transport Pilots and Dogs Keep Out." That should give you some idea what kind of operation they ran. I watched one big fellow who must have weighed 300 pounds straightening out a bent propeller. He laid the bent end onto an anvil and, with a large sledge hammer, proceeded to bang it with mighty blows until it was more or less back into its original shape. They then installed it on a Waco duster!

Hook's furlough from the police department expired, which I considered a good thing, as that allowed him to survive. At home he showed me a little bottle full of boll weevils that he used to convince the farm owners that their cotton crops really did need dusting. "Picked them this morning in your south field."

I had a girl student that caused me a lot of razzing from the guys. She was perfectly round, in all directions, had red hair of a shade between red and orange, and wore glasses that looked like the bottoms of coke bottles. Man she was ugly! She couldn't drive a car, so her Daddy brought her out for lessons. I think they picked me for her instructor because I have such a kind, compassionate face and demeanor. Well we got started using a Taylorcraft. She was quite nervous: normal banks and turns shook her up. After several hours of this, I came to the opinion – influenced by my extreme lack of experience in such matters – that I should give her some spins, so that she would no longer be worried by normal flying. I climbed to about three thousand and headed out to our old field, Hog Waller. This particular airplane had one bad habit. In a spin with the power off, it was necessary to occasionally goose the throttle to keep the engine running. I told her to follow me through on the controls, and kicked it into a spin. She squealed and seemed to enjoy it, so we climbed up again and I told her to try it. She did nicely but I had to goose the throttle for her. I explained why and told her to do it again. She did, and again I had to goose the throttle for her.

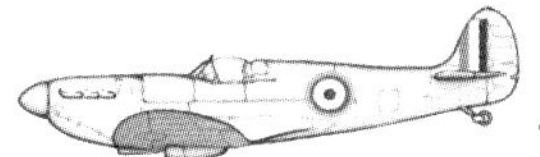

Well I know how to impress it on her mind; so I told her to spin again. This time I didn't touch the throttle so naturally the engine quit.

She grinned, "How was that?"

"Fine spin and recovery, but look at the prop; we will have to land at this airport below us and crank it." Well, Hog Waller hadn't been used in several years, so I touched down in about three-foot-high weeds. After cranking up I had to run up and down the field a couple of times to knock down enough weeds to let me get off. This was a Sunday and all the guys were sitting out in front of the hangar when I taxied up. My student and her Dad departed, and I went over and sat down on the bench. We had a boy around named Preacher. Somebody called, "Preacher, go out there and bring us some of those long weeds hanging all over that airplane."

Well, I knew I was in for it now. There followed a long and serious discussion about what kinds of weeds and where they usually were to be found growing, which was certainly not on an airport. I wouldn't have minded so much if she had been a pretty little thing. My 'girlfriend' never came back.

U.S. Air Force photo

The Army Air Corps Reserve established a detachment at Memphis under the command of Captain William H. Tunner. He was a West Pointer with over twelve years' service. It took at least twelve years to make Captain in those days, and then only if someone senior to you either died or retired. Tunner later became famous as the commander of the 'Hump' operation in India and, after that, the Berlin Air Lift. His final command was MATS, the Military Air Transport Service. Red and I served under him in all three commands. He retired as a three star General. He got Red promoted to Brigadier General after the war. I had been a bad boy a few times, so couldn't make it, for which I'm glad. I have noticed that when someone makes General, his IQ suddenly jumps several octaves. And who would I be trying to kid?

We had completed all our required studies and were given a date to report to Atlanta. We cranked up Red's airplane and shoved off. On arrival we were met by John B, who advised us that we were staying at his house that night. It seems that he was having a party and required a couple of bartenders. We were further advised that every time he took a drink, we were to have one as well. We reminded him that we were due for a physical exam at 8:00 the next morning and we ought not be doing that. His comment was: "If you want to be in my Army, you gotta be tough." The party lasted almost all night so you can imagine what shape we were in when we staggered in to see the Flight Surgeon. He looked us over and asked where we had been. We told him we had spent the night with John B. He felt our pulse and that's about all. I couldn't have even seen the eye chart.

That afternoon I was slated to fly first. John B took me to the hangar. He pointed out a rather large open cockpit biplane with a big Pratt and Whitney engine of about 450 HP, and asked if I had ever flown anything like that. Naturally I said no because if I said yes he might roll out one of those vicious looking things parked in the back. So they rolled out the old BT-2 and we went flying. What he wanted was exactly what I had been teaching students for years. I made only one mistake. When I opened the throttle on that humongous engine, I forgot to shove in full right rudder to take care of

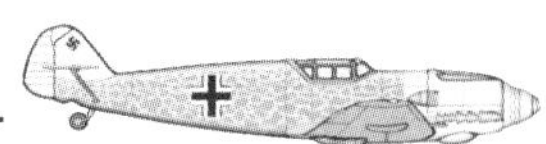

the torque, so she started to turn to the left. I slammed in full right rudder and from there on everything went fine. When we got down he had only one comment to make:

"Well, it's just like I thought. You're nothing but a hayfield pilot. I put you out on a concrete runway and you immediately head for the grass. But I guess you fly as well as the average Second Lieutenant we're getting today."

The date was August 26, 1939.

I phoned Eleanor, "You can call me Louie."

U.S. Army Air Corps photo

"Call me Louie."

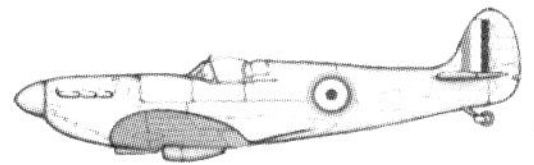

Recruit Haun in Boeing P-12 over Shelby County, Tennessee

U.S. Army Air Corps photo

Haun family photo

1939

chapter seven

SECOND LIEUTENANT, RESERVE

1939: "CALL ME LOUIE"

Now that I was a full fledged Second Lieutenant in the Army Air Corps Reserve, I was eager to get on with the flying end of the business. I rushed out to the airport and reported smartly to Captain Tunner as prescribed in *Customs of the Service*. Then I got my first lesson in that time-honored routine of 'hurry up and wait'. It seems that before I could even get in an airplane I must first have in my hot little hand an order rating me as Pilot and then another one stating that I was required to participate in regular and frequent flights when so authorized by competent authority.

Know when I finally received these two documents? Two months later! By this time I had devoured the Operations Manuals for both the two types of aircraft we had in the Reserve at that time, the BT-9A and the BC-1A ("Texan"). The BT-9 was a low wing, single engine, two place monoplane with a two-position prop. By that I mean the blade angle of the propeller could be changed from low for takeoff and climb, to high for cruise, like shifting gears in your car. The BC-1A was a more advanced type, with retractable landing gear, a constant speed prop and all the necessary radios and instruments for instrument flying. A stripped down model of this airplane became known as the AT-6 (Advanced Trainer), the airplane most all Services used to prepare pilots for combat, before sending them on training in the combat types.

The long awaited documents finally arrived. As I write this, I am looking at my original Form 5, Pilot's Individual Flight Record, which states that I was given 30 minutes dual instruction in a BT-9A, with two landings – and then flew for an hour, with 8 landings, solo. Of course you already knew I was a hot rod pilot! Actually the bird was very easy to fly, stable and light on the controls. I forgot to mention that both airplanes had hydraulic flaps. Remembering how many people had been killed by slipping with flaps down, I avoided that procedure. The Form 5 says I put in ten hours in the BT-9 and then started on the BC-1A. What a lovely airplane! Brand new with that new smell! All the new instruments I was learning how to use and why I needed them. If the thing could cook I would have married it! I'd sit down in that cockpit and just shiver all over with delight, and when I opened the throttle on that big Pratt & Whitney, sometimes I would actually scream for joy!

One of the officers in the unit was an American Airlines captain named Slim Paine. He saw how eager I was and offered to help with instrument flying. I jumped at the chance, so he went to work on me. Because I was strictly a stick and rudder, by the seat-pants pilot, I had an awful lot to learn, and it came hard at first. As I gradually improved he put me on flying the range, then making range letdowns and approaches. I learned to use the ADF (Automatic Direction Finder) and all that good stuff. I practiced and practiced.

The Army was scheduled to hold maneuvers in Louisiana that summer. That is when they assemble all the available forces and practice moving and maneuvering large bodies of troops and material over a large area. This is particularly valuable in training staff officers in the intricate coordination necessary to have all the troops, munitions, food, transportation – all the myriad details – come together in the right place at the right time. It was on this maneuver that Lieutenant Colonel Dwight Eisenhower so impressed his superiors with his organizing and planning ability that he was jumped over many Generals who were much his senior when WW II started. Captain

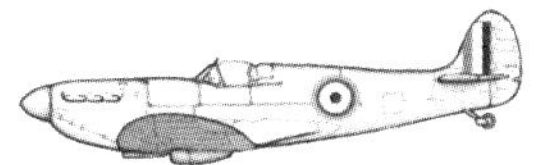

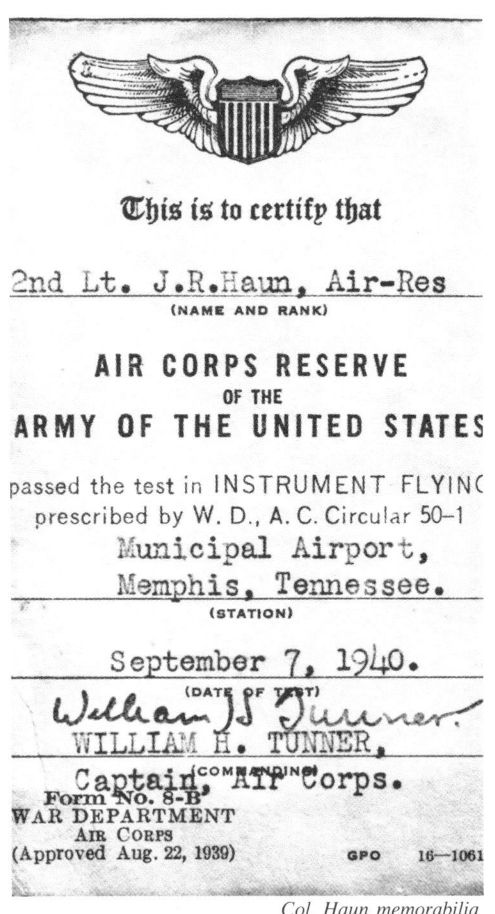

This is to certify that

2nd Lt. J.R.Haun, Air-Res
(NAME AND RANK)

AIR CORPS RESERVE
OF THE
ARMY OF THE UNITED STATES

passed the test in INSTRUMENT FLYIN(
prescribed by W. D., A. C. Circular 50-1

Municipal Airport,
Memphis, Tennessee.
(STATION)

September 7, 1940.
(DATE OF TEST)

WILLIAM H. TUNNER,
Captain, Air Corps.
(COMMANDING)

Form No. 8-B
WAR DEPARTMENT
AIR CORPS
(Approved Aug. 22, 1939) GPO 16—1061

Col. Haun memorabilia

Tunner offered to have us called to active duty for two weeks if we could manage to get away. Red and I both requested this duty and in due course received our orders to report to Natchitoches, Louisiana – pronounced Nach-o-dish.

I flew a BT-9 and I think Red did too. The camp was near the airport in a grove of trees. We lived in the usual 8-man squad tents and were well fed on the usual Army rations. The opposing forces were the Red Army and the Blue Army. I learned that the Blue Army always won the battles. I suppose this was for sentimental reasons. It was quite apparent that the United States was in no condition to fight anyone at that time. I saw trucks with big white signs painted on the sides reading TANK. All sorts of equipment was simulated as there was very little of the real thing available. I heard that most of our field artillery and .30 caliber rifles had been shipped to England. I bombed some troop formations with one pound flour sacks, which created much panic in their ranks. Captain Tunner sent me out to find a field long enough for a BT-9 to land in safely. I found one that was long enough except it had some trees blocking one end. Tunner said he could get the money to buy the trees and have them cut down, which was done, so we moved in there and set up camp. I was told that this was the first time the Army had built a Forward Air Strip. This was repeated hundreds of times during the coming war.

Of course the Blue Army won the battle and I went back to Memphis. On the way I stopped at Barksdale for gasoline – and who should I meet on the ramp? None other than the great John B. Patrick. I was wearing a fine pith helmet I had purchased somewhere. John B looked me over and advised me in no uncertain terms to "get rid of that lion-tamer's hat!" That was the last time I ever saw John B. For some reason I had trouble with headgear frequently in the Service. Perhaps it was the rakish angle that bugged people, especially my superiors.

Our son Jimmy was born March 16, 1940, which made his arrival about four years later than originally scheduled. I don't remember why we saddled him with 'Junior'. Probably Eleanor's idea. My two grandfathers were named James and Robert, maybe that's why. We had an apartment in Eleanor's parents' home, which was a good thing as I was gone so much of the time with my traveling job, and the Welches were a close-knit loving family. We were very lucky, especially with a war coming on.

Haun family photo

The Reserve detachment had received two more airplanes. One of them was a P-12. This little fighter had been front line equipment during the thirties, but now had been replaced by much later types that far exceeded its performance, so they were given to the Reserve. It was a short-coupled open cockpit biplane with a big

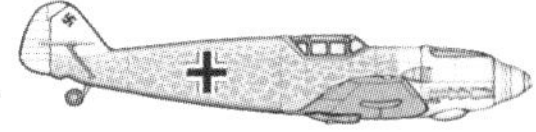

U.S. Army Air Corps photo

Pratt & Whitney engine. Anything you could think of, you could do in this feisty little bird: square loops, eight-point rolls, you name it – except for inverted maneuvers. It had no inverted fuel system, so the engine would always quit when you rolled it over on its back; but it would immediately restart when rolled upright. I had it up one day practicing rolls with great enthusiasm and sort of lost track of the time I'd been up. The fuel gauge was a long glass tube mounted on the left side of the cockpit with a cork in it. As the gas tank was directly in front of the cockpit this gave the pilot an instant and accurate reading of the fuel quantity remaining; that is, if he bothered to glance at it from time to time. Well, I finished an absolutely perfect eight point roll and leveled off. The engine stayed quiet and a glance at the gauge showed why. That's right – empty! Really no sweat as I was within easy gliding distance of the airport. Trouble was, I was going to be quite embarrassed when it became known that the world's most greatest pilot had run out of gas! The ban on grass landings was still in effect but I decided I had rather face the wrath of old man Albricht than the condemnation of my peers. So I plotted a course that would put me on the ground where I could roll up to the gas pump with my dead engine and no one would be the wiser. With the fantastic skill honed by many hours of spot landing practice, I touched down exactly where I wanted and rolled quietly up to the gas pump. Only a slight touch on the brake and I was home. When I walked into the office Captain Tunner was on the phone with a most irate airport manager. After he hung up, Tunner looked at me for a minute: "Ran out of gas, didn't you?"

"Yes, Sir." He finally got that law revoked as the P-12 had a tail wheel and loved the grass, but was a real handful on concrete.

Red wanted to fly the P-12 and I was sent to check him out. I gave Red some awful good advice: "You land this thing three points, in the grass, and stay off the runway!"

Well, Red shot half a dozen landings in the grass and did fine. Then he got hot and lined up on the runway. I was jumping up and down and waving like mad, but he went by me, grinning like a jackass eating cockleburs. You guessed it. He made a smooth three-point landing and that beautiful little airplane disintegrated so fast I couldn't tell which part hit first. It was a world-class groundloop and the little bird was a complete wipeout.

Captain Tunner crawled all over Red and ordered him to go to Atlanta and pick up a replacement for the wrecked aircraft. Red said he wouldn't get in another P-12 for love or money. Tunner told him he would either do as he was told or else turn in his suit. I had to drag Red out of the office. As it turned out, I flew Red to Atlanta and he flew the new P-12 back to Memphis. He flew around the airport for maybe fifteen minutes and finally came in, on the grass, and taxied slowly up to the hangar. He walked into the office and slammed his helmet on the counter. "There's your damn airplane!" and walked out. I made him apologize later and Tunner graciously forgave him.

Hook was in the unit by now as well as half a dozen other new pilots. No trouble now getting enough people for formation practice. In my civilian life I still instructed some students but this ended quickly one day. A stranger accosted me and inquired if I had an Instructors' License. I had never heard of the thing. Seems he was with the CAB, whatever that was, and would give me a

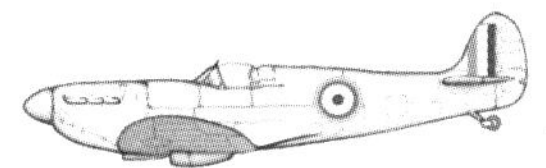

flight check to see if I was qualified. So off we go in a Cub. The first thing he wanted me to show him was a Chandelle. My near-Immellman didn't please him at all, so he demonstrated a rather anemic little climbing turn, which I laughed at. Advice…never laugh at a government bureaucrat. So we returned to the airport and I didn't have an instructors' rating. Not that I cared as I was getting a lot of flying in big, powerful aircraft and it didn't cost me a dime.

I was still traveling for the Bottlers Supply Company, but my heart wasn't in it. My Grandmother Carroll was getting well along in years, so I often stopped by Henderson to visit with her, realizing that each visit might be the last. I dressed up in my Army uniform for this visit. She was in bed, but her usual chipper self.

"What are you got up as?"

"Granny, I'm a Second Lieutenant in the Army Air Corps."

"Well, I hope you're in the Cavalry; I'll have you know your Grandfather…what's that on your collar?"

"The U S stands for the United States and the little wings mean I fly airplanes."

She thought a minute and came out with, "Well, I never thought a grandson of mine would ever turn out to be a goddam Yankee."

She told me to look in the chifferobe and get a sword. It was a long heavy Cavalry sabre. She said, "This was your Grandfather's; wear it with pride!" That was the last I ever saw Granny. She died shortly afterwards.

That was the summer Hitler overran France and the Low Countries. We listened to his ranting and raving over short-wave radio with its distorted sound rising and falling. And of course not understanding a word he said. The Battle of Britain was being fought; Captain Tunner gave us all the information he received from his sources. FDR had called for Congress to enact a draft law, which was passed, only it was called The Selective Service Act. At the appointed time I joined several hundred young men at Rozelle School to be registered. It seemed quite a lark as we lined up, and there was a lot of horseplay. I received a big hand when I presented my identification card showing that I was already a Second Lieutenant in the Air Corps.

Captain Tunner was making almost weekly trips to Washington on some mysterious business that he didn't discuss with us, but he returned from one trip wearing the oakleaf of a Major. He told us that there was no way we could stay out of this war, despite all the talk to the contrary. He advised us to apply for active duty as soon as possible, and added that this would also give us seniority over the coming masses. That made sense to me, but I had a wife and son, so I hesitated. Red went on and asked to be called up, requesting Bombers, on Tunner's advice. He was assigned to Kelley Field as an instructor in B-17s. I suppose they taught him to fly the thing first. He later brought one of the forts to Memphis and let me look inside once. I flew them much later and found them very easy to fly. Just a big old Cub!

The Battle of Britain was over, or so the papers said, and now little Britain stood all alone bracing for the invasion that Hitler threatened. We listened fascinated to the magnificent oratory of Winston Churchill as he mobilized the English language to brace his people for the coming 'blood, sweat and tears'. His 'So Few' speech sends shivers down my spine to this day. I consider him to be the greatest statesman of our era. These sentiments seemed to pervade our whole nation. Quite a few pilots from around Memphis packed their bags and headed for Canada and the CRAF, some to fighting units and some to ferrying bombers to England, which was buying anything that could carry a bomb. One of our boys, Watt King, was aboard as a passenger returning from a delivery when the airplane hit a mountain in Scotland.

All this was tearing at my insides and I knew I must soon come to some decision. To be honest, I think it was the knowledge that I would be absolutely miserable if I didn't become part of all this. I don't recall discussing any of this with Eleanor, as I already knew what her reaction would be, so I came home one day and told her that I had requested Active Duty for a year with duty in a Fighter Group. Stout fellow that she is, she took it a lot better than I had expected. In due course I received orders assigning me to the 12th Observation Squadron stationed at Fort Knox, Kentucky. For a period of one year, effective November 6, 1940. I was devastated. Observation?? For the world's most fantastic acrobatic pilot?? Unthinkable! But there it was. Later I realized that the Army didn't consider a Second Lieutenant who was pushing thirty years of age the ideal candidate for the high aggressiveness required for the Fighter Pilot business. And they were right.

I went to Fort Knox in the P-12 to get some idea of what I was in for and see what the housing prospects were like. I met the Squadron Commander, Captain Robert M. Lee, a fine gentleman of the old school, who to this day I hold in the highest esteem, and used as my role model from that day on. There was no housing available on the base so I was given a car to go into Louisville. On the way back I stopped at a bank in the little town of Shively to see if they might help me with the housing problem. There I met the manager, a Mr. Hillary, who turned out to be our landlord. He had converted what had formerly been a hen house into an apartment. It had one bedroom, a tiny kitchen, and indoor plumbing. The heat came from a pot-bellied coal stove. You could see the ground between the gaps in the floorboards, but we loved it.

I returned to Memphis the next day and started winding up our affairs there. The back seat of our old Ford easily carried all our worldly possessions, and Eleanor held Jimmy in the front seat. She kept a stiff upper lip until we were out of town, but then I saw she was quietly crying, and sobbing, "What are we doing, what are we doing?"

For maybe a second I was tempted to turn back.

We moved into our new home the next day.

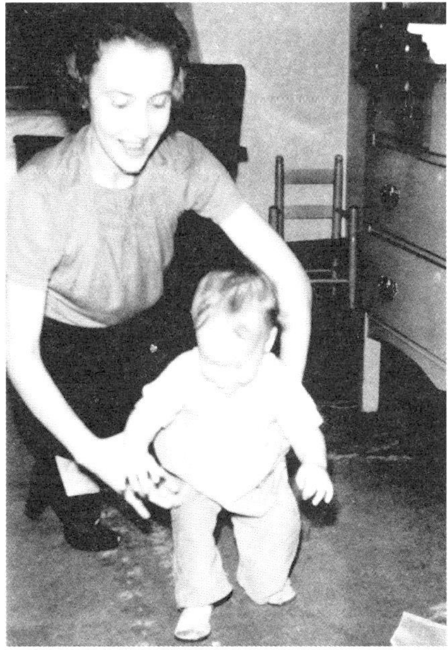

Haun family photo

Home Sweet Chicken-house

12th Observation Squadron - December 1941

U.S. Army Air Corps photo

Haun family photo

Committed and Ready

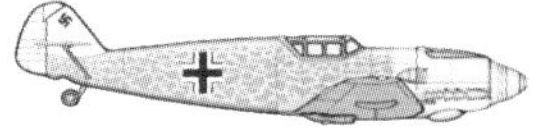

chapter eight

FORT KNOX

1939 – '41: "ROOKIES ON THE RAMPAGE"

Bright and early on the 6th I dressed up in my uniform and found my way through massive traffic and construction equipment to the Squadron area on the airport. There was a flagpole in front of one of the better buildings, which I rightly judged to be the headquarters. I had re-read the bit in *Customs of the Service* on how to report on arrival to a new station and was all set to do it right. I walked into the office that said "Adjutant." There was only one person there behind the desk. I failed to notice that he was a Master Sergeant. I marched up and saluted smartly.

"Haun, James R., Second Lieutenant, reporting for duty, *Sir!*"

The Sergeant sort of tucked his head and almost whispered, "You don't have to do that."

Very old Sergeant Moore; they made him a Colonel shortly after the war started and he was a good one. I spent the rest of the day checking in with the various offices, but I didn't salute any more Sergeants. I learned that the 12th was an old Regular Squadron that had seen service in WW I and was quite proud of it. All the officers were West Pointers with many years' service, and most were about my age. The motion was awfully slow in the peacetime Service. As the only Reserve officer aboard, I decided best I keep both eyes and ears open and my mouth shut. Seemed to work out fine.

The Squadron had four or five old airplanes that they flew once in a while, mainly on Saturday mornings. Fort Knox was an old Cavalry post that was gradually turning into Armoured Force post, and the Air Corps was there to act as the eyes of the Division; we were considered as more or less part of the Division. We even wore the high, peaked caps of the Cavalry! I had to buy a Sam Brown Belt that you hook your sabre to, although I didn't have to buy a sword or spurs. Our mission was exactly the same as it was in WW I. That was to photograph the battle area and act as spotters for the artillery when they were firing.

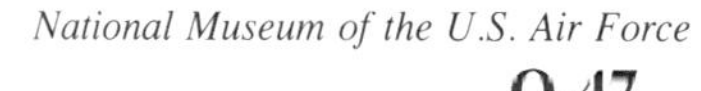

National Museum of the U.S. Air Force

O-47

I got checked out in the O-47 Observation airplane. This was a rather nice flying bird and had been considered quite advanced in the thirties. It was a pot-bellied job with one pilot, a radio operator/photographer in the belly, and a gunner/observer in the rear cockpit. It had a 900 horsepower Wright engine, retractable landing gear, and for weapons two .30 caliber machine guns, one mounted in the left wing and the other for the gunner. Awesome fire power!

Well, I flew that thing around a little and was then told I must take an instrument check. There were no published let-down charts available in those days, so I made my own, using the Louisville range with an approach to Bowman Field. The check pilot, Lieutenant Bagby, took me up to about two thousand feet and told me to pull down the hood. This was a canvas thing that I pulled over my head and covered the cockpit completely so there was no way I could get a glimpse of the outside. I was quite used to this from my training at Memphis. Bagby flew around for a while to get me sufficiently lost and then told me to turn on the radio, orient myself on the range, and locate the station – all of which I accomplished quickly, with extreme accuracy, and even if I do say it myself,

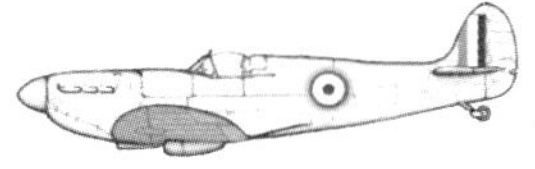

faultlessly. I hit the station at exactly two thousand feet and turned to my outbound heading to start my letdown.

Then Bagby popped the hood and said, "Return to the field."

I was completely confused. What could he possibly have found wrong with my performance? When we got out, I asked Bagby what was wrong.

He said, "Nothing, you did good."

"But I had just started my letdown when you pulled the hood."

He whipped out the regulation covering instrument flying. "Here, read for yourself... ***Instrument Check Ride:*** *Pilot shall orient himself on the range and locate the station.* You did it." That was all there was to it in the year of our Lord, 1940, in the US Army Air Corps!

Martin B-10B

National Museum of the U.S. Air Force

The squadron had one old B-10 bomber that wasn't flown much and the idea of getting some twin engine time appealed to me. I approached the Operations Officer and broached the idea. He asked, "How much time do you have?"

I said, "Fifteen hundred hours."

"I mean, how much time in military aircraft?"

"Three hundred and ninety three hours."

"Well, you must have 400 hours before you can fly a twin engine aircraft."

So I got busy and volunteered for any trip available or anything nobody wanted, and in due course came up with the magic figure. "Captain Revard, I've got 400 hours now and I would like to get checked out in the B-10."

"Go ahead, the crew chief will show you the systems."

"Won't anyone come along to show me what I need to know about how it flies?"

"Look, Lieutenant, the airplane has room for only one pilot and there are no duals in the rear cockpit. There's nothing to it. Just shove in both throttles at the same time and off you go!"

The B-10 was the first bomber built that was faster than the fighters, or 'pursuit planes', of its time. It had retractable landing gear, flaps operated by the pilot using a crank on the right side of the cockpit, and engines mounted in nacelles on the wings. The engine instruments, such as oil temperature, oil pressure, RPM, etc. were mounted on the nacelles and readily visible to the pilot from inside the cockpit, after he learned where to look for this vital information. There was room for a crew of three: The pilot, under a sliding canopy on top of the fuselage, a bombardier in the glassed-in nose, and a gunner in the rear cockpit. It was covered with a corrugated metal skin. I hadn't been able to locate an operations manual for the ship, so the crew chief helped me get both engines running, while showing me all the taps, buttons, and switches.

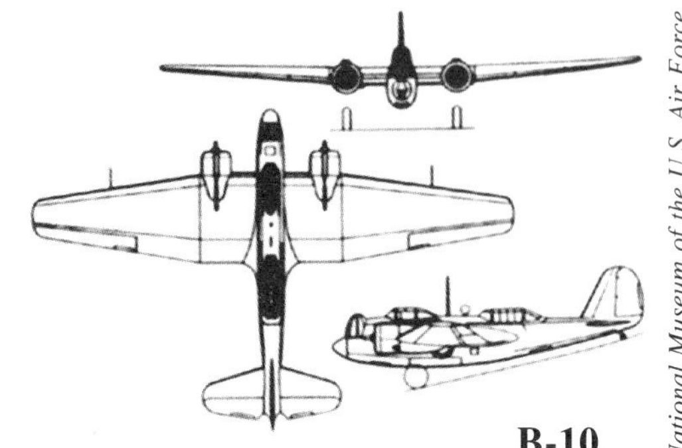
B-10
National Museum of the U.S. Air Force

I taxied out, using the engines separately to make turns plus a little brakes and it acted like any other tail dragger

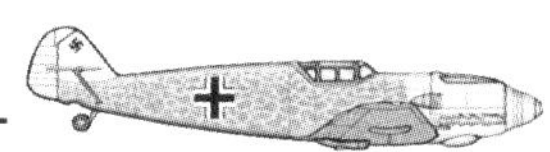

would. The crew chief had advised me not to use any more than 30 inches manifold pressure, as more might damage the engines. Comforting thought! I got it lined up in the middle of the runway and slowly advanced the throttles. I left the tail on the ground until I had good rudder control and she lifted off nicely; then I picked up the gear. I reduced power slightly but had trouble reading the instruments on the right side as the sun was in that direction but I got the left engine reading right and set the other up by sound. At two thousand I leveled off and reduced the power some more. I certainly didn't want to put any strain on those ancient engines.

Haun family photo

The old bird actually flew rather nicely, sluggish on the controls but nice and stable. I was enjoying it…looka me, Joe, in this great big twin engine airplane! I was crossing the Ohio River and happened to be looking out at the left wing tip when I hit a little bump, or thermal. The wing tip flexed at least a foot – I quick reduced more power and headed back toward the airport. I got the gear down and used some flaps on approach. I made a nice smooth wheel landing and parked the airplane; then I went in to see the Engineering Officer, Captain Alness.

"Captain, the wings are loose on that B-10. I hit a bump and they flapped!" He laughed and told me to wait until I hit real rough weather and watch them flap. Well, I was now officially a twin-engine pilot!

Captain Lee put me to work first in the office with the Adjutant, learning all about morning reports, how to find any regulation, correspondence, and all that good stuff. After a month there I was moved around to Supply, Maintenance, Motor Pool, the whole bit. The Squadron was organized to be self-sufficient and could be moved at a moment's notice and operate independently on a bare field. After I had spent about six months learning all the inner workings of the Squadron I was at least partially prepared for the responsibilities that suddenly fell on my head when the war started.

The Army was suffering a money crunch, which meant that we were allowed to fly four hours a month, which qualified us for an extra fifty dollars' Hazardous Duty Pay, but very little more. I played a dirty trick on Hook, because misery loves company. I wrote him about all the flying I was doing and what fine duty this was and sure wished he was here to enjoy it with me! Well, he bit and applied for duty at Fort Knox! Naturally he got his request in record time, and I barely escaped with my life when he arrived and saw what was really happening. We finally made up and decided we would set about reforming the Air Corps into something resembling a fighting force. You know, we actually did do a little good in some areas.

We had to go through the Armed Forces School, where we learned to use all the various weapons and become familiar with their tactics. I was out trying to drive a tank one cold, very dark night. I had seen the tanks knock down trees and ride right over them. With half a dozen other tanks we were crawling through a little woods and I decided to see if I could knock down a tree. I picked one about six inches in diameter and rammed into it full bore. I knocked the tree down all right but then crawled right up on top of it, and there I sat. I was straddled on the downed tree and my tracks were both off the ground, spinning like mad but going nowhere. One of the other tanks came up with a chain and pulled me off. I wouldn't have made a good tanker.

We got to fire all the weapons, including some light anti-aircraft stuff, tommy guns, and the flexible .30 caliber machine gun. Hook and I spent most of our time on the skeet range at the

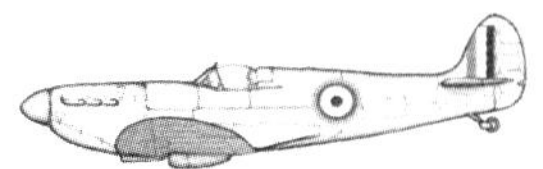

airport. We burned up case after case of ammo. Very few of the other pilots seemed to be interested in shooting, so we had all theirs as well as ours to burn up. Really wasn't much else to do.

I got one job that I approached with some reservations. The ground forces were given a certain amount of ammo to use firing on aerial targets; our squadron was to tow the targets, using the B-10. The target was a cloth sleeve maybe ten feet long on a cable that was let out of the rear cockpit of the airplane, seventy-five or a hundred yards. You would think that was enough distance to make this a very safe operation, but one pilot came in with only three feet of cable remaining. He advised the Operations Officer that if he wanted any more targets towed, it would be necessary to find another pilot. Guess who was assigned that duty? Right. Me. I didn't mind when the ground pounders were using machine guns, as I assumed they would at least be looking through the sights on the gun and would no doubt recognize the difference between the sleeve and the airplane; but when they started using stuff that exploded, I'll admit I sat as far forward in the seat as the seat belt would allow. I felt sorry for the guy in the back operating the cable drum as he was some ten feet closer to the action than I was. Luckily we never took any hits.

Legends Archive photo by permission

I saw General George Patton for the first time as he was climbing into the back of one of our 0-47s for a ride back to Fort Benning, Georgia, where he commanded the Second Armored Division. He was only a one star General then but he looked just as fierce as he did later. He was hawk-faced, gray haired, and had the most icy-cold pale blue eyes I have ever seen. To me he looked like 'Authority' personified.

Time dragged on and finally we were ready for the annual fall Louisiana maneuvers. The Squadron packed up and moved to our first camp at Marshall, Texas. The Red Army and the Blue Army were at it again, hot and heavy. This time they seemed to have more equipment than before, but not much. There were still trucks with 'TANK' painted on the sides, but there were some real ones as well. I saw artillery pieces that I hadn't seen before, and heavy trucks to pull them. Also there seemed to be far larger numbers of troops in the marching formations. There had been some promotions: Major Lee was transferred to Washington and Major Alness was now the CO. We did the usual flying around over the whole operation and dropped a few messages, but didn't take a single picture, at least not from the air. I did have one new experience though. I was sent over to Esler Field to pick up two old Colonels and deliver them to Tullahoma, near Camp Forrest, in Tennessee. Because the weather was a little iffy, they wouldn't go, so we delayed until the next morning. When my passengers showed up the next morning there was a solid overcast, that looked to be quite low. As they climbed aboard, complete with parachutes, they informed me in no uncertain terms that I was to stay under the clouds and under no circumstance was I to enter that gray stuff.

One reason I never made General came out right there: "Colonel, I have orders to take you to Tullahoma, and I will. The weather may force me to enter clouds. Also if this engine quits, I'll give you time to bail out. If you don't, you'll find yourself there alone!" They shut up.

There was no weather station at Esler and no reports were available, but I had good visibility on the runway, so we blasted off in the old 0-47. As soon as we lifted off, I leaned over to reach for the gear handle. When I looked over the nose I was on solid instruments. I glanced over the side and

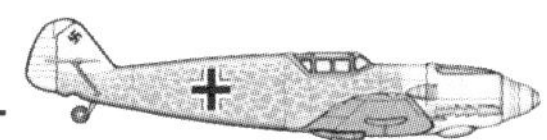

back at the instrument panel. Big mistake! My first case of vertigo and at only about 50 feet off the ground! All my instincts told me I was in a turn to the left, but the instruments said I was in a level shallow climb. Hardest thing I had ever done was to obey old Slim Paine's admonition, "Always believe your instruments: they are right, vertigo can kill you."

We came out on top at about one thousand and the rest of the trip was uneventful. When we landed, the two Colonels got out and never said a murmuring word to me.

After a couple of weeks we moved to a strip in North Carolina. My log book doesn't give it a name and I don't remember. I should, as it was there I met General Patton for the first time. I use the word 'met' advisedly. Returning from a death-defying and most perilous flight over the battlefield, I landed and taxied to my usual parking spot, but found a small civilian airplane right where I wanted to park. Hard right brake and lots of throttle and I blasted me a clear spot. Damn civilians! I shut down and unbuckled but before I could get out, up the wing came the maddest and meanest looking man I had ever seen. General Patton! Seems he owned his own little Stinson that he used to run around the battlefield in by himself. Well, he discussed my parentage, the legality of my birth, the level of my intelligence, and some of my other missing attributes. Then he stomped off. I hadn't hurt his little bird, just got it all dusty. I was to come in contact with him again.

U.S. Army Air Corps Photo

Our next move was to Greenville where we pitched camp on the nice airport there. I got the job of flying General McGruder and General Scott around over the area and keeping up a running commentary on what we were seeing below us. I gave them a nice quiet ride at a little over a thousand feet where they could identify the various types of arms and equipment on display. When we landed, they invited me to have lunch with them and their staff. After a lot of small talk, General Scott called on me.

"Lieutenant, in actual war would you have flown that mission the same way you did today?"

Well, he asked me. "No Sir, we wouldn't have lived five minutes. If I should have the extreme misfortune to show up over a real battlefield in that airplane, there wouldn't be but one way to handle it. That would be to go over as high as I could and then stick it straight down and come across as fast as I could. Anything else would kill you."

General McGruder growled: "We're not interested in casualties."

"No Sir, you're interested in getting information. One way I might get you a little, the other way, nothing at all."

Before McGruder could explode, General Scott bailed me out: "Lieutenant, what sort of airplane do you think we need for that job?"

"General, we need the fastest little fighter-type aircraft available with vertical and oblique cameras mounted in the fuselage which can be automatically operated by the pilot."

General Scott was all smiles. "That's exactly what I told Hap and he agrees." (Hap Arnold was the Chief of the Air Corps.)

I got out of there in a hurry.

The Red Army under General Patton was trying to build a pontoon bridge across the Pee Dee River so they could outflank us Blue Army guys, and naturally we couldn't stand for that! So those two famous fighters, Hook and Haun, armed with a full load of one pound sacks of flour leapt aloft in their trusty 0-47s, and sped to the attack! We tore into them Reds with furious, slashing attacks that turned their tanks white and had their troops leaping off the pontoon bridge to escape our whirling propellers! Then we returned to receive the plaudits of our admiring comrades. That night

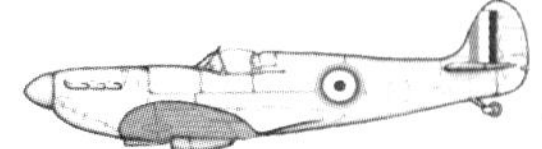

as we sat around the supper tables recounting our exploits, someone yelled, "ATTENTION!" And as we jumped to our feet, standing smartly braced, in walks General George Patton! He looked us over for a while and didn't seem much impressed with what he saw. Locking his gaze on our CO he addressed him thusly: "Harvey, your boys did a good job out there today, very realistic; but I want you to tell the little bastards to stop knocking the aerials off my goddam tanks." Then he walked out.

The Blue Army had won the war and we packed up to go home. Orders came down stating that due to the increasing tensions between various nations, all reserve officers presently on active duty would remain on duty for an indefinite period. For Hook and me that meant the entire war. After awhile you have it memorized: "Officers presently on active duty would remain on such, would not be released, but would be extended."

When we arrived at Fort Knox things began to change rapidly. All but one of the original officers left for other duties, forming and staffing new units. Some of the old sergeants and airmen went to form cadres, and we received a large group of pilots right out of flight school. Dick Morrison became CO and I was made Operations Officer. The draft was in full swing; the 1st Armored Division was flooded with recruits. They were called 'selectees'. The word 'draftees' was not to be used. There was a tremendous amount of construction going on. Hook and I drove together each day on the only road from Louisville to Fort Knox; that was one mad ride. With thousands of cars bumper to bumper and pedal to the metal all the way. It soon got where we paid little attention to the screaming of brakes or the rending of metal.

Someone from the Fort came over and approached us with the bright idea that maybe the ground troops could be supplied by parachute. I saw that this might work, so we set about working out the details. The old B-10 could drop bombs out of its bomb bay – why not bundles using parachutes? Trouble was there were no parachutes available except those reserved for our own tender rear ends; and when we asked Wright Field if there was anything available, they laughed at us – naturally, as it wasn't their idea. In fact, during the war and probably even today the Air Force cannot get any piece of equipment that has not been invented or approved by Wright Field. In England during the War, I saw a display of combat equipment some enterprising Group Commander had made with a big sign that read, "The Wright Field Follies of 1943!" More about that later.

Well anyway, with natural American G. I. ingenuity, the 'gravel agitators' came up with their own big chutes they had made using TOW SACKS! We tried dropping the stuff, weighing up to three hundred pounds, with only fair results as those home-made chutes didn't work very well. But the Brass saw the potential and put pressure in the right places, and you know the rest. I hope the lad that thought it up got the recognition he deserved, but I'll bet it was his boss that got promoted… Goes with the territory.

A couple of factory men brought us a fine little airplane for our evaluation as a light liaison aircraft. As a two seater with a lot of power, it could take off and land in a very restricted area. I jumped in and leaped off. It was a dream! After five minutes I knew this was one for the books. It handled very much like Red's old Clipped Wing Monocoupe, so I turned her loose and let her show her ability. Eight point rolls, square loops, the works. The whole Squadron was out watching, so naturally I put it to its limit. When I landed the two tech-reps swarmed all over the bird. All the cowling and inspection plates came off; they really went through the whole aircraft with a fine tooth comb. They told me that it had been

L-5

U.S. Army Air Corps Photo

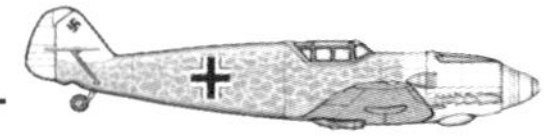

flown only twice and then only straight and level! They were afraid I had overstressed it, but the G-meter showed I had only put 3.5 Gs on it. They cowled it up and Hook insisted that we go up and let him see what he could do with it. Hook was a very good pilot and learned quickly. We had a lot of fun with that little bird – until we had to give it to Wright Field. That ruined it. They added on everything but the kitchen sink and changed this and that. Then they named it the L-5, and many were built. Some are still flying, but you should have flown the original! That was one fine little bird!

We had one of the first C-45 transports. Today they are called the Beech 18, and there are still a lot of them around. Being the high-time pilot in the Squadron, I used it to haul the Brass around. Boy, was I proud of myself! I might have let Hook fly it, but he was off somewhere. We didn't have it long, as someone ranked us out of it.

Then we got orders to go to Buffalo, New York, and pick up some new airplanes made by Curtis-Wright. I think someone drew the plans and the Army bought it sight unseen. Couldn't have been any other way. It was a two-seater observation airplane designated the 0-52, sometimes known as the Owl. A miserable bunch of junk. High wing with the gear retracting into the belly, and an antique hydraulic system that required the pilot to grasp a long lever in his right hand and give about 50 strong pumps to get the gear up, and the same to get it back down. It was overweight and underpowered, and didn't have enough wing either. A killer by design, it killed a lot of pilots, as you shall see. Nine of us went by rail to Buffalo and picked them up. Brand new. At least they smelled good.

Our first stop on the way home was Cleveland, Ohio. As we circled the field I saw a large crowd lining the fences. Must be an air show or something. We all landed successfully and the crowd dispersed. I asked someone what was going on and he replied that they knew we were coming and wanted to watch us tear them up on landing. Seems there was a large stack of the wrecked ones on the field. They were a bit tricky to land, and it's too bad we disappointed the crowd. I played around with one a little and found that it would spin out of a sixty degree bank if you tightened it a bit. I warned the others, but it must not have sunk in.

We also got a pair of Douglas A-20 light bombers. We were told to go pick them up at Bowman Field. Hook and I went over to get them and found them sitting all alone at the end of the field. There was nobody around that knew anything about them. One fellow said he had noticed they always taxied with the cowl flaps open and that they closed the upper ones before takeoff. I could see this was a good idea as the nacelles were flush with the upper surface of the wing, and open flaps would cause the loss of a lot of lift. With this wealth of information we climbed into the cockpits and tried to figure out how to operate the beast. The master switch was located and the batteries were up. There was plenty of gas in the tanks and everything was labeled and arranged right where you might expect to find it. We both cranked up and checked all the systems.

I made two bad mistakes. I put the elevator trim tab wheel in "neutral" and didn't tighten the throttle lock. Can you see what's coming? Hook did the same thing. Taking the lead I tore off down the runway and she lifted off nicely. I reached for the gear handle but the nose pitched up so that it took both hands to hold it down. When I took my left hand off the throttles to grab the wheel, the engines slowed down to almost idle! I was as busy as a one-armed paperhanger for a few minutes but finally got the trim set and the throttles both locked down. Then I looked back for Hook and

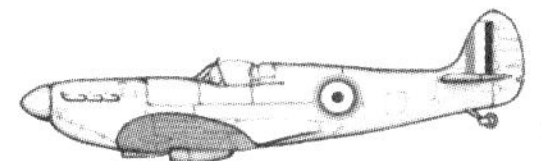

saw his airplane going through all the gyrations I had performed. He got it under control and we arrived at Godman without further problems. The entire Squadron was out to see our landings, and we got all the usual questions tossed at us, but we were in too big a hurry to get to the hangar to talk. I told Hook to grab a couple of Cokes while I got my locker open. I had a fifth of Baccardi which fortunately was already opened. I think we flew those two airplanes once or twice more before someone came with orders to take them away. Things were sure well organized around that time.

It happened to us again shortly after the A-20 foul-up. One day twelve twin-engine Lockheed Hudsons landed and the ferry crews said they belonged to us. Actually they had British markings on them, and they had an open hole in the top of the fuselage where the gun turret was supposed to be installed. Some clerk had hit the wrong key and they came to us by mistake. I asked one of the ferry pilots to check me out but he acted like I was crazy, and the whole bunch were set to leave in a hurry. Naturally, before they were taken away I was going to fly one of the things. The operations manual was written in the King's English, but I could figure it out. The airplane used 'petrol' instead of gasoline, the propellers must be in 'fine' for takeoff and the radios had 'valves' instead of tubes…things like that. Hook gave me a blindfold test to see if I knew where all the controls were. I passed and told him I was ready to try it. I expected him to get out but he buckled in. The airplane had only one pilot's seat, but there was a folding canvas one on the right where the bombardier sat until he was ready to fold it up so he could go down a tunnel to the nose. I got the engines running and they sounded good. They were big Wrights and you should hear the roar they let out in 'fine' pitch. I checked Hook and several others out before they came and stole our toys. You should try checking a pilot out in a strange airplane without duals! Par for the course.

Haun Family Photo

"So those two famous fighters, Hook and Haun, armed with a full load of one pound sacks of flour, leapt aloft in their trusty O-47s and sped to the attack!"

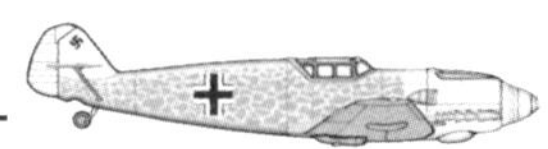

chapter nine

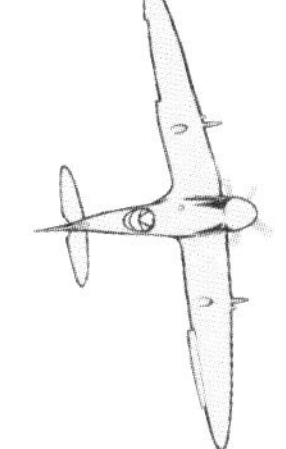

WAR

1941: "ANTICIPATING THE INEVITABLE"

December 7th, 1941 was a nice, warm, cloudless day in Kentucky. Our little henhouse home had a back yard around a mile deep where I often spent time shooting at tin cans, or whatever offered. My .22 Colt Woodsman was hot and the tin cans were jumping most satisfactorily. Eleanor came to the back door and called for me to come listen to the radio. A place I had never heard of out in the Pacific Ocean had been attacked by the Japanese! It was called Pearl Harbor in Hawaii. My first reaction was surprise. What could the little 'slope-eyes' be thinking about, to attack the mighty U S of A? We all knew from reading the intelligence summaries readily available in the Squadron that their equipment was copies of our old and obsolete ships and airplanes. Even their front line fighter aircraft had fixed landing gear. We had pictures of all their stuff. We had sold them the plans for their battleships that were guaranteed to turn turtle when they were launched! (One did.) I didn't know that all our summaries were at least ten years old like everything else we had to fight with.

I called Hook, jumped into my uniform and we headed for the Field. Most of the Squadron had arrived, and we just sat around wondering what we could possibly be expected to do with our four 0-47s and six 0-52s. The entire fleet mounted eighteen little .30 caliber machine guns and nothing else. Someone had forgotten to put the wheels down on the B-10, so we didn't have that thing to worry about.

The British had a saying that covered the situation nicely: "When in doubt, run about, wave your arms, scream and shout."

We didn't do that; we sat around and played poker – for the next week or two. Then we got half a dozen officers from the Armored Division who were to be observers, as they were familiar with all the equipment and tactics of the ground forces and therefore could make much more accurate assessments of what we would be seeing from the air.

Someone up the chain decided that we should be flying all day and all night to hone our skills and make out like we were really doing something besides playing poker. So we divided up into shifts and started in. As Operations Officer I scheduled the airplanes and crews. Every airplane must have a full crew when it flew. I also acted as the control tower operator most of the time.

One night we had all the available ships in the air, and I was about to leave the tower when a frantic call came from one of the 0-52s. He reported that he had a fuel pressure warning light on and was returning to base. I told him to reduce power and be ready to use the "wobble pump" if the engine started losing power. I saw him coming with his navigation and landing lights on. He made a steep turn to final; the airplane whipped into a spin, and hit just short of the runway. There was some fire but not as much as you would expect. We were using Hook's car that night, which was parked close, so I jumped in that. The fire truck had already gone. When I arrived, the fire was still burning but was a little away from the fuselage, as the wing containing most of the fuel had been torn away at impact. A few rounds of ammunition were popping off but doing no damage. The fire truck was doing no good at all as the old brittle hoses broke when they were pulled out, and only succeeded in making a mess under foot. Someone said that the pilot looked like Hook, and I would

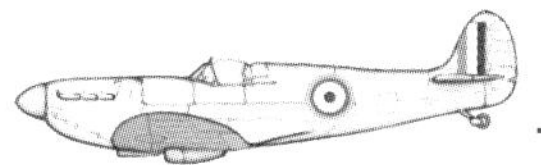

have to tell Jewel, his wife. The fire was spreading toward the cockpit, which was split open, so I walked up and got ahold of his parachute harness and pulled him out. He was dressed in the issue fur-lined leather flying suit, and he sloshed inside it. I'll bet every bone in his body was broken and the top of his head was gone. There was nothing left inside. For some reason I said, "I always knew the bastard never had a brain in his head." The nameplate on the jacket said CAMP. "Oh boy, Camp – and Hogan in the rear cockpit."

National Museum of the U.S. Air Force

While we were standing there waiting for the ambulance, another of those damn 0-52s came in and circled to see the wreck. He tightened his turn for a better look and spun in and hit within fifty yards of the first one. Two more dead. I believe that was Drew. Hook came in a little later and was somewhat upset when he saw what a mess I had made of his car dash trying to find the light switch. I had pulled everything off that would come loose. I don't remember if we got a new fire truck or not. Of course it wouldn't have made any difference anyway.

A few days later one of our new Observers and I were pulling OD (Officer of the Day) duty when we heard there was a big promotion party scheduled at the Officers Club that night. Of course us Fly Boys were not invited and probably wouldn't have gone if we had been. Kwoleck, however, had a bright idea as to how to liven up what would no doubt be a most tiresome affair. Somehow he sneaked into the hospital supply section and came out with a gallon of pure grain alcohol! The Club had prepared several large punch bowls of the usual non-alcoholic brew, into which Kwoleck divided his contribution in equal measures. Making my after-midnight rounds, as prescribed, I went by the Club at just about sunup. What a sight! Full dress uniforms and lovely evening dresses, each containing a body, were draped over and under shrubs, or sprawled over the lawn. Definitely a most memorable party. A diligent investigation failed to identify the culprit.

Hook came up with a solution to the night flying problem. He took one of the 0-52s at around two thirty or three one morning and, with the propeller in flat pitch and wide open, proceeded to practice strafing over the officers' quarters. In flat pitch and wide open that engine screams like a banshee. Orders came down the next day that eliminated the requirement for the night practice as we had reached a state of training that made it unnecessary to continue. So we went back to poker playing. What else?

The spring of '42 was a most frustrating period. People were transferred in and out at such a rapid rate, it was difficult to know who would be around each day. I was flying the Brass around in the C-45, visiting practically every Army base in the South. I wrangled one trip to Washington and went over to the Air Corps Headquarters to visit Major Tunner. This was before the Pentagon was built and the HQ was located in a wooden building on Pennsylvania Avenue, along with all the rest of the military. Tunner introduced me to the officer in Personnel in charge of assignments. I was hugely anxious to get out of Observation and asked for either Fighters or Transports. He didn't have a word to say but shook his head and walked away. That night I got a cab and told the driver to show me the places of most interest. That is an exquisite city at night with the Capitol, the White House, and all the monuments flooded with light. I can't describe the feeling that came over me as I stood in front of the Lincoln statue. I suppose it was a dedication, or love of country, or a resolve to serve with the very best in me. Maybe all of that. A most solemn moment for me, coupled with the knowledge of our repeated defeats in the Pacific.

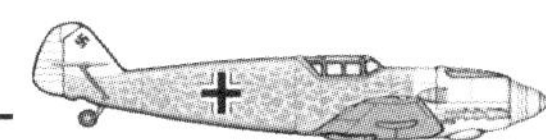

Word came down that the 12th Squadron was to leave Fort Knox and move to Esler Field, Louisiana, near Alexandria. There we would join three National Guard Squadrons to form the 67th Tactical Reconnaissance Group. There was the 107th from Michigan, the 109th from Minnesota, and the 154th from Mississippi. Lieutenant Colonel Anderson had been the Squadron Commander of the 107th and was now to be the Group CO. He had joined the Canadians during WW I, flown a Sopwith Camel for one mission and was shot down. Or so he said.

A quick trip to Esler showed there was very little housing available, so Hook and I left our wives in Memphis and drove down. We found a Tourist Court that had one room available upstairs over the office and I took that. There were five or six other rooms as well, which I reserved for our Squadron as they became vacant. There was one bathroom at the far end of the long hall. I went back to Memphis and brought Eleanor and Jimmy down. We were real cozy in that one little room, in the summer, before air conditioning had been invented.

Hook and I were both promoted to First Lieutenant. We had grown some really magnificent mustaches to differentiate us from the baby-faced Second Lieutenants who made up the bulk of our unit and bought new caps that we crushed down over the left ear after removing the inner plastic ring. Real 50-mission jobs. We even soaked them in a rain barrel to help the reshaping. You see, I was 31, and nobody really knew Hook's age. We had slipped into the courthouse basement one night back in Memphis and made him up a birth certificate so he could get in the Army in the first place! A man's gotta do what a man's gotta do.

That summer continued to be one of mass confusion. People came and went, and where they went nobody seemed to know, or care, really. The turnover in our airplanes was much the same. I am looking through my log book and can count twenty-six different types that we had. There were four kinds of fighters, five kinds of bombers, three transports, and the rest could charitably be called Observation…and I had the job of checking-out the pilots – that is, after I had learned to fly them myself! If they had only one cockpit for the pilot, the best I could do was give them the old blindfold test and tell them what to expect as to their handling characteristics. We had great success and didn't break a single one! In fact I think we set a record.

I came in from a two-day trip and found the Squadron practically deserted. All the old heads had been transferred to other bases. Someone said Hook was over in the Carolinas someplace. Colonel Anderson sent for me and I reported to HQ. There I was informed that I was the new Squadron CO and must be ready to go overseas within a month! Well. Back at the Squadron I looked around to see what I had left to form a squadron with. Fortunately they had left me with three old sergeants who had been in the outfit a long time, so I got them together and we had a serious talk. They knew as well as I did how ill-prepared I was for this job. I told them that I could handle the flying end but they would have to handle the rest, which included training the officers who would be the nominal heads of the departments. Asked where we could find a good First Sergeant, they came up with a guy from the motor pool. He was a great big bruiser who said yes he could handle the job – and he did. We had little or no disciplinary problems. I think he handled those out behind the shed in the Old Army fashion.

A bunch of newly commissioned pilots right out of Advanced Training reported in to fill us up to strength, along with a large number of enlisted men. Some had previous training but most were raw recruits. The old sergeants had their work cut out for them, and they did an excellent job.

We were now equipped with six A-20 light bombers and six P-43s. The A-20 was built by Douglas and was a very nice flying airplane. It carried a crew of three, with one pilot, a bombardier, and a gunner – an airplane that we had no use for at all! I liked the two Pratt & Whitney engines

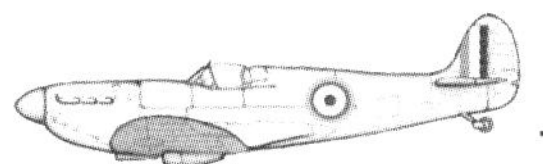

and the speed, and I enjoyed the two forward guns at ground targets down on the Gulf, where Gulf Shores is now. The P-43 was a beautiful little fighter, the forerunner of the famous P-47. It was fairly fast and had two .50 caliber guns firing through the propeller and two little .30 caliber guns in the wings. It had a turbo supercharger under its belly like its big brother, but you couldn't turn it inside two city blocks in spite of its little short wings. At first I thought it was going to be ideal until a P-40 out-turned me. I still thought about aerial combat in the terms of the legendary 'Dawn Patrol' dog-fighting, at which I absolutely knew I would be the world's most greatest. Was I in for a surprise!

We were told that we would shortly receive P-51s with cameras. We had one P-51 that was a dream. It was one of the early ones with the Allison engine and had four .20 mm cannon in the wings. Unfortunately it also had an electric prop. I'm glad we never got that model.

The new guys had to be checked out in the P-43, although they had never flown anything hotter than the T-6, which was very docile and forgiving. I took the whole crowd out beside the runway and sat in the shade of a B-25 wing to watch the other squadrons turn the little birds into scrap metal, which they did on a regular basis. I explained why they were not to attempt a three-point landing, but must always make wheel landings. I explained that with those little short wings a stall would cause the left wing to drop so sharply that the wingtip would beat the wheels to the ground.

As we sat there we saw one guy coming in with the obvious intent to three-point it. I yelled, "Watch this!"

And sure enough the left wing dropped, the airplane cartwheeled and was a complete washout. The boys took the lesson to heart, and when we finally left Esler, all six of our P-43s were still sitting there intact. They were lovely little airplanes but would not have been able to compete in the real world. I believe some of them may have been given to the Chinese. Ding How!

U.S. Army Air Corps photo

I had an interesting experience in the B-25. For some reason I took it to Monroe, Louisiana one day. The airport there had a brand new blacktop runway. A rain squall was over the field when I arrived so I had to wait awhile before landing. The B-25 had a nose wheel but no steering other than the brakes. After touchdown I was rolling along nicely and had to use a little brake to slow up. One of the brakes must have been a little stronger than the other because we made the nicest, smoothest ground loop on that wet runway you could imagine. We ended up sliding backwards down the runway and it took some power on both engines to stop. The tower called to ask if we had any trouble.

I replied, "No, we always land this way on wet runways." I really liked that airplane and would like to have flown them in combat.

The Squadron had by now taken over the Tourist Court; most of the married officers lived there. A number of the single ones had a large house in town they were well pleased with. They told me it had mirrors on all the walls and ceilings, but I never saw it. Our Court had a nice lobby downstairs where we gathered. One afternoon I came home and found the ladies had four or five tables of Bridge going. Jimmy and I had a regular routine of going to the John together when I came home. Upon our return to the lobby, and during a moment of absolute silence, Jimmy in a loud voice informed the gathering that, "Jimmy has a little bitty wee wee, but Daddy has a great big one." Eleanor didn't tell me if there was any further discussion of the subject after my hurried departure.

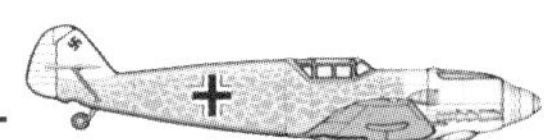

I had been a First Lieutenant only a month when I was promoted to Captain, and most of my young pilots were up to First Lieutenant. Not all of them. There was one named Delmont J. Sylvester III. He got out of an 0-47 and told the crew chief the battery seemed low so he was leaving the battery switch on to let it charge up! Another time he narrowly avoided landing downtown one night because a well lighted street looked like a runway. I decided Delmont needed a little more time.

We were very short of administrative officers to take over the various sections, but I got one that I just couldn't accept. He was a breezy, extroverted cat, and a Captain. I told him I needed an Adjutant, but he said he had only been in the Service for one week and had no idea what being an Adjutant entailed; he had Public Relations in mind. He claimed his daddy knew a Senator who had secured a direct commission for him. I called Group and told them to get him a set of orders to somewhere else. A couple of years later I heard that he was the acting Occupation Mayor of some town in Italy.

Orders came down to prepare for an overseas move. The ground echelon was slated to go by ship while the airplanes were to be flown to our destination. We had the six A-20s but our P-51s had not arrived, so it was decided the air echelon would remain at Esler until we got them. We were told to take only winter clothing, which was a dead giveaway on where we were going. It had to be England. We had a lot of equipment to be packed and crated – that was quite a hassle. We received masses of literature, or 'poop-from-the-Group', which we mainly ignored, as we were quite familiar with the drill, thanks to our experience on maneuvers. I had one unpleasant experience that I was in no way prepared for. The MPs brought in one of our radio operators who had been apprehended downtown in a homosexual act. I asked the First Sergeant if he or anyone knew anything about this guy; everybody denied knowing a thing. I decided he had figured out a way to get out of going to war, and I wasn't buying that. I told him I knew I was supposed to court-martial him but we were so busy packing up there just wasn't time; for all I knew, we might end up in the desert where his talents might be appreciated! That guy hated my guts. In England we had no need for gunners or radio operators, so they were all sent to bomber units. I doubt that many survived 1943.

When the time came for the move, our new airplanes had not arrived, so the ground echelon left by rail, and the rest of us sat around waiting and waiting. I told Eleanor there was no way we could know when I would have to leave, so we had to make plans for her and Jimmy to go to Memphis. It had been settled; they would stay with her parents for the duration. Finally we got word that our airplanes were not coming so we would go by ship. We were graciously given several days notice as to our departure date, which was rather unusual during wartime, even though we would leave by rail. Eleanor's parents drove down and stayed until I left. Eleanor and Jimmy drove me to the station that night. We were not to see each other again for three years.

Haun family photo

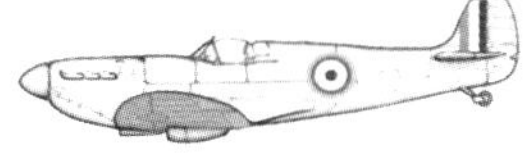

New Zealand
Fighter Pilots Association

U.S. Army Air Corps photo

With enchantress at last.

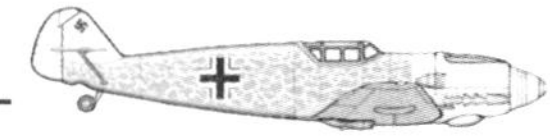

chapter ten

TO ENGLAND

1941 - '42: "DODGING U-BOATS & MEETING THE SPIT"

The train ride lasted a couple of days but we were allowed, or ordered, to get off several times to stretch our legs. There were no bunks, even for such a high ranking hero as me. It was the typical troop train: not the most ideal mode of transportation, especially for a bunch of fly-boys, but eventually we arrived at Fort Dix in New Jersey. There we were marched through some very muddy company streets to our tents, where we stayed a couple of days, strictly confined. Then we were moved to the dock area somewhere in New York City, and straight to our ship. As I approached the gang plank, or whatever they call the stairs used to get aboard, I stomped the ground once for good luck and went up. I have been blessed with a most vivid imagination! It was at this time (I learned later) that the U-boats were having their greatest success in the Atlantic.

I don't remember the name of the ship, but it was a Dutch passenger liner about the size of the old *Joliet* and had diesel engines. There must have been at least five hundred of us aboard. I shared a tiny stateroom with three other guys. The door was locked open in case we were torpedoed and we wore Mae Wests all the time. We had it good compared with the troops packed in below. We could at least walk out on the deck, while those poor guys had to stay below all the way over. Us officers ate in the large dining room and were waited on by little brown men from the Dutch East Indies. The food was excellent.

We left the dock at daylight and moved out into the Bay. There we were joined by a large number of other ships that made up the convoy. Our ship took up its station, which was number last on the left outside column. Passing the Statue Of Liberty, we were on our way. There was some air cover, and a small blimp went along ahead. The mighty battleship *Texas* led the parade, with several destroyers ahead and on the flanks. We headed in a general northerly direction for several days and came to anchor at Halifax. There we waited for three more days while more ships arrived. Then we headed out.

In a convoy, the speed is regulated by the slowest ship, so everybody can keep station. Every fifteen minutes or so the *Texas* would send out a blast on her horn and change course either left or right with no set pattern or degree of turn, called zig-zagging. The leading destroyer would rush full speed to where we were headed and then stop dead still and sniff around for U-boats. Our old tub would be left quite a way behind when we made right turns and had to hurry to catch up during the left turns. I'll admit to feeling rather lonesome when we were left so far behind. There were two destroyers on each flank but one stayed way ahead. We must have had company, as every day just at dawn or just before dusk the destroyers would be seen working as a team with much rushing about; then both would stop, rather close together, and after a little we would hear depth charges going off. We didn't have any air cover after the second day. We were lucky; no ship was lost from this convoy.

I did get one scare after we had been out about a week. I went on deck early in the morning, and there within fifty yards on our right was a black U-boat, complete with the big ugly cross on its conning tower! I tried to yell, but nothing came out. It turned out that the British had captured the thing and used it on various spy missions. He stayed with us a couple of days and then disappeared.

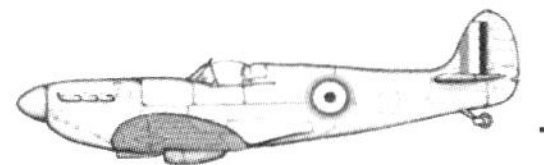

There was plenty of fire power to have handled a U-boat on the surface, including both 5-inch cannon and anti-aircraft stuff. On clear days they would sometimes send big balloons up, and the whole crowd would cut loose on them with everything they had. They were terrible shots.

U.S. Army Air Corps photo

We had fine weather all the way across. Finally, having passed close enough to Northern Ireland to see it, we started getting some air cover as we approached Scotland; and I saw my first Spitfire. I was amazed at how quiet it was. All our airplanes are quite noisy, but that little thing just sort of hummed as it circled around ahead of us. When we entered the bay, or wide river that leads to Glasgow, we got a wonderful look at the countryside of Scotland. Passing the dockyards I saw many ships under construction and some that obviously had battle damage. The largest one I saw had the bow all 'stove in'. Maybe one of the Queens.

We disembarked and loaded directly onto a train that pulled out almost immediately. That train had more speed than any I had ever ridden. It ran flat out but had the most pitiful whistle. During the night we came to a screeching halt and sat there for maybe thirty minutes. The Conductor came through…"Not to worry. Old Jerry is out tonight, but the lads will deal with him shortly."

The rest of the trip being uneventful, we arrived at the little town of Newbury, where we were met by a fleet of trucks that took us on out to our brand new airfield named Membury. We went to the mess hall and got our first taste of Spam, mashed potatoes, peanut butter and jelly, with powdered milk. And that was one of the better meals. We were to become quite happy with things that came out of cans. We were shown the showers and were delighted we could have one hot bath a week. There's a war on, chum.

Our squadron living area had the usual tar paper construction. For heat each room included a little pot-bellied stove with a ration of coke for fuel. I could see that we were going to be snug enough in our new home away from home. That night we were listening to Berlin Radio, as they had the best music, and 'Lord Haw Haw' came on and welcomed the Air Echelon of the 67th Group to Membury. Made us feel so welcome!

U.S. Army Air Corps photo

I am going to find it hard to write about the next six months, as there was nothing going on really worth telling. There we sat, an entire Group of four squadrons with nothing to do, in weather that was cold and damp. We had classes on various subjects, like 'Escape and Evasion', which I attended religiously, inspired by the thought of spending years behind barbed wire. Of course I was quite confident that no German could shoot me down, but there was the possibility that an engine could quit, as I had had that happen many times in the past. We had one exercise where we were sent out into the country in a sealed truck and turned loose to see if we could get back to base without being captured by

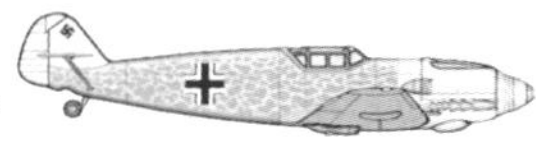

the local constabulary or the MPs. We could carry no money or other identification. The only restriction was that we could commit no mayhem. Russ Berg and I teamed up. We wore our Trench coats and no insignia. A lorry stopped for us and we crawled in with the driver. He found us to be the most uncommunicative people he had ever met, as we were forbidden to speak English. We got out at Reading and failed to thank him. In the town market square we spotted a jeep with an American driver. We stuck our hands deep in our coat pockets, mobster-like, and approached the kid. I made a vicious growl, "*'Raus mit uns*," with my cruel, beady eyes boring right through him. He got the message and jumped out right smartly. We broke various restrictions on the return trip, like failing to obey the orders of the police to halt. We were first two back, and Colonel Anderson upbraided us for breaking the rules. We pleaded 'not guilty', as the simulated shots fired at us were all clean misses!

We had no movies, and if there were any USO groups around, they avoided us non-combatants. We had a few dances at the O-Club, attended by WAF and WREN women brought in from nearby stations. I doubt if any serious romantic attachments were made. We did get two little airplanes to fly. They were Tiger Moths, the primary trainer that practically all RAF pilots learn to fly on. I had flown the earlier model at home but these had a larger engine and handled beautifully. As all pilots are required to fly at least four hours a month in order to draw the extra pay for 'hazardous duty', there wasn't time for much extra flying. We also got in twelve Piper Cubs to store. Naturally we didn't leave them in storage, especially since they were in flying condition. One day I organized a formation using all twelve and we had a ball. Out on the Downs north of us I spotted a horse-training farm complete with jumping hurdles all neatly lined up. I went down and found that by bouncing the wheels just before reaching a hurdle you could clear the hurdle and had room to repeat at the next one and so on. Having completed the course, I looked back and saw all the rest, in line astern, doing the same. The property owner was watching from the sidelines and seemed to be enjoying the show, so we all landed and were invited to the house. He produced a quart bottle of very fine Scotch, and the whole assemblage toasted the inevitable victory.

U.S. Army Air Corps photo

I was sitting at the end of our runway in a Moth when I saw a real live Spitfire circle the field. I cleared the runway to watch his landing and got quite a surprise. Approaching on a high final and fast, he pulled up a steep climbing turn, kicked the gear out while practically on his back, put down full flaps, and turned final in an almost vertical side slip! I knew for sure he would spin in right on top of me! Anything we had would have certainly snapped into a spin. But he dropped in, fishtailed and greased on a three-pointer. I couldn't believe my eyes. That airplane flew just like the old ones I had grown up on. It was love at first sight.

We started receiving Spits until we had more than our compliment. The spares were for breakage, which as it turned out, we needed. The Spit didn't have a hydraulic system, but instead used compressed air to activate the gear, flaps and brakes. The control stick had a spade-grip on top that had the firing button and the brake lever. When you squeezed the lever you got brakes in

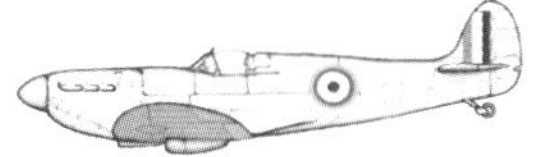

U.S. Army Air Corps photo

whichever direction you pushed the rudder bar. You had five or six squeezes before the air supply was exhausted. The runway was built five or six inches above the grass, so there was a drop-off at the edge. Several fellows ran out of air and off the runway and ended up on the nose. Russ forgot to lower his gear and slid in on his belly. The airplane was built as light as possible, with lots of power and plenty of wing, with nothing that wasn't absolutely necessary to weigh it down. Ours were the old Mark V-B and earlier. Some had two 20 mm cannon plus four .30 caliber machine guns, all in the wings. The only thing that restricted the airplane was the small fuel supply. It carried 87 imperial gallons and was intended to fight over England as an interceptor, which it did, with outstanding success against the Luftwaffe. Of all the airplanes I've ever flown, that was far and away my favorite. It was beautiful on aerobatics, would turn on a dime, and climb like a homesick angel.

We also received some maps of the British Isles which caused a little trouble, being of a much different scale than ours. These showed as a river what we would call a creek. Every little town and patch of woods stood out. I flew time and distance, so I had no trouble, but some of the guys would get lost and take several days to get back, having landed at many fields to ask directions. There were no radio aids, but that didn't matter as all the ship had was one little four channel VHF set. But we learned, and were soon flying all over the country. Fly east or west, and when you see water, turn around! Especially if you were going south!

It took us a while to get used to the frequent air raid warnings. When the siren began its moan, we were supposed to head for our bomb shelters and remain there underground until the 'all clear' sounded. We had several shelters in our squadron areas, within easy sprinting distance. After taking shelter on several nights when no bombs had fallen, we became rather slack in responding to the siren's wail. One night a large poker game was in progress, and that thing started up again. Someone came out with the statement, "It won't hit you unless it has your name on it." There was silence for a moment until a small voice in the rear said, "I wonder what method they use to put names on bombs." We all departed for the shelters. We learned to listen to where the guns were firing, and then decide if the raid was coming our way; if not, go back to sleep. No bombs ever fell near our base, but if you went to London, raids were a frequent occurrence.

Haun family photo

Several of us had planned on going to London to see a play at one of the theaters, arranging to meet at a little hotel, the Erie Mansions, on Germaine Street, just off Picadilly Circus. I was late leaving the base and took the train by myself. On the English trains, after buying your ticket, if you have any luggage – which I seldom had other than a musette bag – you tossed your suitcase into an open baggage car without checking it. Nobody

would steal it. Also no one checked to see if you had a ticket, which would be taken up at the exit gate at the London station. I forget the name of the station, but the name 'Waterloo' comes to mind, or maybe 'Paddington'. I took the Underground and got off at Picadilly.

There was an air raid on and the Underground was packed with people, some sleeping or just sitting it out. I went outside into a total blackout and listened for the guns. The raid seemed to be after the dock area, so I started walking. There was sufficient light from all the searchlights reflecting off some lower clouds to make walking easy.

A girl's voice said, "Hello Yank."

I stopped and asked her how she knew I was a Yank.

She said, "You have rubber soles on your shoes."

I went on down to Germaine Street. In the middle of the street an old fellow was banging away on a barrel organ, which is, or was, a common sight in London. I never saw one anywhere else. He was playing *The Warsaw Concerto*, and yelling at the night sky: "Barstards!" accompanied by the guns and the searchlights. An Air Raid Warden walked up and suggested that we get under cover, with the reminder that, "All that goes up is bound to fall down," and there was plenty going up. But I elected to stay with the old man until the 'all clear' sounded.

Col. Haun photo

Stuka Dive-bomber

Bob Walker and I took a taxi to the Savoy Hotel for supper. On the menu I spotted 'Scottish Quail'. My taste buds quivered and I told the waiter, "That's what I'll have." He sort of whispered, "You don't want that." I kept insisting, so he shrugged his shoulders and departed. My quail turned out to be two pitiful little English Sparrows! Bob had some sort of meat that I'm sure had worn shoes on its four feet. The waiter rolled up with his little cart and made up, with many flourishes, a fine sauce. Bob asked him if he had any A-1! He didn't ask if we wished any dessert. We went to the theater. The play was most forgettable. There's a war on, chum.

I did scratch the paint on another airplane. We had several very early model A-20s that had belonged to the French but had been flown to England when France fell. There was one that had been rigged up as a night fighter by sawing off the nose and installing a huge searchlight, with the bomb-bay filled with batteries. I can see why that idea didn't go over very big, especially for the pilot. But there was another one that hadn't been modified. With nothing better to do I put one of our new pilots in the nose and two others in the rear cockpit. We played around the countryside for a while – did a little ground strafing on the Downs, etc. The only entrance to the front, or nose compartment was from outside, through a trap door in its floor. After we took off, the lad up front somehow got that door open and couldn't get it closed. When I lowered the landing gear, the nose wheel would not go to the down-and-locked position because the door, folded back by the wind, got in the way of the wheel strut. I flew around for a half an hour trying to see if the boy could either get the door closed or jettisoned. Nothing worked. Well: If I landed with the mains down and the nose wheel retracted, I would slam that boy on the ground pretty hard; and if I made a wheels-up landing the door would be blocked, he would have no exit, and there might be fire. So I told him he would have to bail out. At two thousand feet over the airport I slowed down to just over a stall

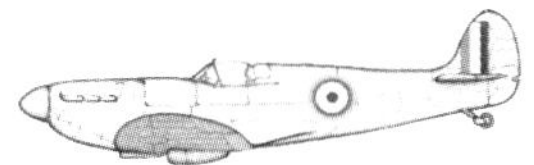

and he left. The two in back asked if they should bail out but I told them to sit tight. I called the tower to send out the fire trucks and they lined up on the runway. I made one mistake I won't make again. With gear up and full flaps down at about twenty feet off the ground, I reached up and cut the switches. That was the mistake. That airplane fell like a ton of brick, but I just barely had enough altitude to cushion the drop and the landing was fairly gentle, except for that awful grating and grinding noise that a belly landing always makes.

U.S. Army Air Corps photo

My parachutist had been drifting badly when he landed: his foot caught in a hole, his ankle broke, he stayed in the hospital several months, married his nurse, and went home!

We had an RAF squadron-leader come to advise and assist in getting us ready for combat. His name was Ginger Neal and we all liked him. He had been in the Battle of Britain, so he knew what he was talking about. Someone higher up had decided that, as we were flying Spitfires, we were therefore fighter pilots and should be used that way until we received our P-51s with their cameras. Ginger told us how the RAF had started flying in V-formation and line-astern and why they had to change to the finger-four that became standard worldwide. We practiced until we had that down pat. We even got to do a little shooting at ground targets! Finally we were scheduled to escort a squadron of British light bombers to a target on the coast of France.

Colonel Anderson had his own idea as to how this job should be done and explained it to the Group in great detail during the before-mission briefing. It was weird. My squadron, the 12th, was to put twelve ships, line astern, on the right side of the bomber formation, with the 109th doing the same on the left side, and the two other squadrons somewhere in the back. If attacked, he, Colonel Anderson, flying by himself out in front of everybody, would direct fire by calling out, let's say, "Scornful squadron, Red section, turn right and fire."

When we started to go out I called, "Twelfth Squadron, I don't want any of you guys turning on your gun switches while you're in this formation, or you'll shoot me right in the ass."

U.S. Army Air Corps photo

Anderson didn't like that a bit. As we walked to our ships, Ginger eased up to me and handed me a strip of masking tape, "Better stick this over your gun camera. We've had some of our chaps get into big trouble over this sort of thing."

It turned out all right anyway because either we were just a diversion, or the British saw what was happening and aborted the mission.

Spring had come and our area was solid mud. When it dried a bit, I got a good supply of grass seed and some rakes and had the troops making pretty designs and planting. I heard some of the guys growling about now we'll have to be cutting it. Colonel Anderson came by and complimented us highly, and I was promoted to Major. (That must have been before our famous escort job, described above.) Well, time went on and one day the First Sergeant came into the office with the word that there was a lady outside with her daughter, wanting to see me. The lady came in, and after some chit chat, informed me that her daughter was pregnant by one of my men. I asked her for the man's name, but the daughter wouldn't tell. I told them that if I didn't know who the man was there wasn't a thing I could do about it, and they left. I asked the Sergeant what he thought, and he allowed that it might be half the squadron, as the pub where the

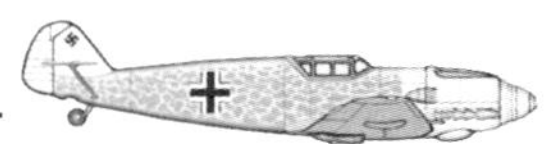

girl worked was a favorite hangout for the troops. In those days the squadron CO paid the troops in cash himself. The next payday I had all the troops line up for pay call and took the opportunity to make a little speech. It went something like this:

"Now men, the Squadron is going to have a baby. I'm putting my hat here on the table and I think it would be mighty nice if every one of you guys dropped in a pound toward the expenses." They all did. I sent all the money to the girl's mother and forgot all about it.

Time went on and one day a big picture of a brand new baby appeared over my desk labeled 'Our Baby'.

He, or she, was as black as the ace of spades! They never let me forget that.

12th over England 8/31/43

U.S. Army Air Corps photos

A-20 save

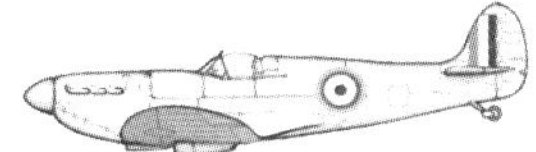

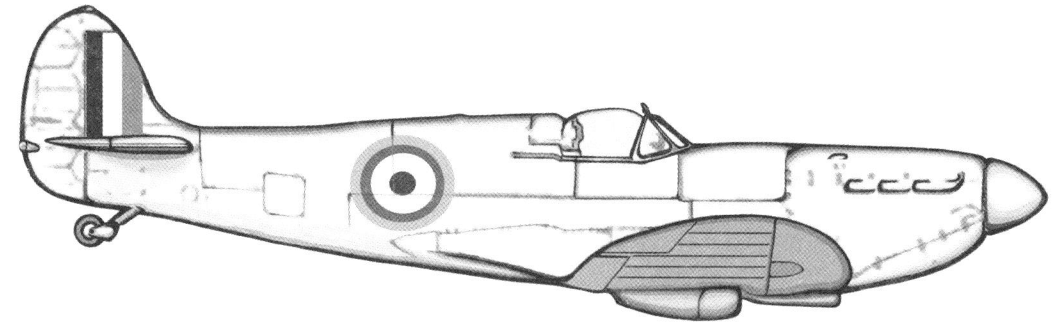

U.S. Army Air Corps photo

"Up and at 'em!"

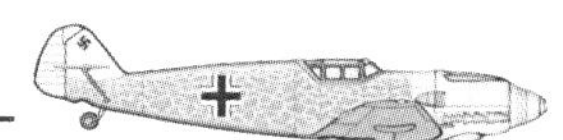

chapter eleven

FARMED OUT TO THE RAF

1943: "HAVE YOU EVER WATCHED A FRIEND STREAM DOWN IN SMOKE?"

After the so-called escort fiasco it was apparent we needed some training in the fighter business if we were to act in that role. Instead of sending us to one of the Fighter Training Schools the RAF used to prepare their pilots for combat, our Brain Trust decided that some of us should go direct to operational units on the theory that one learns fast when the bullets start flying around! This may be true, but not highly recommended as the ideal. So the 8th Air Force made a deal with the RAF to take some of us. I requested and received orders assigning me to the 485 New Zealand Squadron stationed at Biggin Hill south of London, for thirty days period. I asked Bob (Pappy) Walker if he would like to go with me and he did. We packed our gear and took a jeep for the trip.

Biggin Hill had been badly knocked around during the Blitz but most of the field had been repaired and retained few signs of damage. We had very comfortable quarters and the Mess was nice. I met Johnny Checketts, the Squadron Leader, who had been advised of our coming and was obviously not overjoyed at the prospect of taking on two rookies. I told him what my experience consisted of, that I had never fired on an aerial target, but I had considerable time in the Spit 5-B. He told me that he had lost six wingmen but I could fly with him under the condition that should we find two Huns and he got one, I could have the other. Naturally I agreed. He further said that, as I would have a fuel tank directly in front of me, a hit could mean I would be sitting in a ball of fire, so I must always keep my goggles over my eyes, wear long sleeves and gloves, and my American parachute was no good at all as it had no quick release like the British ones. He demonstrated why…if my hands were badly burned I would be unable to get rid of the chute in case I was going down in the Channel, in which case I would certainly drown. I was supplied with the proper chute and fur-lined boots.

248

R.A.F. STATION BIGGIN HILL

OPERATIONS SECTION

CELEBRATION PARTY

to commemorate the pranging of

1000 HUN PLANES

at

THE ROOKERY, BROMLEY COMMON

on

Thursday, 29th July, 1943

From 8.30 to ? ? ?

Refreshments Dancing

Col. Haun memorabilia

I was then introduced to the Wing Commander, Alan Deere, one of the ranking aces from the Battle of Britain. He was a handsome man who looked like he had been carved from stone. He had been shot down nine times, but not a scratch showed on him. He was very cool and aloof, and I began to get the message: they had orders to take us but it was under protest. Al took me to see the Group Captain, Sailor Malan, who was also a top ranking ace. He was a South African, large, who never looked at me, only straight ahead. Well, I had orders sending me there, so I would just have to make the best of it. I don't recall ever talking to another member of the squadron except Johnny, and him rarely.

I can understand the cool reception we received. No squadron likes to get new men who cannot be depended upon to perform as team members in the deadly game of combat, where every man's life is at stake. My job was to fly on Johnny's wing and keep him covered so he could concentrate

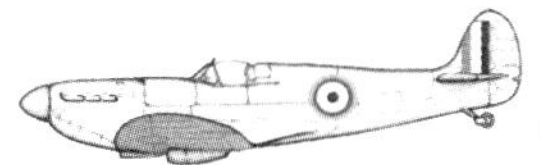

U.S. Army Air Corps photo

on the attack, and he knew I wasn't trained to do that job. When I told him I had never fired on an aerial target, he said, "Just run your gun barrels up his arse and pull the trigger!"

That sounded easy if they would just sit still while you do that!

The Squadron was equipped with the late model Spit 9-B, which was much improved, having more power and better performance at altitude. It would out-climb and out-turn anything flying in Europe, which ability was to save my neck that month.

Our first mission was to escort a few light bombers to the Le Havre area. The object was to get the Germans to come up and fight, but they didn't choose to play that day, so the flight was uneventful. We were at eighteen thousand feet; I was amazed to see how dark the sky is up there. I had never been over ten thousand before. The next day it was an escort to the St. Omer area, where there were several fighter airfields. We crossed the channel at 'naught feet', which means you don't let your prop touch the water and it keeps you off the radar screens. When you get close to the coast you can hear the radar when it sweeps over you. Makes sort of a 'whumppp' sound. That's when you go to full power and climb like mad to get above the light flack before crossing the coast, but the Germans throw up a lot of light stuff anyway. It looks like white golf balls and seems to float up real slow until it gets close and then it really whips by, or explodes. They didn't waste much of the heavy stuff on us but saved it for the bombers. Naturally we stayed a fair piece away from the bombers! Again there were no fighters, and that was strange, as this was the home of the famous Yellow Noses.

U.S. Army Air Corps photo

The next day was July 14th, Bastille Day, 1943, and the B-17s were going to Paris to help the French celebrate. As we were suiting up Pappy was acting sort of strange. He didn't speak and had a faraway look about him. When we cranked up I looked over and gave him the high sign, but he didn't answer, just sat there looking straight ahead. We crossed the coast and climbed up to the bombers. You don't get close to them and you certainly don't point your nose at them or out will come a red cloud of tracer. I know the German pilots must have had a lot of guts to dive into that storm…but they did.

As we neared Paris Johnny started a dive and I went wide open after him, but he drew away and I couldn't keep up. I saw another airplane diving off to my right, and when I looked back, Johnny was gone. I looked around and found myself all alone in an empty sky. I've heard of many pilots reporting the same thing. Look around and everybody disappears. That happened to me several other times. I heard Johnny call for us to regroup on the port side of the bomber formation, so I headed in that general direction. I was weaving, trying to see under my tail all the time and climbing. Off to my left I saw a lone Spit climbing straight away, without weaving. Suddenly from above a FW-190 dived on that Spit. I yelled "BREAK!" but there was a lot of chatter from the French squadron in the Wing, and the pilot probably didn't hear me. I turned toward him but it was too late. The 190 fired a short burst…a small streamer of white smoke came from under the belly of

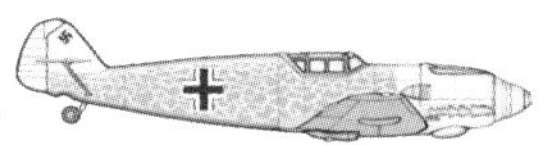

the Spit. The 190 and I were on a collision course and came so close I almost hit his tail with my prop. There was a big black eagle or hawk painted on the side of his fuselage. He disappeared under me, so I looked for the other Spit, but it was gone; I was again all alone. I stuck the nose down and ran wide open all the way back to England. Pappy didn't return, and someone reported seeing a Spit go in near Beaune.

Johnny was upset at me for breaking formation, and so was I. I couldn't understand why he could pull away from me every time he went in on an attack. It happened several times. Al Deere had me in his office while he called someone in 8th AF Headquarters, suggesting that I was going to get killed from breaking formation. Whoever it was he talked to said that to make an omelet you had to break some eggs. By this time I had my back up and kept flying.

artistic rendering from photo on Supermarine pilot's handbook

One day I was scheduled to fly as Al's wingman. It was an ordinary sweep over France. We were at eighteen thousand, and after a while I saw that we were by ourselves. I thought, well, we are the bait and the rest of the squadron must be up in the sun.

Someone called: "Brutus, you are being bounced by six."

Al replied, "Yes, I see them. Now Major, stay in close and I will call the break. Then it's through the gate and a climbing left turn."

I was thinking, "The gate, the gate." From somewhere in my subconscious it came to me. If I push the throttle to the left and shove it hard I'll break a wire that restricts the forward movement of the throttle and the engine will develop its War Emergency horsepower, which can be used for only a few minutes. All this flashed through my mind in the time it took me to slide over into close formation. Now I knew what the trouble had been. Johnny always went 'through the gate' when he attacked! I think I actually laughed out loud. Now I can fly as tight a formation as the best – I was practically scratching the paint on Al's airplane. He called the break and we started a slow left climbing turn. In the thin air at high altitude all turns must be slow and shallow or the ship will stall. After a bit Al said, "You may look back now." I did and looked right down the gun barrels of the leader, with the others strung out behind him.

U.S. Army Air Corps photo

"Now watch me spin that first Barstard in; tighten it up a bit."

We did…the fight was over, and we headed home. I didn't open my mouth about what had happened, although I was tempted, and Johnny didn't lose me again!

The next time I flew with Johnny we were in the Poitou area. He called, "Major, today you get a shot; there are two of them." We went down in a diving left turn and lined up under them. I slid over to the right behind mine. When we were almost within firing range, they slowly rolled over

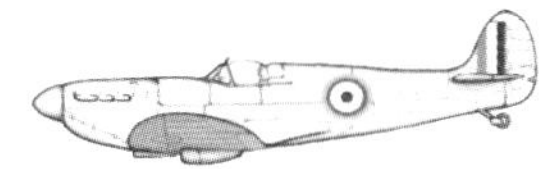

and dived. Johnny yelled, “Go home!” When we got home I asked them why we let them get away; it looked like we had them cold. He said, “They saw us, therefore they had a chance. That’s not the way you play this game. We’ll try them again tomorrow.”

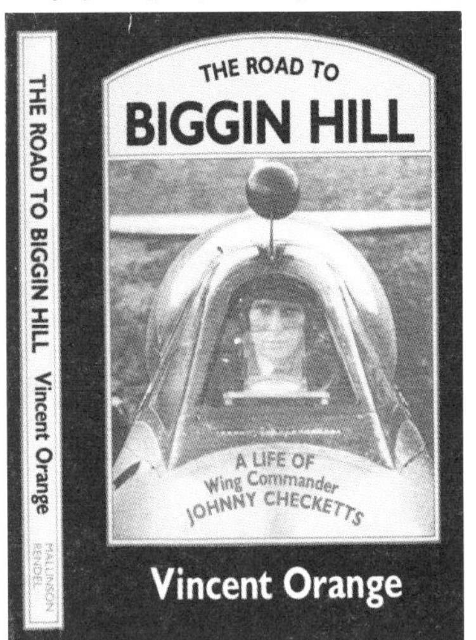

by Mallinson Rendel permission

My month was up and I had flown twenty-three missions with them. I had certainly learned a lot, so I went back to Membury. Johnny was shot down about three weeks later and was badly burned. His story is detailed by Vincent Orange in the book, *The Road to Biggin Hill,* in which Johnny describes his fight, and how the French underground helped him escape and return to England. I met him again in France after the invasion. He told me that an intensive search of the Beaune area failed to find any trace of Pappy Walker. [*Editor’s note:* Major Haun and Captain Walker are introduced on pages 85-6 of this publication from Mallinson Rendel; Wellington, New Zealand. In 1987 Johnny Checketts sent a first-run copy personally inscribed to ‘my friend Jim Haun’.]

Another pilot from the squadron, Johnnie Houlton, in his book, *Spitfire Strikes*, describes the same fight when Johnny’s plane was hit. Houlton was coming out of France by himself and spotted another Spit down low chasing an ME-109 and went to join up. High above he spotted fourteen FW-190s. Twelve came down and two stayed high. In that climbing, turning evasive action Johnny taught me, they reached the two top 190s but one of them got Checketts, who bailed out of the burning airplane, and Houlton escaped. It would appear that I was not the only one who got separated at times. Both of those fellows, by the way, do a better job of writing than I can. [*Note:* Houlton characterizes Major Haun as ‘a quiet, impressive man’ on page 110 of *Spitfire Strikes*, John Murray Publishers Ltd., London, 1985.]

by John Murray, Ltd. permission

U.S. Army Air Corps photo

I had one last adventure with the old 12th Squadron. The Germans were making some nuisance raids on the south coast. The papers called them “Tip and Run” raids. FW-190s would come across from the Cherbourg area, each carrying a single heavy bomb. They would stay right down on the water to avoid the radar, pop up over some coastal town, drop their one bomb, and run. They killed a few people, and then one day hit a crowded theater. The 12th was moved to an abandoned field named Ibsley, near the coast. We tried patrols, but that never works, so we went on what is called ‘runway alert’. We kept four aircraft sitting at the end of the runway so when we got a call from Sector we could scramble and then follow their vectors to the target. I had the Sergeant in Ops get a flare gun; when the phone from Sector would ring he would fire a red flare out the window even before he

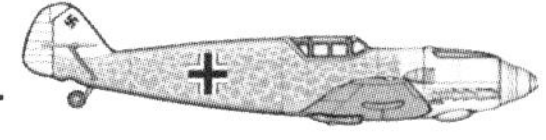

answered the phone. You didn't have to warm up the Spit, which had one tiny radiator under the wing. Even taxiing could cause it to overheat. This day I was sitting there reading a book and smoking my pipe when the red flare went sailing out the Ops window. I threw the book one way and the pipe the other and hit the starter button. As the wheels came up I called Sector (I forget the call sign): "Red section airborne." They gave me a heading and said, "Make angels," meaning get all the altitude you can.

Haun family photo

The Channel here is about seventy miles wide, and I was approaching Cherbourg. Sector called again and asked for my altitude. I told him twenty thousand. He said, "Good, he is under your left wing." I banked up to look and the engine quit. I mean it got real quiet! I looked around for my trusty three other airplanes, but there wasn't anyone in sight. Sector called and said, "He has seen you, you can come home now." I kept my mouth shut as I knew the German controller was listening, so I set up a glide for England. The prop was still windmilling, but the engine stayed quiet.

I had been warned that it's not a good idea to try to ditch a Spit because immediately after touchdown it will point its nose straight down and head for the bottom. I don't know if that's true or not, but I wasn't going to find out. At two thousand feet I'm going to roll upside down and leave it. I had the usual Mae West and a one-man inflatable dinghy attached to the parachute. I was sitting on that RAF parachute, which I had somehow forgotten to turn in. The Spit has an excellent glide ratio when it's clean, and I was getting along fairly well. About half way across I figured I could risk a call, so told Sector I was having a little engine trouble and asked that they keep an eye on me. There's a lot of water down there, and I sure didn't want to bail out, knowing my chances of being picked up were slim at best. At three thousand I got unbuckled and had the canopy open, and the engine hit one or two licks! It hit a few more times and a lot of black smoke belched out of the exhausts. At two thousand it was lurching along enough to keep me flying, and the coast was getting closer. I made it back to the runway, but had to be towed to parking.

We found that a diaphragm in the carburetor had ruptured, allowing the engine to have such a rich mixture it wouldn't run until it got down into thicker air. The other three guys had various excuses as to why they turned back. I knew what had happened. I had taken off and headed immediately on course, wide open, and they didn't have a chance to catch up. Don't blame them a bit. Of course I didn't apologize!

U.S. Army Air Corps photo

We were not having a bit of luck stopping the raids, so one day an RAF squadron leader landed at Ibsley in his

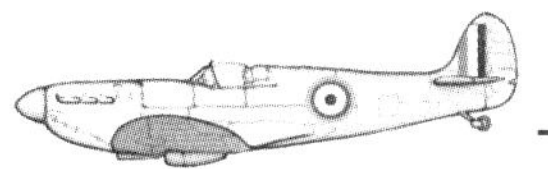

Haun family photo

Typhoon. He asked if I would object if he and some of his boys came down and had a go at the raiders. I thought that was a very nice way to convey Sector's orders! That Typhoon was quite some airplane. The ones I saw had a twenty-four cylinder X-type engine and bags of power, or so I was told. They put a stop to the raids in short order. Their tactic was to lay low out in the middle of the Channel and wait for Sector to call. Then they popped up; that's all she wrote. We folded our tents and returned to Membury, and I still hadn't got a shot.

The Eighth Air Force in England was a Strategic Force. That is, it was mainly composed of long range bombers and escort fighters. Their mission was to hit the industrial strength of Germany and thus impede that country's ability to make war. The planners believed that bombers armed with ten or more heavy machine guns could fight their way to targets which would be destroyed in daylight with pinpoint bombing. This plan required that they be sent beyond the range of the then available fighter escort, where they suffered terrible losses from German fighters and anti-aircraft fire.

The Ninth Air Force was being formed in England as a Tactical Air Force. Its mission was to support the ground forces in the immediate battle area; it was composed of light and medium bombers, plus fighters and fighter-bombers. Our 67th Tactical Reconnaissance Group was transferred to the 9th Air Force. At that time we were about the only unit available from which to draw personnel to man the new headquarters. When we heard that Brigadier General Quesada from 9th AF was coming to pay us a visit, I knew that a lot of changes were coming.

We had a parade and some of us were decorated with Air Medals and such for our heroic conduct in the face of the Enemy! Then we assembled at Colonel Anderson's office where he was to present his idea on how a Tactical Air Force should be organized. If you think his escort plans were weird, you should have seen this! When he put up his first chart I started slinking down in my chair. He had every Division with its own Air Arm! It was awful. I believe his thinking was dated 1916 or earlier. I rather liked the old man, but he didn't have a clue! Although the General didn't interrupt, I could see his face getting red.

After the meeting, Anderson was brimming with great expectations. "Jim, this is my year. I can feel extraordinary things coming for me."

He was transferred to 9th AF HQ and given command of the map room in the basement.

U.S. Army Air Corps photo

"That plan calls for WHAT?"

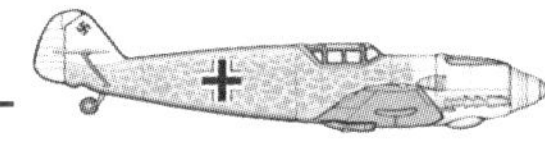

chapter twelve
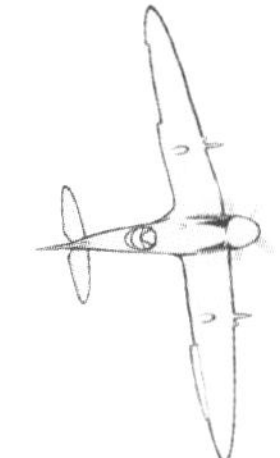

100th FIGHTER WING – PROVISIONAL

1943 – '44: "DIVEBOMBING: EMBARRASSMENT & FRUSTRATION"

U.S. Army Air Corps photo

George Peck became the Group Commander, while our 109th CO, Al Defer, and I went to 9th AF to learn our fate. I was told to form a Fighter Wing HQ using personnel drawn from the 12th and 109th Squadrons. Al tried to protest but I saved him from the firing squad by punching him in the ribs. I became the CO of the 100th Fighter Wing Provisional, with Al as deputy…talk about the blind leading the blind; but there wasn't anyone else available. I made one of our Observers, Sam Carter, Adjutant. We got some equipment and moved to Boxtead and then down to Aldermaston.

A new BG named Tex Sanders showed up, all slicked up and looking real sharp. I was wearing my old 50-Mission cap pulled down at its most rakish angle and a pair of black RAF flying boots, with trousers tucked in top. He took one look at me and said, "Buy yourself another cap." After looking through our records, he told me, "You will be Operations until I get a man I have asked for from the States; he's really on the ball." I requested that upon the arrival of this paragon I be shipped to one of the Groups. He grunted.

We got orders to send someone to Italy for thirty days to study dive-bombing. Who better than ole Jim. I hopped a ride to Prestwick, Scotland, where all the overseas trips operated from. This was the first time I had ever seen a C-54. It was a large four-engined airplane with beautiful lines. This one had regular passenger seats instead of the usual buckets. Up front, there were two large gas tanks strapped to the floor for extra range. The take-off worried me because of the very long run it took to get airborne. It was night and I couldn't see what was going on. I'm a terrible passenger anyway. We flew west for quite a while (the North Star was out my window) and then turned south. We were far out over the Atlantic beyond the range of German interceptors. After flying for several hours, to my surprise we turned around and went back to Prestwick. The tanks in the cabin were not feeding properly, so we had to change planes. Since it was nearly daylight, we had to wait until dark to try it again. This time everything worked right, and after flying all night and part of the next day we landed at Casablanca. The next stop was Algiers. There were still signs of the fighting, especially in the harbor. Someone told me the old *City of Joliet* was sunk there by bombing.

I rode a C-47 (Gooney Bird) to Fogia and another on over to my destination, a field outside Naples. I don't remember the name, but it sounded something like Campachino, or words to that effect. The squadron I was assigned to was equipped with P-40s, painted with desert camouflage, which had faded into an almost pink color. The Squadron CO was a very young Lieutenant Colonel

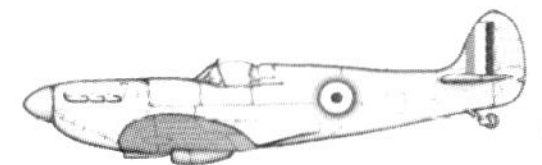

U.S. Army Air Corps photo

covered with ribbons. This was the Squadron that had pulled off the so-called Cape Bon Massacre. That was when the Germans were trying to evacuate some of their best troops to Italy using their JU-52 Transports. As I recall, some fifty or sixty were shot down. I don't believe I would have been very proud of doing that…but that's war.

The Anzio beachhead was bogged down with the Germans pinning them tightly to the beach. The landing had been well planned and executed; but the General commanding the operation had failed to take advantage of having no opposition, to push on inland, which gave the Germans time to gather forces to seal him in. Churchill commented that we thought we were flinging a tiger ashore but it turned out to be a dead whale. Of course the General was fired, but it took several months and many lives to correct that blunder. Our job was to drop 500-pound bombs on the German positions and also fly cover over the beach.

I was asked if I had ever flown the P-40 and I modestly assured them I could handle it. I would be flying someone's wing again, but that was what I was there for. Of course I had never flown any type of fighter with a big bomb hung on but didn't have any trouble. We avoided the battle north of Naples by swinging out over the Mediterranean. I was in the second squadron and looked down at the squadron below. That pink paint stood out against the bright blue sea, making them look like a bunch of butterflies. It also made the hair on the back of my neck stand up: From above that's exactly what I look like! Apparently there were no Germans around; I was told the Group had never been attacked.

Our target was what looked like a supply dump, just back of the lines, going in at eleven thousand, in line astern. We pulled the arming lever and, when directly over the target, rolled inverted and dived straight down. With the gun sight on the target we released the bomb and pulled out in a steep climb… I did not experience the expected blackout. We then circled the beach for about an hour. When this pattern took us over the German lines, they put up some AA fire, but for some reason they always picked on only one aircraft. The rest of us eased away from that hapless individual and made rude comments about his flying technique as he jumped about dodging the stuff. No one was ever hit.

U.S. Army Air Corps photo

Before going to Italy I had never even seen a bomb, much less carried one, so I had to study them now. When a bomb is loaded onto an airplane it does not have a fuse installed, so it can be handled safely. After it is secured to the shackles, then the fuse is screwed into its nose. Now it is hot, and if dropped, will explode. To prevent that from happening accidentally, a pin is inserted in the fuse that prevents the plunger from striking the detonator. This pin is attached to a cable running up to the cockpit to the arming lever. When the arming lever is pulled, the cable is locked so that, when the bomb is released, the

pin is pulled out and the bomb is hot. So you have two levers near your left hand: one to arm the bomb and the other to release it. More about that in a minute.

We were sent to hit various targets – gun positions and the like. We always used the same procedure. At eleven thousand feet over the target, roll inverted and dive straight down wide open. You would think this would be very accurate bombing, but for some reason the hits seemed to scatter all over the place. The P-40 had six .50 caliber guns in the wings, and the Group always fired them during the diving run. On the first mission I didn't fire mine; after landing, the flight leader remarked, "The old Major doesn't seem to want to fire his guns."

I got the same treatment here as I had at Biggin. I asked him what I was supposed to be shooting at.

U.S. Army Air Corps photo

P-40 Trainer

He said, "There are troops down there and it makes them keep their heads down so they can't shoot back."

That made sense, so from then on I would give them a good long squirt on the way down.

We hit the area in front of the Monte Casino Abbey a couple of times, being careful to stay well clear of the Abbey, for political reasons. Later the place was flattened by the bombers when it was suspected the Germans were using it as a strong point.

Meanwhile I learned that during the fighting in the desert each side captured grounded airplanes that could be put back into flying condition, and were. As a result it was wise not to let any other airplane come up behind you, regardless of the type. I saw an order from HQ that stated: "There have been numerous instances reported of combat between Spitfires and P-40s. This practice will cease immediately!"

We were returning to base when someone called, "Bogey, three o'clock, low." We eased over for a look and spotted a pointed-nosed, square-wing-tipped little bird. The Spit and the P-40 both have elliptical wings, so we started down. A distinctive Southern voice came over the radio, "This here ain't no Bogey. This is a P-51." And so it was. A Negro squadron, trained at Tuskegee, Alabama, was in Italy and equipped with P-51s. They did a good job and several outstanding officers came out of that outfit.

At the head of the Anzio Peninsula was the little town of Cisterno de Roma, through which ran the main north-south highway. Facing this road was a tall building. Someone had the bright idea that if we could put a 1000 pound bomb, with a ten second delay fuse, through the roof, it would go clear down to the basement, the building would collapse, fall over and clog the highway, and we would win the war. So it was set up. I decided to fly in the number last position so I could get a good look at the results. Now a P-40 with a 1000 pounder hung on is really sluggish; we pretty much staggered up to the beachhead. I pulled off to one side to watch. We were at the usual eleven thousand. Our ships rolled in one after the other, but they didn't hold the dive but a few seconds before dropping and pulling out. They were scattering bombs all over the country. Of course the flack was heavy and making a column of smoke clear up to eleven thousand. After everybody had bombed, the building hadn't been hit, so I figured old Jim had better show them how it was done. The wind was drifting the flack smoke away so I had a clear view of the target. I rolled over and went down and down and down, with better than 400 on the clock. When I got as low as I dared I jerked the bomb release hard, grabbed the stick with both hands, and pulled. Instead of coming out of the dive, I went into a high-speed stall and was flopping around going down, the bomb still hanging on. I got control and pulled out at around three hundred feet. That's much too high over

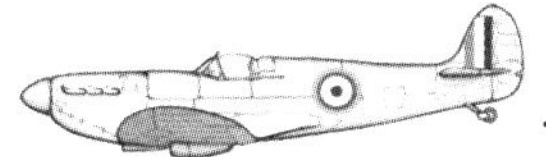

U.S. Army Air Corps photo

enemy territory, so I dove to tree level and started out. Fortunately I was headed in the right direction, all the while jerking the release lever like crazy, but that bomb wouldn't come off and the poor old airplane was staggering along, wide open with black smoke belching from the exhaust. The Germans threw a lot of stuff at me but it all seemed to be passing in front of me and I didn't take a hit. When I crossed the lines, the Americans cut loose on me! When one guy shoots, everybody shoots. I made it out over the water, and then the Navy got in the act, splashing big stuff in front of me. I sure was lonesome! When I got close to Naples, I called the Base and asked if I should bail out or try to land. They told me to put the arming lever in "safe" and land. I made the smoothest landing of my life on that PSP (pierced steel plank) runway. I taxied to the revetment and climbed out. A crowd was standing around, looking disgusted. The Armament Sergeant climbed up on the wing and pulled the release lever. The bomb hit the ground and the crowd walked away. I had been jerking on the *arming* lever all that time! Why try to explain; they wouldn't believe me anyway. Maybe I had been a little nervous. My logbook reads, "Returned with bomb. No mission."

I only flew eleven missions here (credited with ten) so I had time to look around a bit. The harbor had numerous wrecked ships, some showing partway out of the water, and some with only tops of the masts showing. The wharf area was quite beat up, but enough had been cleared so as to handle the military supply shipping. The city was almost deserted, having been badly bombed. The streets had been bulldozed so the convoys of trucks could move easily. The place had that distinct odor of death that is common to all bombed-out cities before the bodies have been cleared from the rubble...a sickly sweet smell. At night there were only a few street lights, and those small and dim. It was very quiet, with only the sound of a passing truck or staff car; that is, except for a man singing a sad, mournful rendition of what sounded like *"O Sole Mio,"* to be joined by someone in the next street with perhaps a slightly different version of the same song. Always men singing, never women, and I didn't see any children.

Mount Vesuvius was smoking a bit; I heard it did erupt some few weeks later. In the meantime I was able to tour the ruins of Pompeii in the areas that had been excavated. Must have been some sort of resort town with many public baths, shops, and – from the looks of the wall paintings and murals – the sex capital of the Roman Empire!

I drove through some of the British camps nearby. There were troops from all over the Empire including Gurkas from India, wearing their wraparound headdress and carrying their long, curved Gurka knives. Every vehicle I saw was chained to something; I was told everybody carried a spare distributor rotor in his pocket. Apparently the only game in town was stealing cars and trucks. I had heard the old saying, "See Naples and die." The boys in the Group had changed that to: "*SMELL* Naples and fly."

My return flight to England was quite uneventful, except over North Africa where I was able to view the residue of the war in the desert. There were burned out tanks, trucks, and airplanes of all sorts strewn about, giving stark evidence of the fighting that had gone on along that route. Also there was a delay at Algiers, where I met one of our former Fort Knox people, Captain Cropper, who drove me around that rather pretty French city. Back away from the waterfront the city had not

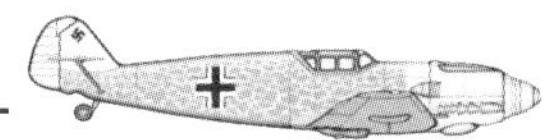

suffered much damage. There I saw my first camel but declined an offer to ride one of the smelly things. The flight from Casablanca rounded the Rock just at dusk; we flew all night and arrived at Prestwick after dawn.

Arriving at 9th HQ, I was ushered in to see the CG, General Quesada, to whom I reported on my trip. He said we would be equipped with the P-47 'Thunderbolt'; I was to go fly one and develop an SOP (Standard Operating Procedure) for using this airplane as a dive-bomber. There was one available on the flight line, which I appropriated for the purpose.

U.S. Army Air Corps photo

Now the P-47 is a much larger version of the P-43 we had used back in the States. It weighed 12,000 pounds, had eight .50 caliber guns, plus racks to carry bombs, rockets, and napalm. It had the same type of supercharger under the belly, which gave it power to operate at very high altitudes where its performance was outstanding. We, however, were going to use it down around the trees! I just couldn't envision this great mass of metal as the ideal dog-fighter, twisting and turning in aerial combat. It flew extremely well – stable, surprisingly light on the controls, and so very quiet with the exhaust being funneled to the supercharger. I saw another fighter, I think it was a Corsair, and 'bounced' him. A few seconds later he was sitting on my tail! So much for dog-fighting. Chastened, I proceeded to open country for some dive bombing. From eleven thousand feet I picked out an isolated farmhouse, rolled over and dived at it. I damn near hit that house with my prop! That airplane came out of the sky like a streak of lightning! I had never seen anything that could dive anywhere near that fast.

It was obvious that the old P-40 method wouldn't work with this airplane. I tried again, this time from twenty thousand, with much the same results. I tried from thirty and went into compressibility; that is, the nose started to tuck under and the controls froze tight. I recovered at around sixteen thousand and flew around awhile to get my brain unscrabbled and some blood back in my head. My first black-out. I tried some straight-ahead dives at more shallow angles. Someone smarter than I would have to figure out the proper dive angle. But the split-S was definitely out.

I went back to tell General Quesada what I had found, but made one big mistake. I walked into his office and reported: "General, we can't use that airplane as a dive-bomber; we must … "

"Get out of this office, you are no longer a combat pilot!"

"But General…"

"Get out of here!"

I left. Outside, I heard him call for the CO of one of the Groups that had recently arrived in England. Nice young fellow. When he came out of the office, he said he was told to go dive a target over on the coast of France. I tried to tell him what I had learned, but he was too fired up to listen. Incidentally, he did hit that target. He and several of his boys – with their propellers.

Throughout the war, the P-47 was used extensively for ground support work. The 'Jug' dropped untold thousands of bombs, but not as a dive-bomber.

My dreams of being a fierce fighter pilot having been so rudely shattered, I drifted back to the Wing to resume my duties there. Al Deefer had just left for Italy to fly with the same Group I had been with. We heard that his airplane exploded during a dive. Perhaps flack had detonated his bomb. We all liked Al.

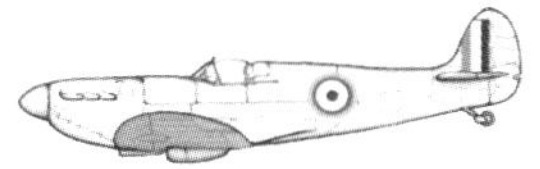

U.S. Army Air Corps photo

Many new Groups were arriving in England. The 9th was to get thirteen or fourteen groups of fighters, all but one of them were P-47s. A Squadron normally used four flights of four, or sixteen airplanes per mission. A Group had four Squadrons, and a Wing had a varying number of Groups. The 9th also had about the same number of light or medium bombers. A sizeable force, packing a lot of firepower. It proved to be a formidable force. The 67th was equipped with P-51s with cameras, and was assigned to the 9th Air Force. They did a fine job all across Europe. My job was to visit the new Groups and give lectures on what they needed to know about operating in the European Theater. I lectured on such subjects as typical weather, navigation aids (which were few), night lighting, escape and evasion, maps, etc. They got a kick out of my dive bombing experiences and maybe it did them some good.

I asked General Sanders when he thought my replacement would arrive, but he said he hadn't been able to get him and that he would have to put up with me! I was promoted to Lieutenant Colonel, which would make it even harder for me to get into a group. Everybody wants new Second Lieutenants, because anything above that means someone else won't get promoted. It looked like I was stuck in the Wing with nothing much to do, and so it turned out. I did get to fly with several Groups on attacks against the buzz bomb sites in France, although we hadn't been told what they were yet. Neither were we told that most of the German Air Force had been transferred to the Eastern front, at least those elements which we would have faced at that time. They came back later.

I was tagging along with a Group, I think it was the 4th, one pretty day. There was no opposition, so we split up into squadrons and then into flights of four. We were carrying two 500s and went looking for something to drop them on. The flight I was in wandered over west to the Cherbourg area, but nothing was moving. Everything looked quiet and peaceful down there. Well, we had to do something with those bombs, so the Lieutenant who was leading the flight suggested we cut the railroad that came down from Cherbourg. I told him the rails looked rusted like the road wasn't being used, so we settled on a pretty little stone bridge that was probably built around the time of William the Conqueror. The guys each wanted to try a different approach to the problem.

U.S. Army Air Corps photo

All three tried with no success, so it was my turn. The railroad was built on top of an embankment some ten or fifteen feet high. As our bombs had ten second delay fuses, I figured I could go in right on the ground and stick them into the embankment right at the abutment and get out of there before they exploded. I went in very fast, released the bombs, and jumped over the embankment in a steep climbing turn. Looking back I saw both bombs bouncing along in the next field, which was full of cows! The farmer was standing, or rather jumping up and down like crazy on the edge of the field, shaking his stick at us. I heard the bombs go off but I

didn't look back as I hate to see a grown man cry. I was told that the bombs went right through the embankment. I didn't ask if the old man got hurt. The bridge is probably still standing.

U.S. Army Air Corps photo

The 9th Air Force began assembling its strength in and around the southeast coast of England on numerous temporary grass fields. The Wing moved near a strip at Headcorn and set up camp at a nice old house in an orchard. The place had a large greenhouse that we used as our mess hall. This area is, I think, the most beautiful part of England, with its manicured farms and orchards. We had built caravans to house our Operations and other offices and had acquired all our other vehicles and equipment to enable us to act as a Wing headquarters. The 9th AF had three subdivisions: The 9th, the 19th (Tactical Air Command), plus the Tactical Bombers. The 9th AF laid on the missions and passed them down to the TACs for action. Occasionally these orders came through us and thence to certain Groups. I felt that the Wing was an unnecessary link in the chain of command and that we had no real mission. In France this proved to be true. The TACs dealt directly with the Groups under their command and we in the Wing just sat there, and sat there, and sat there – as useful as teats on a boar hog.

I don't know how many Fighter Groups were packed into our general area, but every morning just before dawn, the crew chiefs started running up their engines in preparation for the day's mission, and the whole countryside would vibrate with the volume of sound. I could tell which Groups they were by the sound of their engines. The P-47s had a deep, muffled roar while the P-51s would pop and crackle through their stubby exhaust stacks. Then the large formations of bombers would start their parade; finally the Groups, one after the other, would take off to go join them as escorts. And I just sat there.

With so many tactical aircraft packed into our small area, the Brass knew this would be an especially lucrative target for the Germans to go after. Some speculated that it might be worthwhile for the enemy to expend a parachute division to knock out this force. In anticipation of any such attempt, a large amount of anti-aircraft firepower was moved in and positioned around each airfield. I thought the attack was at hand when one night the whole sky suddenly erupted with our fire. The first V-1, or buzz bomb, came over. The firing stopped as suddenly as it had started. I strapped on my trusty .45 caliber 1911 model Colt automatic and ran to the nearest gun emplacement. This was a truck with a Quad-.50 mounted and a rather shook up private sitting in the saddle. A Quad-.50 is a mount having four heavy machine guns and a saddle for the gunner. It can pump out a terrific amount of fire with all four guns going. (I vaguely recall that one of the guns can fire some eleven hundred rounds a minute.) Every fifth or sixth round is a tracer so you can see where the bullets are going.

The firing started again and here came another one of those things. At night all you can see is the flame from its exhaust and

U.S. Army Air Corps photo

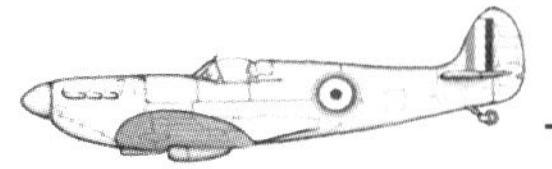

U.S. Army Air Corps photo

hear the distinctive pop-pop-pop sound of the little ram-jet engine. I was standing behind the gunner and watching his tracers miss the target by at least a hundred yards behind. I kept yelling, "Lead him, lead him!" But the kid was locked on the gun handles and kept firing long after his rounds were falling below the target. In fact, he was firing right into the little town of Headcorn.

This kept up the rest of the night. Nobody hit anything, except the English countryside. No parachutists arrived, for which I was duly grateful, especially after witnessing the skill of our gunners. The V-1 was a 1000-pound bomb with little short wings and a small jet engine to push it. The

missile was launched from an inclined ramp and always followed the same path at the same speed and altitude, guided by an autopilot. When the fuel was exhausted the engine quit and down came the bomb.

I thought they should be very easy to shoot down, so that morning I took a P-51 and climbed up

to five thousand feet over a town that was right on their path. I told our tower to call me when one was directly over the center of that town and I would give it a try. He called me and I dived wide open down to three thousand where it was supposed to be… I couldn't pick it up in the daylight so went back up to wait for the next one. This went on all day, and I had yet to spot one. It's just as well, as the first pilot that got one had it explode in his face. The RAF had some success against them using the Typhoon, which had the speed necessary to overtake them. Pilots would fly alongside and when they were over open country use their wing to tip the thing, which would upset its gyros and it would go down. AA fire got a lot of them; some were snagged on the cables of the balloon barrage that was raised south of London. Too many got through though, and killed a lot of people.

The glass roof of our greenhouse/mess-hall was in sad shape from all the falling shrapnel, but we continued to eat there. We also had to dig individual foxholes where we were expected to sleep. }We dug the holes, but I slept on the grass beside mine. We learned to listen to the little putt-putts coming and knew that if they quit right over us they would still glide on a little farther before coming down; it was the ones that quit just before they got to you that made you roll over into that hole. They were fueled to reach London, so all we got were the malfunctions. I flew a couple of missions in P-47s after the launch sites, but I never got to see the strike pictures the old 12th was taking. We didn't seem to put much of a dent in the number of bombs coming over. The Germans built those things by the thousands.

Before the buzz bombs ever started coming, I had toured the country at fairly low altitude so I could see what the Invasion build-up looked like. Each staging area was loaded with every conceivable kind of war materiel. Trucks, tanks, guns, gliders – plus stacks and mounds of supplies tied down under canvas. As someone has remarked, the island would have sunk but for all the barrage balloons holding it up. We all knew that the curtain was about to rise.

U.S. Army Air Corps photo

chapter thirteen

INVASION

1944: "A BIRD'S EYE VIEW"

We were having breakfast in our greenhouse when someone came rushing in and yelled that the Invasion had started! The General called for his car and left; the rest of us sat around trying to look cool, calm and collected. Apparently we were not needed for this undertaking. I hung around the Operations Office to see if the phone might ring, but it didn't. The suspense got the better of my good judgment. We had a brand new P-51 on our flight line that hadn't been flown since its arrival from the depot, so I jumped in and checked the fuel. The two wing tanks read full, so I cranked up. There was a group of P-51s forming up nearby so I joined up with them. Someone called, "Who is that guy?"

I answered, "Don't worry about it fella, I'm from Wing."

U.S. Army Air Corps photo

We headed across the Channel and saw the most fantastic sight in the annals of warfare. The Invasion Fleet! We had to stay at two thousand, as there was cloud cover above, while every ship had a captive balloon tied to a cable and floating at around one thousand to keep dive-bombers away. We kept well clear of the parade as we knew there were thousands of itchy fingers down there. As we neared the coast it was obvious from all the smoke that there was a lot of activity on the ground. The heavy battleships were lying further out and keeping up a steady fire with the big guns, while the destroyers were in fairly close to the shore. There was a tremendous amount of traffic, with hordes of landing craft going back and forth from the freighters and troop transports.

We were just crossing over the coast when my engine sputtered and quit. I had been burning out of my right wing tank; now that gauge showed empty after only thirty minutes. I switched to the left tank and the engine started up again, so I turned for home. As this was a new airplane, I figured there must be a loose connection in the right fuel line. I didn't much like the thought of raw gasoline sloshing around in the wing or belly, so I cut off all electric power and got back to Headcorn without further trouble. We found a loose hose connection.

The next day General Sanders told me to follow him in another P-51 to look at a strip that was being built on the bluff behind the beach, to see if it was ready for use. We dodged around the various shipping and their balloons. None of the fleet fired at us, so we had time to get a good look at all the activity. Bulldozers were working on the strip, so we didn't land that day. Back behind the beach we saw the wreckage of the glider operation. Those poor guys sure took a beating. The Germans had planted heavy posts in all the fields that could be used and these hadn't shown up on the Reconnaissance photographs. Some of those gliders carried jeeps and light guns which had slammed right out through the front end when the glider came to a sudden stop. There were parachutes hanging from trees, scattered all over the ground, and I saw one hanging from the steeple of a church.

The next day the two of us went back and landed on the new strip. It was rough, but we got away with it without damaging the airplanes. The Germans had the range of the strip and sent the occasional 88mm shell screeching in. The General went off somewhere, but I found a nice abandoned foxhole and sat there most of the day watching the bulldozers working. The Luftwaffe

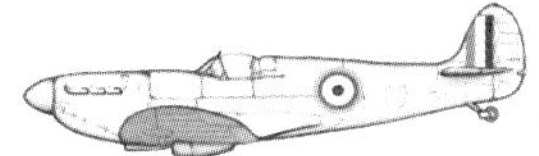

never did show during the daylight hours, except for one lone ME-109 that buzzed the beach and nobody paid him any attention.

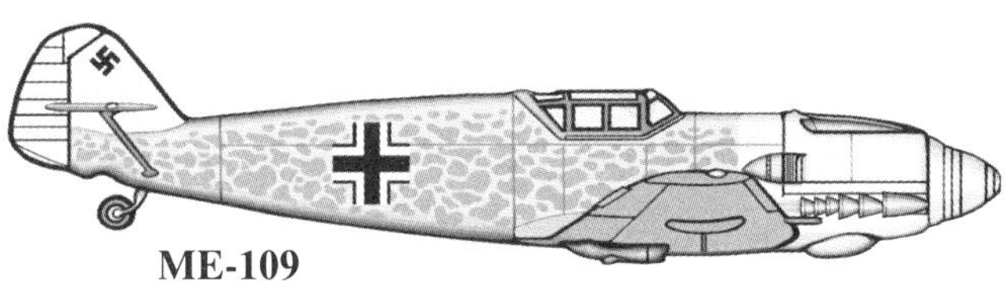
ME-109

We spent the next few days packing up and waterproofing our vehicles. We were issued some heavy, stinky coveralls meant for protection against gas attacks. We wore this garb for one day and then threw it away, under the assumption that if they didn't use gas to stop the Invasion, they wouldn't use it at all. Everything was declared expendable, so I drew a new watch, a new Colt .45, plus a .30 caliber carbine. I felt a lot more comfortable with that little rifle than with the old .45.

That new P-51 we had was the latest model, with bubble canopy and an extra gas tank behind the pilot that held eighty or eighty-five gallons. I wanted to see how it flew with that much weight located that far aft. Well I found out! I played around for a while and it seemed to fly good, so I dived the field and pulled up in a slow roll to the left. The airplane took complete control, going into some wild gyrations. Just what happened I couldn't tell, as I was being sloshed around all over the cockpit. As you can see, I did finally get control and brought it down. That extra weight in the rear upset the balance. I heard of another instance where a pilot rolled his airplane and the whole tail group snapped off. It became standard policy to fill that tank only half full, and then burn it off first.

It was decided that I would take two of the Operations Sergeants and go set up a temporary tower at the new strip that had now been declared usable. We had no portable radio, so I would use the one in the airplane. We had a UC-78, sometimes known as the Bamboo Bomber, that I would use. The three of us loaded our worldly goods, plus several days' supply of K Rations. One of the boys had an arm in a cast, and took along his pet mongrel dog. The other had a guitar that he played the whole trip. His favorite piece seemed to be *I Love Life and I Want To Live*. We wove our way through the shipping without getting entangled in balloon cables or shot at. A pair of 51's was dispatched to check us out and flew alongside for a few moments, flaps extended so as to slow down to our speed. We waved, the dog barked; the two pilots shook their heads and departed.

I parked in one of the new revetments and told the guys to find a foxhole. I found a dandy with a heavy barn door lying beside it. I knew that the Germans would have their bombers over after dark, which they did, with a vengeance. Every gun in the invasion force cut loose on them. I wanted to watch the fireworks, but everything that went up turned into small pieces that came whistling down again. I tried to get my shoulders in under my helmet, but that won't work, so I crawled into my foxhole and pulled the barn door over me. The next morning I crawled out and went to look at my airplane. It looked like a sieve. This is a fabric covered aircraft that offers very little resistance to any sharp object. I didn't count the holes, but sent word I would need a gallon of nitrate dope and a yard of Grade A Flitex.

The next morning I was blasted awake by an explosion the like of which I had never experienced. Finding myself still alive and in one piece, I carefully raised the door covering my foxhole and peeked out. During the night the artillery had moved a battery of 155mm guns into position almost over my head. It was the muzzle blast from that gun that had so rudely disturbed my slumbers. Seeing that they were still reloading, I jumped out of my hole and, waving my arms madly, got the gunner's attention. They held fire long enough for me to get behind the guns. One of those guys had heard talk of snipers being left behind hidden in holes. I understand some had

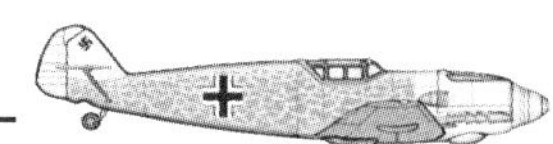

actually been found by using metal detectors, and cleared by dropping a live hand grenade on their heads. Saved the trouble of burying them. A few hours later the battery moved again, so I could still use my cozy little bed.

Just at dusk that day, one lone P-38 came over and quietly circled our strip. Obviously he wanted to land, as he had his landing gear down and his landing lights burning bright. The most peaceful looking P-38 imaginable, and there is no other airplane that remotely resembles it. Invasion stripes on the wing. But somebody took a shot at him. As usual, when one gun shoots, everybody in the area gets in the act. The poor guy disappeared in a cloud of smoke and flame. Word must have spread around because we got very little trade at that strip, and then only if someone was having engine trouble.

P-38

National Museum of the U.S. Air Force

The French make a liquor called Calvados from apples. This is 100 proof pure alcohol and must be used very sparingly, like a thimble-full at a time. As the troops advanced further south, they found some bottles of this elixir and, as was to be expected, proceeded to toss it down. They were found dead. I tried a thimble-full of the stuff and it was indeed quite potent.

The Germans left another nasty little trick behind by stringing electric cables through the creeks and shell holes that had rainwater in them. Now when two or three men walk up to a shell hole that is only half full of water they will instinctively try to raise the water level. If it so happens that there is a hot cable in the water, you have an instant dead man. That happened rather frequently. Of course there were all sorts of booby traps left everywhere, and mines of all types, big ones and little ones. For some weird reason they sometimes left little signs marking these locations, probably to protect their own troops, and forgot to take them down. *Achtung: Minen,* or words to that effect.

The rest of the Wing personnel arrived at the beach in landing craft – most of them seasick from the rough crossing. But they remembered to bring me the dope and fabric to repair the Bamboo Bomber. We moved into a former German bunker area that, because it had been only partly destroyed, was sufficient for our immediate needs. This was situated near the little town of St. Mere Eglese, overlooking the sea, a rather nice location with a small grove of trees adjoining that the General selected as the site of our mess tent. I didn't take too kindly to that, as the grove had a lot of those little signs still posted. The General demonstrated his utter fearlessness (I called it something else) by walking into the woods and spotting the trip wires. He stood behind a tree and kicked the wire, causing the little mine to jump up about three feet and explode. He cleared out the woods, at least to his own satisfaction, and bowed to the plaudits of his captive audience. I never liked the guy, but he did have guts.

After we got settled, the General told me to go up to a maintenance base in England – I can't recall the name – and pick up a Gooney Bird we had been assigned. I took a mechanic to act as engineer and we got a ride over in the Bamboo Bomber. (I only recently gave all my maps of England to the Warbirds of America, Inc., to adorn their club house, so I will have to guess at a lot of the places. Chilton comes to mind, but I'm not certain.) Anyway I found the Gooney and someone to show me how to operate the landing gear; everything else being fairly standard. It

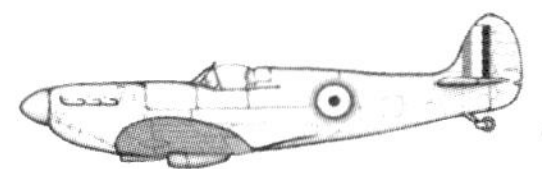

handled much better than the old B-10, so I didn't have any trouble with it. I was in such a hurry to get back that I didn't stay over there long enough to take a bath, which I surely needed. We wore winter clothes, and it was getting fairly hot in France. As we were not allowed to use any water in France, all of our water had to be brought in from England, and that for cooking and drinking only. We were getting rather ripe.

Although the buildup of our strength continued, the troops were making agonizingly slow progress pushing the Germans back further from the beaches. The enemy still held Cannes and had the British ringed with their armor; also the Americans were having trouble advancing through the hedgerows that bordered every little field. It was murderous work. And Cherbourg still held out, so the harbor could not be opened to handle our much-needed shipping. Everything had to come in over the beaches, in spite of the artificial breakwaters and docks being severely damaged by storms.

Have you ever been a month without a bath? I have, and it got to where I couldn't stand to be around myself. Then I came up with a bright idea. Back in the little town of Headcorn there lived a baker who baked good bread and would sell us some on occasion. The General didn't enjoy the stuff that came out of cans any more than I did, so I suggested that I could run over there in the Bomber and pick up a load of that fine stuff. He agreed and off I went.

Arriving at our old abandoned strip, I had the most unusual experience, and have never heard of it happening to anyone else. It was a hot sunny day and no wind. I drifted slowly in and just as I closed the throttles and flared, that little bird leaped up a few feet in the air, turned ninety degrees to the left, landed, and came instantly to a full stop! Nothing was hurt as there was no side load put on the gear. Maybe what I hit was something like a little dust devil. I can't explain it. I got a good bath at the local pub, put on clean clothes, got a lot of bread, and tooled happily back to France.

Cherbourg was captured and all German resistance in the Peninsula cleared. The port, however, had been so thoroughly demolished that it was unusable for many months, so still all the supplies for the invasion forces had to come in over the beaches. This slowed the buildup considerably, so a pipeline was laid under the waters of the Channel to supply the Army with fuel. From our perch up on the bluff we could watch all the activity on the beach. Occasionally there was a big explosion down there, caused by someone running over a mine that had been overlooked, or else the Germans firing a long range gun that could reach the beach. A local priest took a group of little French children down there to play in the surf and one of them tripped a mine and was killed.

The American forces had slowly fought their way through the hedgerows until finally coming to the St. Lo road or highway. This is a long straight road that is plainly visible from the air. The Germans had dug in on the south side and had a clear field of fire across the road and the nearby fields, making this a very strong position. The Americans had fought their way up to this road and stopped. Stalemate!

The "Breakthrough at St. Lo" has been well documented, but I will tell you what I saw of it. The plan was to use the combined strength of both the 8th and 9th U. S. Air Forces together with all of the RAF, including all of the available heavy, medium and light bombers, plus all the fighter-bombers of both forces – in fact anything that could carry a bomb. Each formation, down to the squadron level, was given a specific area to hit. The fighters were assigned the space closest to the road with the heavies going a bit deeper. I don't recall how long or how wide an area was covered but it was certainly sufficient. The attack started around mid-morning. The Third Army under General Patton was in place close to the jump-off. After this tremendous force had completed its attack, the ground force, after some delay from having the lead elements hit by one air outfit

dropping their bombs short, pushed through the bombed-out area and headed south through France. Nothing stood in their way.

I drove through there the next day in a jeep and saw the devastation. It looked like the whole area had been plowed fifteen or twenty feet deep, with the bomb craters overlapping. There was no sign of life. You history buffs know that Patton went south to LeMans, where he detached some forces to go west into Brittany and capture Brest, while the balance of his force turned east toward Germany.

The Germans had some twenty or thirty thousand troops down south of Patton's route to the east, which would come up and try to cut his supply lines if they were not stopped. Patton chose to leave the job of stopping that force to the 19th TAC under General O. P. Wyeland, who had five or six Groups of P-47s to do the job with. Patton was headed east with his right flank completely exposed, so the fighter bombers went to work on the German columns trying to come north. Nothing can move on the ground in daylight with fighter bombers overhead, and their hiding places were so thoroughly beat up that there wasn't much left to move at night. What was left of that force finally came riding up the road with white flags flying and surrendered to four P-47s circling overhead. The 19th TAC had held the right flank!

General Sanders called me in and showed me on a map a little abandoned airfield down where General Patton was heading. (This was shortly after he had turned east.)

"See this little river that circles the field like a horseshoe? And at this end of the field there's this hill. I want to set up a fighter control radar on top of that hill. The equipment and the people are over at the airport. I want you to take the Gooney Bird and haul this stuff down to that strip so it can be set up."

U.S. Army Air Corps photo

"Hell, General, that's German territory!"

"Well it won't be by the time you get there."

I grabbed my .45 and carbine and headed for the airstrip. The radar people had a big pile of stuff to load, what with a jeep and trailer, tents, stoves, heavy boxes and whatever, plus eight or ten people. I didn't have much time in the Gooney yet, but I had heard that it would fly with everything you could put in it. I didn't take a co-pilot or engineer. I had to use a lot of power to taxi. On take-off it used almost all the runway but finally staggered off with a few feet to spare.

I found the little field without any trouble, right where the map said it was. There was a lot of activity on the ground, with tanks, trucks and guns making clouds of dust. They looked American. The field didn't look very promising, with the grass, or rather weeds, a very bright green, like an area wet from the river getting out of its banks. I came in with full flaps and plenty of power, as slow as I dared. I hit three points near the middle of the field and rolled maybe 50 feet. The tail came up and I thought we were going to nose over, but it hung there and the tail dropped. We crawled out and saw the wheels mired up to the hubs. We started unloading and hauling the stuff up the hill. After the airplane was completely empty it was still impossible to power it out of the mud, so I was stuck.

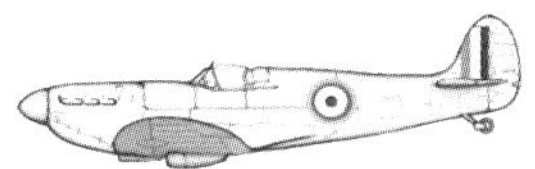

From up on the hill I could see that all the vehicles over on the road had the big white star, so I felt easy about starting a little fire to warm up some of our K-Rations. As we sat around eating, two Frenchmen in civilian clothes with FFI arm bands and carrying rifles came in out of the dark. One of them spoke very good English. He told me that there were a large number of Germans close by that wanted to surrender. I understood him to say "Thousands," and I promptly banished any thoughts of being another Sergeant York. I told him to accept their surrender, but he replied that they wouldn't surrender to the French Underground (for obvious reasons) but would surrender to the Americans. I told him I had seen plenty of Americans on the road and I was sure they would handle the details. They left and we put out the fire and spread out a bit. I kept thinking there just might be a few of those Germans that might not want to surrender. We passed a rather sleepless night.

The next morning I went down to walk the field to see if there was any dry area, but it was all soaked. After a while a jeep came roaring up with some Combat Engineers aboard.

"Looks like you are pretty well stuck." We talked about it awhile as more trucks arrived. They asked me how long a run it would take me to get off if they put down a wire mesh strip. I figured five hundred feet would be enough, so they started to work. They used a tractor to pull me out of the mud and up to the far end of the field. The wire comes in rolls about fifteen or twenty feet wide. They had truckloads of it. They rolled out five hundred feet and staked it down with spikes. I cranked up the engines and put down about half flaps, then with full power on, released the brakes. I raised the tail a little and at the end of the wire mesh she lifted off nicely. After picking up the gear and flaps I came back across the field for a little buzz job and they were already busy rolling up their mesh. The Combat Engineers did wonderful work all during the war. They built runways out of pierced steel plank (PSP) where there would be a lot of heavy traffic; they also had one method where they scraped out a runway on dry ground and covered it with tar paper! Those were not meant to last long.

I got back to base before dark and walked into our mess tent, where I was greeted by the General with, "What took you so long?"

"Well General, you see I met this pretty little French gal and..." Actually I never did get around to telling him what I had done. He didn't even ask me if the radar all arrived safely. Made me wish I *had* brought in a few thousand prisoners.

We packed up our gear and moved south to LeMans. There we took over a chateau for our quarters. The old Count and his wife were also living somewhere in the house, though we seldom saw them. They complained about the American bombers always missing their target and killing Frenchmen instead. This was the first time we had come in contact with the French; we had a lot to learn about them. They seemed rather indifferent to our being there and obviously wanted us to move on. I had as little to do with the French people as possible.

We stayed at LeMans for about ten days and moved on east to Saint-Dizier. Here was a large airport with concrete runways, packed with three fighter groups plus various other units. I found a spot for our Gooney Bird, the P-51, and the P-47. There were no living quarters that had not already been commandeered, so we moved about a mile away and set up a tent camp in a meadow that we shared with a large flock of sheep. That was the first time I had seen a sheep dog work and was quite fascinated how he controlled the flock without any commands from the shepherd that I could see or hear.

The meadow, despite being terribly wet and muddy, was long enough to accommodate our little L-5. The General decided to keep the L-5 parked in front of his tent so he could commute to the 9th

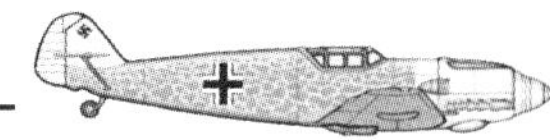

AF headquarters in a hurry; that is, if they ever had any business whatever to discuss with us. Since leaving England they seemed to have forgotten our existence. We certainly hadn't done anything to further the war effort, with the possible exception of moving the radar unit. The General called me in and directed that I procure enough wire mesh to make a little runway in the meadow for the L-5, so I took some troops down to the airport and raided the Engineer's supply dump for the necessary supplies. I'll confess that I didn't bother to ask anyone if I might have the stuff. We made a nice runway five or six hundred feet long and a parking spot right in front of the General's tent. The weather had turned off cold and rainy but we did a fair job.

U.S. Army Air Corps photo

A few days later a group of officers from the Engineers paid us a visit. I was told to report to the meeting room immediately, if not sooner. The General gave me a vicious tongue lashing and ordered me to pull up the wire mesh and take it back to where I had stolen it – much to the enjoyment of the Engineers. Well, we went out there in the rain and rolled up all that wire and returned it to its proper owners. When I reported the job completed, the General told me to take the Gooney back to the beaches and get some more, where it wouldn't be missed! So I gathered my detail of happy troops and flew back to the beach. There we found a sufficient supply with which to rebuild the strip. I don't know if the General ever used the strip. One reason was that I tore up his airplane… It happened like this:

I went over to the airport to get the little bird and had trouble digging it out of the spot where it was buried in with a number of other airplanes of various types. That airport was packed and jammed. I was taxiing slowly around the perimeter toward the runway when I approached a P-38 in a revetment with its tail toward the taxiway. The crew chief was running up the engines so I stopped to wait until he had finished, as I would be passing within a few feet of his tail. He ran both engines up to max power a couple of times and then throttled down to idle. I figured he had finished so I started slowly ahead. The little rascal must have been watching me in his rear view mirror. When I was directly behind him, he threw both throttles wide open and the L-5 was blown upside-down in a twinkling. It takes awhile to get out of an airplane that is on its back, so by the time I had extracted myself from the mess, there wasn't a soul to be seen in the area. The General had a lot to say about my busting up his pet airplane, but I didn't lose any sleep over it.

I visited around to several of the Groups that were supposed to be in our Wing and watched for an opening that I might be allowed to fill. They were taking heavy casualties from the German ground fire. In the first three months of the Invasion, the 9th's losses had equaled the number of airplanes they had started with! Of course the pilot losses were not that great, as some had bailed out, bellied in, or returned with aircraft so damaged they had to be scrapped. I flew a few missions with them until the General found out about it. I had asked him several times to send me to one of the Groups, but he once said, "Look, Second Lieutenants are expendable, but you are not!" From that time my military bearing, demeanor, and general attitude began to deteriorate to below the standards outlined in *Customs of the Service*. In fact I was hanging on the verge of a court-martial.

During this time Patton was pushing hard toward Germany, and it seemed he would break through far ahead of the armies on the northern flank. The political situation couldn't allow that, so Patton's supply of fuel and ammunition was curtailed to stop him. All supplies were still coming in

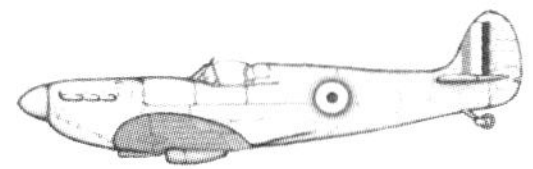

over the beaches as no ports had yet been opened. The Red Ball Express was organized by pulling as many trucks as possible from all units and placing them in the hands of the Transportation people. They loaded at the beaches and, like the Pony Express, ran day and night to the front. Even some of the Bomber Groups were used to haul five-gallon Jerry cans of gasoline to the forward areas.

I found gainful employment by using our Gooney to go to the beaches to pick up food that I would then drop off at the various Groups. The supplies were piling up back at the beach depots and I had no trouble picking up loads of steak or turkey – whatever the guys had. I would just ask for five thousand pounds of loot, and they would fill me up. That was about all of my contribution to the war effort at that time.

One time I took a full load of fighter pilots to London for a three-day pass. The weather was bad and they wouldn't be doing any flying anyway. When the day of the return trip came around, I went out to the airport a little early to see if I had a full load. I had given a definite departure time but didn't really expect to find a full load ready to leave. I told the Operations people I was going to sit in the airplane out of the rain and they could load on as many as showed up. I told the crew chief to stay in the back and lock the doors after we were loaded. I heard quite a few people come aboard, but I was reading a paperback and didn't look back into the cabin. When the door light went out, I cranked the engines and started to taxi. The airplane moved rather sluggishly, which I attributed to the wet, soggy field. The takeoff run took quite a bit longer than I expected, but we were off. The ceiling was around three or four hundred, which was alright as that's where we always flew anyway. I headed west for awhile to clear the balloon barrage, which I wouldn't be able to see, and then turned south to the coast. I wasn't worried about the weather closing down, as there was a radio range set up at Paris and several new ones in England, and I had all the information about them in my little book, plus eight hours fuel in my tanks. When I landed at Saint-Dizier, it was raining rather heavily, so I decided to stay seated until the rain slacked up. Of course there is no way to stay dry in a Gooney, as they leak all around the windshield anyway. When I decided that I might as well get out, I couldn't push the door to the cabin open. When I shoved a little harder I got angry yells of "Hold your horses!"

When I did get it open far enough to see to the rear, I found more people jammed in than I could count. The crew chief, who had stayed in the back, said he estimated we had about seventy people aboard. Not bad for a thirty-seat airplane…and speaks well for an eager bunch of pilots.

I lost the Gooney shortly thereafter. One of the Wing pilots had been checked out in it and was sent to England for some reason. He landed at Heston, a grass field, came in too fast, landed long and slid on the wet grass out of the field, slamming into a building. As a replacement for the Gooney we received a Norseman. This was a single-engine highwing cargo airplane that will carry a good load. Ours was the six-passenger job. That didn't last long either. Our Flight Surgeon was also a pilot; he got the job of flying that airplane in his spare time, which was all the time. He had an engine failure on takeoff and killed a couple of passengers with some damage to himself. After the war he was to do me a great favor. His name was Patterson – which reminds me of a story about him when we were stationed back at Membury, shortly after our arrival in England:

Each squadron had its own Flight Surgeon. One night all four of these docs were in my room playing poker and trying to think of something more exciting to do. In walks Delmont J. Sylvester, Third. There was something about Delmont that seemed to bring out the devilment in people and now it was working with a vengeance. Patterson spoke up: "Delmont, have you been circumcised?"

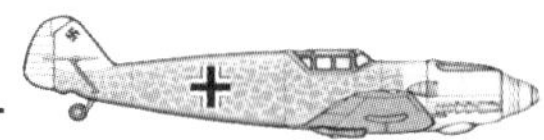

His reply in the negative caused dismay among the four and it was decided that this oversight must be corrected immediately. They hauled him off, kicking and screaming, to our little dispensary where he was strapped to the operating table and given enough ether to knock him out. They didn't actually operate on Delmont, but they did scratch him up enough to cause a little irritation, then bandaged him up nicely. Poor Delmont lay around for several days worried about what had happened to him until he was allowed to remove his bandages.

A former 12th Squadron pilot, Meserve, had been transferred to a P-51 Group and had done real well. He had four confirmed victories and was given a thirty-day leave in the States. When he returned he came to me and asked to be transferred to the Wing. His thirty days in the States had ruined him as a fighter pilot. He said people back home were moaning and groaning about the hard life they had, what with rationing and all, plus they had to work so much overtime, etc. – that he just didn't feel like risking his neck for them anymore. I gave him a job in Operations. We had a new L-5, which Meserve promptly wrecked.

U.S. Army Air Corps photo

"I heard quite a few people come aboard..."

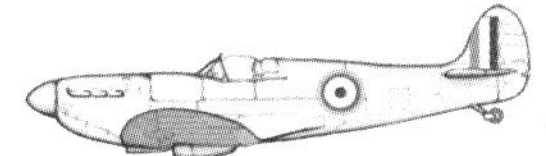

U.S. Army Air Corps photo

Haun family photo

"So I jumped into my own personal P-47 and took off for Brussels."

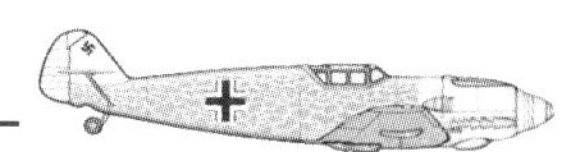

chapter fourteen

NINTH AF HQ AND BRUSSELS

1944 – '45: "THE VIEW SOMEWHAT WIDENS"

The 9th Air Force HQ had moved to Luxembourg, so we hauled our unit to a small town near there. We had been there two or three days when I received orders assigning me to an infantry division with duty as Forward Air Controller. The 9th had used this system with great success in cooperating with the ground forces. There was always a flight of P-47s patrolling near the head of all the ground troops. When the ground forces came against strong opposition, they called for air support. The air controller was in touch with the patrolling aircraft via radio and would direct them onto the enemy position. The Germans would sometimes bury their tanks with their guns almost flush with the ground, then cover each over with camouflage netting, making them impossible to locate from the air. In such cases the air controller would ask the troops to throw smoke shells to mark the target for the pilots. With the target thus spotted, the 47s would attack with bombs, rockets, napalm or whatever was needed, then return to base as soon as a new flight arrived to take over the patrol. The controller was usually a pilot from the Group he was controlling.

I suppose I should have taken the job, but I figured the General was just giving me the shaft by putting me in another ground job; so I decided to go over his head. Captain Bob Lee from the old Fort Knox days was now a Major General and Deputy Commander of the 9th AF, so that's where I went. I told him I just wasn't cut out to be a Gravel Agitator and perhaps he could use me somewhere in the flying business. It turned out they needed someone with my qualifications at Brussels to act as the American member on the Combined Operations Staff. Staff Officer or not, that was where I was going. I went back to the Wing and packed up my gear and – without telling anyone what I was up to – put my stuff in our P-47 and went to the 9th AF flight strip; there I asked them to transfer the P-47 to their flight line and detach it with me to Brussels, as the Wing had no use for it. The Lieutenant in charge bought the idea, so I jumped into my own personal P-47 and took off for Brussels. After the war I was at the Pentagon trying to get a Regular Commission, and a friend in the Records section said that he had torn up the Efficiency Report General Sanders had made on me; otherwise I would have been out on my ear! I expected that.

The British Tactical Air Force, TAF, had their headquarters in the Grand Hotel. I was given a room with a bath on the fifth floor. There was hot water once a week, but of course no central heating. The Operations Office was downstairs; I was given a desk and a telephone. The Brits were polite, if not actually friendly, and were quite helpful in getting me settled. I hadn't been told what my duties would be, so I just kept quiet and waited to see what transpired. I attended all the staff meetings and learned a lot about the planning that goes on at the higher levels of command. I was a bit surprised to see as many as a hundred officers gathered in one auditorium to discuss the details of a planned operation. I had supposed that this was all done in strict secrecy. It was amazingly laid back and relaxed.

There were two Russian officers hanging around whose duties seemed to be to determine if all the information given them was in fact the truth or just an attempt to deceive them. I watched them try to peek into various file cabinets, apparently to ascertain if what they were given matched what they could find elsewhere. For our part, there was the obvious need to know where the Russian

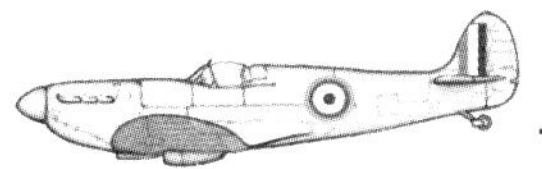

U.S. Army Air Corps photo

forces were located in order to prevent the Allies from accidentally bombing them. This was known as the 'Bomb Line', beyond which the Allies were not supposed to go. The two officers were given this information every morning but would never provide any information concerning the Russian forces. Consequently as the two forces came closer together, there arose numerous instances of combat between supposedly friendly allies.

I found that many benefits came with being assigned to a headquarters such as the 2nd TAF. For one, there were the 'Situation Maps' where the Big Picture was displayed, giving the location and strengths of all the armies and air forces. Each morning there was a well attended gathering to be shown what action was taking place, any changes in the situation, and what was planned for that day. There was a summary of the air action of the previous day, with the results claimed, known as the 'profit and loss' totals. I began to understand the vast logistical problems involved in maintaining a large fighting force in the field. I finally realized that wars are not won by killing the enemy's soldiers but rather by destroying his ability to make war. Thus our concentration on destroying his supply and transportation systems, which allied air forces were doing with a vengeance. I was a bit worried by the presence of the two Russians at these meetings, but no one else seemed bothered.

There was another room with the situation in the Pacific displayed. I knew absolutely nothing about that theatre of operations, except what little had appeared in the newspapers. An old codger who must have been a college professor was in charge of keeping this room and its maps up to date; he provided me with information about the state of the war worldwide. I began to appreciate the fact that I was now in an enviable position to really learn what wars are about. I was too old to be a fighter pilot, anyway!

I went on a bombing mission, but I didn't know I was going until I climbed into the cockpit. There was a big burly South African squadron leader who had been pulled off Ops and assigned to the same office I was in. He was extremely unhappy about being assigned to an office job and made no bones about his opinion of those who would stoop to such low-life activities! He was flouncing around the office and slapped me on the back – "Come on, let's go fly."

Naturally I jumped at that, and off we went. He was driving a jeep and not giving out any information about where we were going. The Brits had an airport close to town named Wavre, where I also kept my P-47. There a squadron of B-25s was stationed which had formerly been commanded by my unhappy companion. The squadron was taxiing out when he pulled the jeep in front of the lead aircraft and jumped out. With arm signals that could not be misinterpreted he ordered the two pilots out of the airplane. Then he and I climbed in and rolled to the runway. After takeoff we headed east so I began to get the idea of where we were going.

I kept a sharp lookout for any escort; there wasn't any in sight. Our target turned out to be a marshalling yard. The flack was fairly heavy but not close. The squadron pulled into a very tight formation and all bombed on the leader, who then bent the bird around in a steep diving turn and we headed for home. The bombs did a good job on the rail yard. At Wavre we parked and jumped quickly into the jeep. As far as I could tell my companion never said a word from the time we left the office until we got back. I never saw him again.

Haun family photo

Late winter of '44, the weather turned off cold and miserable, with snow or freezing rain. The Situation Board showed very little movement or action. There was considerable talk about the spring offensives and the supply build-up that had to be organized and accomplished before much could be done. It was a quiet time. On days that were flyable I visited around various fields where there might be someone I knew. As long as I could promote gasoline and oil for the old P-47, I could go anywhere I pleased. I visited the old 12th Squadron down in France. They had been strafed by 190s that day and had some aircraft damaged. Shortly after the attack one of their own P-51s came in from a mission. The machine gunners stationed around the field were trigger-happy from the recent raid, and as the pilot flared for his landing, they all opened up on him. He was killed right there on his own runway. He was a new boy that I hadn't met yet.

The Ardennes is a hilly, heavily forested area with only a few secondary roads – the last place you would expect a large scale armored attack. There was one American division covering that part of the front; it was considered more or less a rest area. Volumes have been written about 'The Battle of the Bulge', so I'll skip the gory details. Suffice it to say it came as a complete surprise, with heavy force and under cover of ugly weather.

I watched fascinated as the picture unfolded on the map. Armies were set in motion to take up their new positions. All our Air was grounded by the nasty weather, allowing the Germans to make deep penetrations through and behind our lines. It looked rather grim for awhile, at least to me, but the Brass seemed to be having a ball playing chess with divisions, corps, and armies. I got a call to report to 9th HQ. They had left Luxembourg and were now at Namur. I borrowed a jeep and headed out. We had about five inches of snow on the ground, which made the driving rather slow, but I made it all in one piece.

The 9th Air Force had been using underground telephone cables to communicate with all its subordinate commands, but some of these cables had been overrun and cut by the German advance. At Brussels I could use the 2nd TAF's network to reach those units that were now out of reach of 9th HQ. There was a radio net connecting 9th and 2nd TAF which could be used. My job was to be a relay station. The field orders would come to me via radio and through the TAF switchboard. Then using the telephone lines, which had 'scramblers', I would pass the orders on to the units concerned. Sounds very simple, until you factor in Murphy's Law.

I rushed back to Brussels with the feeling that now at last I was going to play at least a small part in the war. The only preparation I could make was to secure a large hardcover notebook and several pencils. Everything that passed over my phone would be recorded by date, time, who, what, where, and when. Everything went fine for a couple of days until I passed an order to the 9th TAC, commanded by Major General Quesada – an order which had not been fully complied with. I called down there and talked with somebody in their Ops Office, but got no definite answer. I did get a call back:

"Haun, this is Quesada. I understand you are very unhappy."

"No sir, I'm not the least unhappy."

"I understand you questioned how we operate here."

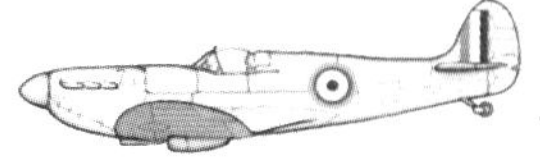

U.S. Army Air Corps photo

"General, this is a telephone relay station, I have no command authority whatsoever – I merely pass on the orders 9th AF addressed to you."

"Who do you receive the orders from?"

"A Lieutenant Colonel Tomlinson in 9th Ops Office."

"Well, you tell Lieutenant Colonel Tomlinson I'm running this show…etc. etc."

Naturally I wasn't going to pass on any such talk as that. The good General was well known to have a hair trigger temper and would be brutal with anyone who crossed him. I had seen that back in England, so I let it slide.

The weather cleared and all the air forces went to work on those German columns, which were trapped on those narrow roads in the hills and slaughtered. The northern armies came down, Patton's army came up, and they cleaned up what the air forces had left. I got a call on the radio from 9th AF which I copied very carefully:

"Put thirteen Bomb Groups on the marshalling area at BRUNSWEIG, and escort them with two Groups from the 9th TAC. Rendezvous 0830 – signed Tomlinson." (I don't remember the real name of the target, so I've used a name I am familiar with from the Berlin Airlift.) I called 'Bombay' and relayed the order, received by Major Smith. I then repeated it to 9th TAC, received by Lieutenant Jones. With times all dutifully logged. This must be a big supply dump if it is worth putting between three and four hundred bombers and two Groups of fighter escort on it. That's almost a hundred. They must be expecting trouble.

Bright and early the next morning, at 0730 hours, I called 'Bombay.'

Major Smith reported, "Thirteen Groups up and forming."

0734: I call 9th TAC regarding escort.

Lieutenant Jones responds: "Uh, the 9th TAC will not be providing escort today. All aircraft with bombs on will be attacking ground targets, by order of CG of 9th TAC." *Quesada!*

0738: I call: "Operator, get me HQ 9th Air Force!"

0740: "Sorry sir, our radio net seems to be inoperative."

"Keep trying!!!"

0745: A most proper British officer marches to my desk, comes to attention and reports: "Y-Service reports four hundred German fighters airborne, destination BRUNSWEIG," and smartly departs. (The 'Y-Service' monitors all German radio broadcasts.)

0750: "Operator, try to reach 9th AF!"

"Sorry, sir, radio net inoperative."

"Connect me with 2nd TAF Ops." When she does, I ask them, "Can the Spitfire squadrons cover the BRUNSWEIG area?"

"Sorry old boy, all Spitfires at limit of their ranges, returning to base."

0800: To 9th TAC: "Can you contact your fighters?"

"Negative, fighters now under the control of RIPSAW." (Ripsaw was the forward radar control for fighter units.)

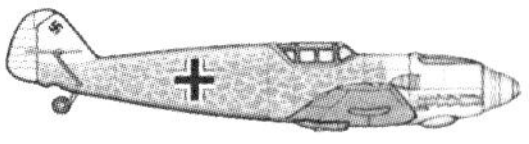

U.S. Army Air Corps photo

They say 'The buck stops here.' I surely wanted to pass this one to someone else. Suppose the Brits were playing games with me? I didn't think there were four hundred German fighters available. So what? Fifty could raise hell with the bombers.

0805: "Operator, try 9th one more time and then get me RIPSAW." I got Ripsaw's Captain Jackson: I identified myself, explained the situation and told them to have the 9th TAC fighters jettison their bombs, safe, and go cover the bombers.

0807: RIPSAW did contact the fighters, the bombs were jettisoned and fell all over our own forces. Fortunately they had been dropped 'safe', so none exploded. That afternoon I called RIPSAW. Yes, there had been quite a fight out there that day. My only problem now was the fact that I, a lowly Lieutenant Colonel, had countermanded a Major General's orders. I should have spent a sleepless night, but with the certainty that the action I had taken was in the best interest of the 9th AF, I slept the sleep of the innocent.

photo by permission of Gen. Hoyt S. Vandenberg, Jr.

The next morning, freshly shaved and in proper uniform, I arrived at the office fully expecting the wrath of General Quesada to descend on my head. What I was not prepared for was something quite different. Into the office strode the Commanding General of the 9th Air Force, Lieutenant General Vandenberg, accompanied by three of his staff officers. I hit a brace.

"What went on around here yesterday?"

For a short period (it seemed like an hour) I unflinchingly met his steely eyes. The BOOK says *"Never apologize or make excuses."* I turned around and picked up the logbook. My turning my back on him brought fire to his eyes. "Here is the log."

He took it and read for a few minutes, while I stood there in a stiff brace like the fine, upstanding soldier that I am; meanwhile I had detected a slight grin flicker over the face of one of the staff. The General tucked the logbook under his arm and said, "When General Quesada arrives, send him into that office."

The four went in that office and I breathed again. Within five minutes General Quesada arrived, exuding apprehension, and I pointed to the office.

They stayed in there for maybe thirty minutes. Of course I have no idea what went on, but when they came out, General Vandenberg handed me the log and kept walking. General Quesada followed in the rear, shoulders sagging and chin on his chest. Couldn't happen to a finer fellow! I remembered those boys who hit the target with their propellers. A few days later I read in *The Stars and Stripes* that General Quesada had been assigned new duties in the States.

There was a big party in the downstairs ballroom New Years Eve. I hung around a while but didn't know a soul. I went to bed and napped a short while, then decided to run over to London to see what I could see. I got to the airport just at the crack of dawn and made a quick check of the P-47. When I tried to crank, the engine hit a few licks and quit. In cold weather you had better get it running the first lick or there is a good chance the plugs will ice up. Figured that was what had happened, so I climbed out wondering where I could find a plug wrench so I could dry off the front row. At exactly that time, across the airport came a flight of FW-190s with all guns going! I had the

P-47 parked close to a low stone wall, which I cleared with one leap and from this vantage point watched the whole operation.

Within a few minutes there were airplanes burning all over the airport. The Germans set up a traffic pattern around the field, which by now was fairly well covered with smoke from burning airplanes. One of the pilots took a particular dislike to my shiny airplane. He made four runs at it, but it didn't burn. I didn't know if he was getting any hits or not, because when I saw the shells kicking up the snow and approaching, I ducked down behind the stone wall until he was past me. I believe I heard only one Borfus popping away at them. The Germans had certainly picked the right time to pull that raid. I learned that they had sent out around four hundred fighter-bombers that morning in an effort to destroy as many of our aircraft as possible. Happily, a large number of them were caught and destroyed before they could get back to their bases.

After the Germans left, I came out from behind my wall and looked the bird over. At first glance it seemed that it hadn't been hurt, but further examination showed four hits with 20mm shells. Two armor-piercing, one through the engine and another through the turbo. There was an explosive hit in the left wing spar and one in the cockpit. Class X! I called 9th Air Force to see about a replacement, but they had lost a large number that morning and were scraping the bottom of the barrel to mount today's missions.

There was a large airport out from town which was used primarily as an emergency strip for ships in trouble. I went out there and found damaged airplanes of all types that had made it to safety. I found two P-47s that, with a minimum of effort, could be turned into one; so, gathering a team of very eager workers, I went to work. The engine on the P-47 is mounted so that with a crane and a few wrenches you can quickly disconnect one and swing another in its place. While the lads were working on the engines, I started stripping weight off. The bomb racks under the wings were the first things I took off. Then six of its eight guns bit the dust. All I wanted was transportation. I got the engine cowling from three different airplanes, each with different paint jobs. With the left gear strut deflated a bit so the ship sagged on that side, and then with a liberal splashing of mud here and there, I had my own personal ugly duckling that I figured no-one would rank me out of. I kept it the rest of the time I was over there.

The 2nd TAF left Brussels and moved to Munchen-Gladbach in Germany, to stay closer to the advancing forces. A few days later I received orders assigning me to Tangmere on the south coast of England, again as a liaison officer. Just what I was supposed to do I never did find out. Tangmere had been one of the most active bases during the Battle of Britain but now seemed to be more of an experimental base. There I saw my first jet fighter, but they wouldn't let me fly it. These were the most likable bunch of people I had encountered during the war. The CO was a famous pilot from the pre-war era named 'Batch' Atcherly, who referred to all lesser ranks than himself as 'colonials' or 'sub-humans', but always with a grin. I remembered pictures of him at the Cleveland Air Races dressed in top hat and tails, astride a saddle mounted atop the fuselage of a Curtis Fledgling and flying it using reins to the controls. There was also a Navy pilot who had been in on the sinking of the *Bismarck*. I traded him my .30 carbine for a .22 caliber Walther he had liberated somewhere.

The war was winding down, but there was still hard fighting going on in Germany, and there I sat at Tangmere with no duties and no prospects of any. I still had my old P-47 to roam around in a bit, so I visited some of the old outfits I had known. Some of the pilots from the 67th Group were now flying Gooney Birds as troop carrier and medical air-evac, and doing a most worthwhile job. In talking to some of them, they invited me to come up and visit. I talked to 'Batch' about my flying some with them, and he agreed.

The Gooneys had litters installed in tiers on both sides of the airplane with plenty of aisle space between. I forget just how many litter patients could be carried, but I think it was around twenty. The ones I flew also carried a nurse and two medical technicians. Most of the airports in Germany had been bombed into rubble, with the runways broken up, so most of the time we used grass strips made usable by the engineers. I remember one trip to a place called Magdeburg. It was a grey, rainy day and the field was pretty well cut up and muddy. There were about a half-dozen Gooneys lined up with a stream of ambulances backed up to the loading doors. We had to wait for the next convoy, so I got out to stretch. Under the wing of the airplane parked next to us I saw a nurse with mud all over her boots and slacks. She was washing her hair using an upturned helmet, half full of soapy water, and sobbing like her little heart would break. I didn't ask her what she was crying about. I already knew.

On the return trip we stayed just under the base of the overcast so we could pull up into it should one of the few remaining German fighters spot us. I had several more trips with that Squadron before I went back to Tangmere.

I was wondering out loud how I might get a quick trip to the States. 'Batch' came up with a brilliant idea. He would get me a set of orders sending me to the Pentagon to determine what progress was being made with the 'stowed fighter' concept. Supposedly this was an idea where the long-range bombers could carry a little fighter along with them. The deal was I should have thirty days delay en-route, provided I return with a dozen new golf balls, which were unobtainable in England at that time. So, armed with a set of orders from RAF Experimental Station, Tangmere, U.K., authorizing priority-1 air travel, I beetled off to Prestwick, Scotland, and, believe it or not, ATC put me aboard the first westbound C-54!

We landed at Washington National Airport, where I caught a cab to the Pentagon. This monster had been built during the war; this was the first time I had seen it. After walking for what seemed like several miles, I found the office that might have something to do with developments. I introduced myself as a British spy in search of the aforementioned information, of which they professed complete ignorance. I'm certain they were telling the truth, so I jumped a cab for the five-minute ride back to National and bought a ticket to Memphis. I had time to call Memphis collect and advise Eleanor of my impending arrival. She sounded happy to hear my voice after almost three years.

Haun family photo

That was a wonderful thirty days. Jimmy had grown a couple of feet. Eleanor was as slim and sassy as ever. When folks asked about what I had done in the war and how many Germans I had killed, I'd get a faraway look in my eyes like it was just too horrible to talk about. The time was rapidly running out; I had to go back, so I bought a dozen golf balls and headed north.

The CO at Washington National thought I was crazy. "You want to go BACK?"

I showed him my RAF orders and reminded him that they were not USA orders and quoted from the BOOK: *"Desertion in the face of the enemy shall be punishable by death or such other punishment as a courts-martial may direct."*

So I climbed aboard another C-54, and went back to Tangmere.

On VE-Day we all got very drunk and had a wonderful polo match on bicycles. 'Batch' made a rousing speech about the coming war with the Russians!

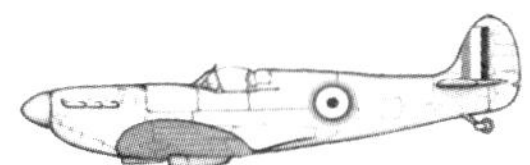

ATC: Allergic to Combat

U.S. Army Air Corps photo

This is to certify that

JAMES R HAUN, lt Col., AC
(NAME AND RANK)

ARMY OF THE UNITED STATES

HAS MET THE REQUIREMENTS FOR THE

INSTRUMENT PILOT CERTIFICATE
(WHITE)

AS PRESCRIBED BY AAF REG. 50-3

21 June 1946
(EXPIRATION DATE)

(CHECK PILOT'S SIG.) Capt, AC — (ORG. C.O. SIG.) Colonel, AC

Key Fld, Miss (STATION) — 347 AAF BU (ORGANIZATION)

TOTAL PILOT TIME TO DATE 1700:00

PILOT TIME LAST 12 MONTHS 250:00

WAR DEPARTMENT
A. A. F. Form No. 8
(REVISED 10-1-43) 16—37015-1 GPO

Haun family photo

"We're poor little lambs who have gone astray..."

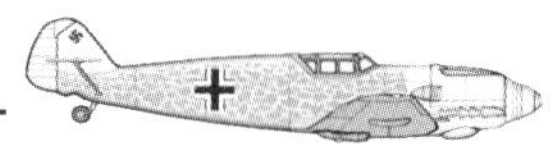

chapter fifteen

TRANSITION

1945: "BIG CAREER MOVE TO A.T.C."

The next day I went to Paris to see if I could transfer to ATC (Arnold's Trucking Company) or ATC (Allergic to Combat) and go join my buddies General Tunner and Red Forman in India, flying the Hump.

I had several good and valid reasons for wanting to get out to India. I was now 34 years old, which is much too old for the Fighter business, and I very much wanted to stay in the Service. As a Reserve officer I would have to stay closely connected to some influential General or expect to be on the first RIF (reduction in force) list that was certain to come out as soon as the war was over. I had been receiving letters from friends out there describing the terrors of the dreaded Hump, and I knew I would be snowed under for the rest of my life if I didn't go see for myself. Besides, the thought of having to go back to peddling bottler caps for a living just made me sick.

So off to the European Headquarters of the Air Transport Command at Paris. Red Forman had written them a letter stating that there was a position waiting for me, so the rails had been greased. I was given orders to report to Homestead, Florida, for transition training in C-54s, with thirty days delay en-route, travel by air authorized. So it was straight back to Prestwick; I was lucky and was put aboard a C-54 flown by some airline. We went to Iceland, across to Newfoundland, thence to New York.

In our Reserve unit before the war we had a likeable young fellow named Charlie Lewellen. During the war he was assigned to a troop carrier and had been on the invasion of Sicily transporting parachute troops. That was the night the Air Force got off course and flew over our trigger-happy Navy, which caused the loss of quite a number of our C-47s. (Red Forman lost a brother on that trip.) I had met Charlie in England before the coming Invasion and Charlie's nerves had become somewhat frayed. The night I saw him he had been standing on top of a piano in the club and crowing like a rooster! He was sent home with a physical discharge. Apparently Charlie was cured as soon as his foot touched good old US of A soil. I bought a ticket to Memphis on American and climbed aboard a well used DC-3 with a pair of clanking Wright engines that sounded like we ought to wait for a replacement. I took the very last seat in the rear. As we taxied out a sign lighted up over the cockpit door that said "C. C. Lewellen, Captain."

I called the stewardess: "When we level off, tell the Captain there is a very nervous passenger back here."

When we leveled off, Charlie stuck his head out of the cockpit door and I yelled in my best parade-ground voice, "Hey, Charlie, have you been cured?"

The rest of the trip was uneventful. Charlie stayed with American until he retired, but lost his disability pay shortly after the war, which loss caused him to scream like a wounded eagle: said he had to get rid of one of his horses!

I enjoyed that month in Memphis, swimming and playing golf with Eleanor's Dad, who was known as P.B. He and I always got along fine together, although he always beat me playing golf. The BOMB was dropped; a lot of people were suddenly out of work, and everybody started making babies – a crop that would far exceed our recent losses in population! Eleanor, Jimmy, and I jumped in our old Ford and headed for Florida.

***

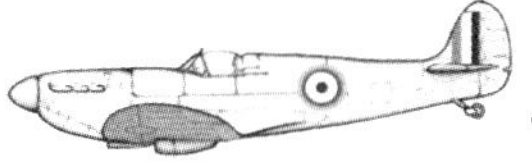

National Museum of the U.S. Air Force

Shortly after the start of the war, the need for long-range air transportation was obvious. The only aircraft available at that time were a few Clippers flown by Pan-Am, plus a handful of B-17s that could be spared. Some B-24s were converted to freighters and renamed the C-109 (or 1-Oh-Boom when converted to tankers). Douglas Aircraft Company brought out the famous C-54, which was to replace all transport aircraft of that time. This was a beautiful, round-bodied ship with four Pratt and Whitney engines that delivered about eighteen hundred horsepower each. The G-model had eight fuel tanks in the wings and has been known to fly for as much as twenty hours. I got 14 hours and 45 minutes out of one once and had plenty of fuel left. ATC had several hundred of them.

Air Transport Command had been formed around a nucleus of airline pilots and administrative personnel. Naturally it took on the characteristics of the civilian airlines. The training was heavily weighted toward instrument and weather flying. There were never any parachutes carried, so the training stressed emergency procedures, such as engine failures, fuel management, cruise control, electrical problems, and the like. The instructors at Homestead were strict taskmasters, and I had an awful lot to learn about things I had never paid much attention to. Before, I had always followed the usual 'kick the tires and light the fires' approach. I was introduced to the sacred 'CHECK LIST'. No move was made until the relevant item had been read off, accomplished, and pronounced completed. Theoretically it required a pilot, a co-pilot, and engineer to fly the bird. On occasion I have flown them solo, as the cockpit is so arranged that all controls, switches, etc. are well within reach of the pilot. After a few take-offs and landings, all my training was conducted with a hood over my head, so I was unable to see outside, while the instructor was busy creating emergencies by failing an engine, cutting off various systems – electrical, hydraulic, or vacuum – and in general keeping me busy as a one-armed paper hanger. The lessons usually lasted around four hours, and I would be wringing wet when I got out. I don't think that guy liked me very much.

A hurricane came roaring through the area while Eleanor, Jimmy, and I were staying in a hotel there in Miami, so we had a grandstand seat in comparative safety. I won't attempt to describe a hurricane, but it is a most fascinating thing to watch. (Storms have always inspired me to want to assume a stance outside and shout *"Odin!"* or some such at heaven's darkly raging turbulence.) As this one was subsiding, we three were standing in front of the hotel when two Navy fighter pilots collided overhead, then hit the street a hundred yards away and burned. I was sorry Eleanor and Jimmy saw that.

When the storm was over I went out to Homestead, only to find that most of it had blown away. As I had not finished the course, we went to Charleston, South Carolina, to complete my training. I took my final check-ride and was declared competent to act as Aircraft Commander in a C-54. For the first time I was actually a legally certified transport pilot! I also knew I was now a far more *qualified* pilot to be hauling passengers around the world than the throttle jockey I had been. I've

never regretted any of the grueling work I'd been put through. But now we bid a fond farewell to beautiful downtown Miami and head for Memphis.

The folks at home had trouble understanding why I was going back overseas while everyone else was coming home from the wars. Though I think Eleanor knew what was driving me, she was nevertheless most unhappy about it. I couldn't blame her, but I was going anyway.

I rode American to Washington and had no trouble at all getting a seat on the next flight east. This airplane was flown by a series of airline crews hopping the same bird all the way to India. We stopped at Stevensville in Newfoundland, the Azores Islands, Casablanca, Tripoli, Cairo, Dhahran, Karachi, New Delhi, and finally Calcutta. En-route the airplane stopped long enough to take on gasoline, a new crew, and those infamous box lunches featuring a hard boiled egg, an apple, and something that I think was fried sea gull. I am the world's worst passenger, sitting way back in the rear of the cabin, listening to every sound the aircraft makes and wondering if the pilots are awake or asleep. I can't criticize their rough arrivals, sometimes called landings, as long as we are at least back on the ground, and I can tolerate their dismal lack of knowledge of brake usage – but I cannot forgive their utter lack of rudder coordination, which sloshes me all over the cabin! It is quite obvious that these clowns were never fighter pilots.

It took two days to get to Calcutta, where we arrived at midnight, and not quite that long to find transportation to my new Base, Bharakpore, a few miles out from Calcutta.

U.S. Army Air Corps photo

"I am the world's worst passenger."

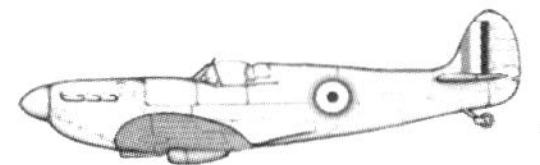

"...those faraway places with strange sounding names..."

Col. Haun photos

"...the buzzards! Hundreds of them circling around at treetop height."

chapter sixteen

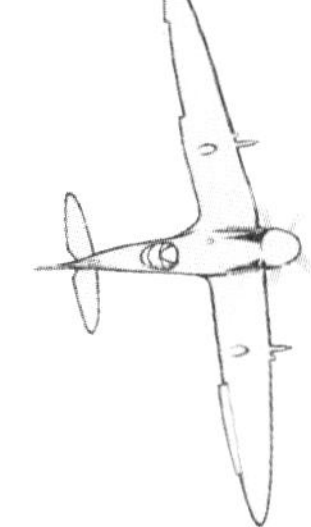

INDIA AND THE HUMP

1945: "RIOTS & BUZZARDS IN DIVERSE PLACES"

The Base was sound asleep. The driver took me to a row of little one-room concrete cubbyholes and pointed out an empty one. It had a cot ready made up and a table and one chair. Home at last! I dropped my clothes in the middle of the floor, put my wallet and Colt .45 under the pillow, and died.

It was still dark when I was awakened by a soft noise. I could make out a shadowy figure moving about the room doing things with my B-4 bag and discarded garments. I slipped my hand under the pillow and watched as the darkness gradually faded. He got my clothes silently unpacked and properly stowed and, with the first glimmer of sunlight, eased out the door and spread a little rug on the ground under my window. I had never seen nor heard a Muslim at prayer, but this boy apparently had a lot to pray about. Turned out this was my own private bearer, or servant, whose duty was to see that my clothes were washed and ironed and my room kept spotless at all times. He was a fine bearer and I was able – very diplomatically of course – to persuade him to perform his crack-of-dawn devotionals a little further away from my window.

That morning I found transportation to take me over to Hasting Mills to check in with the command headquarters. My inquiry as to where I might find General Tunner's office was met with a surprising reply:

"General Tunner and his entire staff left here last week for the States. I understand he is now CO of the Ferry Command, located at Cincinnati, Ohio."

I was introduced to a Colonel Barksdale, a really nice fellow who, incidentally, was the same officer that had been so surprised at my returning to Europe from Washington National several months before…small world. He said he was delighted to have me aboard and certainly did have a job for me as Director of Operations at Bharakpore, as the present occupant of that position was frantic for a replacement so he could go home! The entire CBI (China-Burma-India) was folding up as rapidly as possible and Bharakpore would be the last and only active base left. I wasn't exactly overjoyed at this revolting development, but there was really nothing I could do about it. So, "Press On."

I was given a tour of the area and downtown Calcutta. What an amazing place! The people appeared to vary between poverty and abject poverty. Everyone wore white, lightweight cotton garments. The men had loose, baggy pants and long coats, while the women wore a long shapeless garment resembling a dress. I saw my first 'Holy Man'; he wore a top hat, carried a lady's parasol, and was otherwise completely naked except for a good sprinkling of ashes and a benevolent smile.

And the buzzards! Hundreds of them circling around at treetop height. I later saw why: By early morning the sidewalks would have acquired quite a crop of people who had died during the night. The buzzards loved to peck out their eyeballs before the trucks could come to pick up the bodies for transporting to the burning ghats. They don't bury people in India. The supply of firewood must present quite a problem.

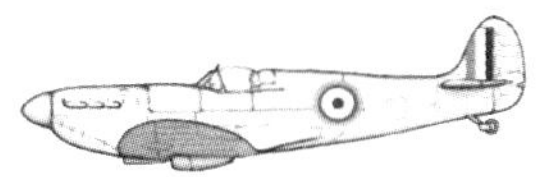

Then there were the cows: They wander around in all the streets and are untouchable. Traffic must make way for the holy animals, which are never eaten in this starving land. Street vendors sold from their carts assortments of fruits and nuts, the only visible sources of food.

Contrary to expectations, I found my job as Operations Director most interesting. The task of winding down and folding up the widely scattered remnants of an entire Theatre of Operations required a sizeable number of people who must be fed, clothed, and transported over long distances; that was our job. We had a fleet of C-54s for long hauls and a number of Gooney Birds for the 'local' work – local including all of Burma and India. Then there was the morale problem with homesick men wanting to be aboard the next westbound plane. I tackled that one with the usual, "Let's get this job finished in a hurry so we can all get out of here." Almost everyone responded favorably to that approach.

National Museum of the U.S Air Force

A nearby base had the job of smashing up all the airplanes that had been left behind. I was over there one day when some Colonel came in with his own private B-25, all shiny and nice. He parked and left the base for some reason. While he was gone, a tractor pulled up and hooked on to tow it to the scrap heap. There the lads collapsed the gear and drove tractors over it until it was properly prepared for sale as scrap. Naturally, the Colonel blew his stack when he came back and saw what was left of his runabout. I gave him a ride to Bharakpore, which is way out in the boonies. I could have dropped him off at Dum Dum, as he had asked, but I didn't like his negative attitude.

The first night I went to the club for a few shots of 'Carrews Brews For Weary Air Crews', I spied a forlorn looking individual at the bar and sat down near him to see if I could elicit any worthwhile information about anything in particular.

"Hi, how long have you been out here?"

He slowly turned to see where such an absurd question had come from and with a glazed look whispered, "They won't tell me."

I rather liked him, and as he was one of our better pilots, I selected him as my co-pilot on my first trip over the Hump to Kunming in China. Of course I had practically memorized the maps and terrain features for the route. There was only one little radio beacon still operating, which was located on top of the last high ridge before reaching the wide Irrawaddy Valley. We were on solid instruments with the bird dog – radio compass – tuned to that beacon and homing nicely on it.

From the right seat my experienced co-pilot instructed me: "Now when you hit the station you must follow my instructions precisely, and I will give you the headings we must follow."

The needle rotated to point straight down, so we were crossing the beacon.

"Now turn ten degrees left…we hold that for twenty seconds…now sharply, twenty degrees right, fifteen seconds…now back to the original heading; I always sweat out that pass," as he wiped the sweat off his brow. I played along with the comforting knowledge that the nearest rock was a good twelve thousand feet below us.

The weather cleared so I could get my first look at China. This is the most rugged terrain – mountains crowded close together with tight little valleys that showed no sign of human habitation, a forbidding place if one were to be forced down. Far to our left I could see the High Hump, with

snow capped peaks piled up to around thirty thousand feet, where the boys had to fly before the Japs were cleared from the area we were now over. Beautiful, majestic, and scary as hell.

There was a beacon at Kunming, where – though the weather was clear – I made the published ADF letdown, just so as to see where it took me, for future reference. The runway at Kunming was gravel, so there was always a large number of Chinese workers lining both sides, ready to repair immediately any damage our landing might cause. The Chinese firmly believe that each person has a little invisible dragon always following at his heels which causes all of his bad luck. They invented firecrackers to be tossed over their shoulders to hopefully scare the little devil away. The arrival of an airplane sometimes tempted them to dash in front of it in hopes that the wheels would run over the dragon, allowing their lot in life to be greatly improved. This seemed to work fairly well with twin engined airplanes, but the four engine jobs caused a problem with that windmilling outer propeller. The resulting little 'thump' didn't damage the propeller – and obviously the dragon escaped scot-free.

U. S. Army Air Corps photo

Our government decided that the military should operate an Air Transport Service connecting all our far flung commitments, by transporting personnel, mail, and supplies. It originated at Washington National Airport, circling from thence through Europe, North Africa, India, the Philippines, and back to the U.S. This circuit was called the Statesman. Our segment ran from Karachi through New Delhi, Calcutta, Bangkok, and Manila. We stationed crews at each stop so that there was no delay except for fuel and service. Another trip was always scheduled to start from Manila in the opposite direction, so that we usually had two planes a day passing through our base near Calcutta – which, incidentally, is almost exactly half way around the world from Washington.

I took the first trip east, to both position crews and get familiar with the route, as I had never been in that part of the world. Our first stop was Bangkok, where we were to leave two crews. The airport was quite a few miles from town, surrounded mainly by jungle. The Thais had set up quarters for us in a semi-palace roomy enough to accommodate a full airplane load of people, should the need arise. It was extremely well staffed, with an excellent chef. Here I had the first real steak I had had in years. It was water buffalo, all covered with what I supposed were mushrooms and other vegetables; about three inches thick and tender as a mother's love. We were treated royally: nice rooms, mosquito nets over each bed – even an indoor swimming pool. The Good-will Ambassador inquired if he should establish, or provide, what he termed a 'harem' in conjunction with the palace. After much soul-searching, lasting perhaps ten seconds, and considering the large

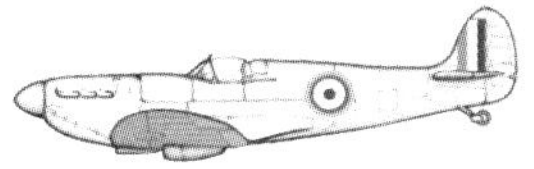

number and varying types of people that would be coming through, I thought it best to regretfully decline his offer.

U.S. Army Air Corps photo

The next day we crossed a lot of water, during which crossing I learned to use an instrument entirely new to me. It is called a 'drift meter'. Out where there are no radio aids, in daytime when the navigator has no stars to shoot – and each wave looks pretty much like any other – it's nice to be able to find where the wind is. The drift meter is a tube pointed down through the floor so you can see the earth beneath: it has a rotatable compass-rose with a 'lubber line'. By simply looking down at the ocean and picking out a white cap, you turn the lubber line until the white cap is moving exactly along that line, then you read the wind drift at your altitude. If you do this every hour or so, you will stay right on course. We used this method on the return trip, as the radio beacon at Bangkok was so weak we couldn't receive it until we were within about fifteen miles, and we still hit the field right on the nose. Our later transports didn't have drift meters, which was a pity.

We had a good look at Manila and the Bay. Not much had been cleaned up at that time; the harbor was still littered with sunken ships and all the usual debris of war. We circled Corregidor and the wrecked city, then landed at Clark Field, leaving two crews there and heading home after a good night's rest. We stopped at Saigon for no particular reason except to see what the field was like. Someone had a Jap Zero that was flying. I saw a number of Japanese soldiers in uniform standing around, acting very friendly. Maybe they hadn't been able to get a ride home. I didn't ask.

Crossing what is now Cambodia, we saw an ancient city buried deep in the jungle with no roads leading to it, apparently uninhabited. On my next trip to Bangkok I asked about that city, but no one seemed to know anything about it. From the air we took a few snapshots of very poor quality. Later, when I was stationed in Japan, we were not allowed to fly over that area.

We had another run that I found extremely interesting. The Japanese had operated prison camps in Java where a number of English civilians from Singapore had been interred. We went down to Jakarta to pick up a load of these unfortunates. There were no quarters at the airport, so we went into the city and checked in at their best hotel. We wanted to get around a bit to see the city, but there was occasional gunfire from the center of town, so we stayed around the hotel. I bought some of their woodcarvings, which I still have. The hotel faced a river, or canal. The next morning I was privileged to witness the natives at their ablutions there on the bank. Some were in the water bathing; others were drawing water for, I suppose, cooking purposes; meanwhile literally hundreds were squatting on the bank with their little brown fannies hung over the water, doing what comes naturally. I normally have coffee for breakfast, but that morning I chose bottled beer.

Our passengers were brought out to the airport in trucks; and a quieter, more subdued bunch I've never seen. I thought they would be jumping for joy, but the best they could do was grin…obviously very undernourished and weak. There were a few men in the crowd, but mostly

Haun family photo

women and children, their clothes old and faded but very clean. We had been told to bring them to Calcutta; I suppose for medical care. There was one little boy who had a little life left in him, so I took him to the cockpit and, with the autopilot on, let him sit in my lap. His mother told me he had been born in prison camp.

Seeing these prisoners brought back a terrible scene. After VE Day I had flown deep into Germany with a British officer who was looking for a friend or relative. Our airstrip there adjoined the prison camp walls. I stayed with the airplane while the Brit went inside. There those walking skeletons had stood and stared at my airplane without speaking. At least our Calcutta passengers now were somewhat better fed and clothed, and would answer if you spoke to them directly. During the war my greatest fear had been of being captured and having to spend years penned behind barbed wire, watching the grass grow. Now I saw the result of dehumanizing people over a long period of time, and knew just how lucky I had been. We had a nice, quiet non-stop flight back to Calcutta.

Word came down that the Air Force was interested in awarding regular commissions to a few worthy Reserve officers who could measure up to their exactingly strict standards. Naturally I jumped at the chance and put my name in the pot. There were to be written exams held on a specific date over at the Mill, so I appeared there bright and early. This exam was the new-fangled type known as True or False; all you had to do was mark the answer you selected. When I was in grade and high school we had to write out our answers in long hand, including the math work where your calculations were done on the test paper itself. I'm sure this was so the teacher could tell if you really knew the answers or were just guessing. I remember my Dad telling me why I must take Latin: "You probably won't have any use for it ever," he said, "But that's not the point. You are exercising your brain, which, like your arms, must be worked hard to have any strength." I think I witnessed in that test the beginning of the decline of the American education system so lamented today. Besides, it must have been written with eighth grade kids in mind. I was told I made the highest score in India!

Next we had to take a physical. I always passed a good physical, so I approached this one in high spirits. When they asked me if I had ever had an operation, I had a sudden rush of truth to the head and told them about my left knee. It hadn't bothered me in years; I had almost forgotten about it. Well, they x-rayed the member and announced, "Sorry, that knee looks like a jumble of rocks. We can't use you."

That was a blow, but I figured there were other ways to skin this cat…which turned out to be true.

My next trip was to Shanghai. Because there were no radio aids on this route, and it was about a twelve-hour trip, we took a navigator aboard and flew at night. Also we arrived in daylight, which was a great help. We planned a twenty-four hour layover in case we had any return cargo or passengers; besides we wanted to see the town. There was a big sign over Ops that said THE CITY OF SHANGHAI IS OFF LIMITS TO AMERICAN PERSONNEL. Now that's no way to treat us valiant airmen. I tried to get some of the crew to go in with me, but they expressed great hesitancy. Shows they were all good well-disciplined troops, so I went in by myself.

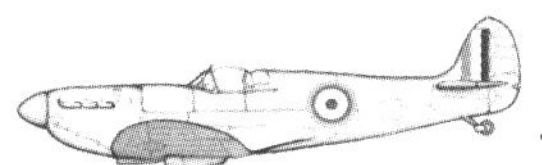

I wandered all over that town but was especially interested by the shipping on the river; big junks and little junks, each with big bulging eyes on the prow to watch for those bad old water devils. I doubt if they were water dragons. Coolies were hand loading and unloading the ships, carrying great loads on their backs. The ever-present police wandered about, each with a long, rather heavy cane which they used to belabor any coolie that came within reach, for no reason I could see. They were not heavy blows, but the coolies dutifully cried big tears. I had stopped at the main hotel to get my Indian rupees changed into the Chinese script, and hired a rickshaw to haul me around all day. That guy had legs like a horse. I'm sure I over-tipped him. I paid 2500 dollars, Chinese, for supper, took in a nightclub, paid 1800 dollars for breakfast, and went back to the airport.

I was ordered to report to the detachment commander, who happened to be living in the same hotel I had just left downtown. I was warned that this Colonel was a real tough guy. I found him to be a drunk. When I arrived he was dressed in a flowery Chinese garment and was, in fact, staggering drunk.

"What are you doing in Shanghai?"

"I brought the scheduled trip from Bharakpore."

"I said, what are you doing in Shanghai? Don't you know there's a war on?"

I scratched my head: "Well I'll be damned, I heard the war was over! The folks in India will sure be surprised."

He poured another drink, and I turned around and walked out.

Back at the base I found that our airplane was gone…just disappeared. Of course the line crew couldn't say where, so I just hung around getting to know the fellows and listening to their sad stories.

That paid off. At the crack of dawn the next morning one of them came around with the information that our airplane was back and was hidden in a revetment across the field. I asked if the boys could get a fuel truck and go top off the tanks, which they cheerfully did. (I figured that drunk Colonel wouldn't have a very loyal following.) That airplane was filthy dirty with old lunch boxes and trash covering the floor. We didn't wait to tell Ops when we were leaving or where bound. We just cranked up the engines – all four of them worked – so off we went. We had been at twelve thousand most of the trip, but I hadn't been using oxygen, as I couldn't smoke my pipe with a mask on. As we crossed the last ridge and started to descend, the co-pilot said he saw the lights of Calcutta in the distance. All I could see were a few pinpoints of light – until I put on the mask and took a deep drag of pure oxygen – whereupon lights bloomed all over the place. I'd just learned another valuable lesson.

At Bharakpore we were having increasing trouble with buzzards over our runway. A Gooney Bird took one through the windshield that hurt the pilot. To do something about it I got a 12 Gauge Winchester pump and a supply of GI-issue double ought buck. There were about a hundred of the nasty rascals funneling down to within thirty or forty feet of the ground, so by shooting at the higher birds and working down, I had time to reload and get another seven killed before they wised up and left. My idea was to take the dead birds over to the fence and hang them there so maybe their friends and relatives would move their flight pattern over there away from the runway. That didn't seem to work, but I had to try something.

That night we heard a lot of singing, drum beating, and what passed for music coming from the village adjoining the Base. "The natives are restless tonight."

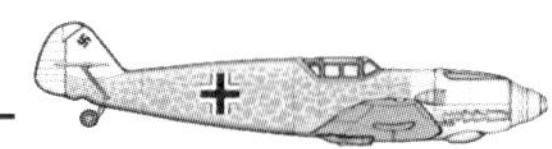

The next morning the local LAW, in the form of a British Constable, arrived. He advised me that the villagers were "extraordinarily upset" at the killing of the previous day. You see, they believed in reincarnation; so when I killed a buzzard, I might in fact be killing old Aunt Susie, who – having by good works risen to a higher form of life – must now become a people again; and you shouldn't wish that on any buzzard. Trying hard not to laugh aloud, I promised to behave.

During my tour there, the Indians were trying to gain their independence from Great Britain. We in the military knew very little about this struggle as we had no radios on the Base, and what newspapers were available played down the problem with typical British understatement. There was no indication of unrest in the nearby village now that I had discontinued my efforts concerning the buzzard blight. So it came as a complete surprise when we found ourselves right in the middle of some shockingly violent activity.

Whenever we went into Calcutta at night, our favorite hangout was the principal hotel there. I vaguely recall the name Shepherd, but that may have been some other town. In front of the main entrance we were accustomed to seeing an old beggar woman, always with a tiny baby in her arms. (She seemed to have acquired a new baby every time I saw her, and I am certain there was a plentiful supply.) Obviously some GI had coached her in pitiful pleading as she always came up with the same whining pitch: "*Bahksee Sahb, Bahksee Sahb*, no mama, no papa, no flying pay, no per diem, no goddam thing." I always gave her a rupee or two so I could check on whether this new baby was alive or dead.

This hotel had the best food, drink, and entertainment in town and was definitely the place to see and be seen. One night five of us took a staff car into town and parked as always inside a secure compound across the street from the hotel. There was a very large park, I would guess almost a quarter mile square, directly adjacent. This was the center of Calcutta. Around ten o'clock we decided to leave so as to conform with that unwritten law, "Twelve hours from bottle to throttle." We made our way with some difficulty through an extremely large crowd of people into the compound. From there we could see the entire square, which was packed with the largest crowd I have ever seen: Fifty thousand, a hundred thousand – who knows. The compound attendants told us we shouldn't leave, as this was a riot we were looking at, and people were being killed. Just at that time a scattering of shots convinced us we were being told the truth.

You've seen a big flock of White Leghorn chickens? When the shots rang out, that entire multitude would flutter away from the sounds and stop, until the next volley sent them back the other way. There were some fires burning in the area. We stayed there until it became light enough to see the entire square. Over on the far side from us we saw a young woman come out of a house with her little dog on a leash and walk right into the park as though there was no one else around. After a minute or two she was jumped by the crowd. We could see her running for her front door; you know how a woman runs, with her head thrown back and her hair streaming. She made it to the door and was beating on it until she was stabbed repeatedly and disappeared under a pile of her attackers. Two small tanks appeared and fired into the crowd with no apparent result as far as dispersing the mob.

By now it was broad daylight. Another woman appeared and walked into the park, her head held high and carrying herself with a quite regal bearing. She was a beautiful girl we had all seen at the club several times. The crowd parted for her and she made it almost to where we were standing inside the compound before she too was suddenly mobbed and disappeared. All of us there rushed out and pulled her away, carrying her into the safety of the compound. She had been stripped and

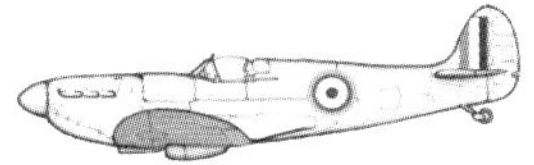

slashed badly with either knives or rocks but was still alive. We wrapped her with some sheets and called for help. Shortly one of those little tanks arrived and took her away.

I talked to an Indian standing outside our fence. He seemed to be of the higher class and spoke the King's English with an Oxford accent. He explained the revolt to me in some detail. I asked him if we Americans were in any danger from the mob, and he assured me that we were considered friendly and could come and go as we pleased provided we remembered one thing: If we were approached by a mob, we should put on a wide friendly grin and, with right fist clenched and arm extended, yell "*YAH IND!*" – which, being translated, means "FREE INDIA!" He assured me that cry would calm their fevered breasts. I talked it over with the others and we decided to give it a try.

I was driving. We had all the windows rolled down as we eased out of the compound. Immediately we were swarmed, but our enthusiastic and highly vocal support for their cause was favorably received; instantly we were waved on our way. We passed a lorry on fire, with a dead British soldier chained to the steering wheel. We saw quite a few 'Anglo' girls who had been hideously killed with red-hot pokers. (These Anglos were part Indian and part British.) The mob surrounded us again several times, but our joyful yells always got us through without trouble. I don't recall any of us going back to town after that.

National Museum of the U.S Air Force

We had one more job that we hated but had to do. There were numerous burial sites over in the Irrawaddy Valley where so much fighting had been. These bodies were to be exhumed and brought to Calcutta for burial in a large military cemetery. Our job was to load our Gooney Birds with twenty-four empty wooden caskets and deliver them to a base out there, whose name I forget, and return to Calcutta with twenty-four bodies. It was a nasty job and some of the boys simply couldn't do it. I found that if I wore my oxygen mask and breathed pure oxygen, I could handle it. The British had a control tower in operation at that field; before I landed, they advised me to land close to the loading area and stay away from the vicinity of the tower. Seems they had a little war going on at the other end of the field. The tower was well sandbagged and the operators didn't seem particularly disturbed. We unloaded rather quickly and reloaded to the sound of some desultory rifle fire, but we were not bothered. After that job was finished, we took those three Gooney Birds over on the far side of the field and set them on fire. They could never be of any further use.

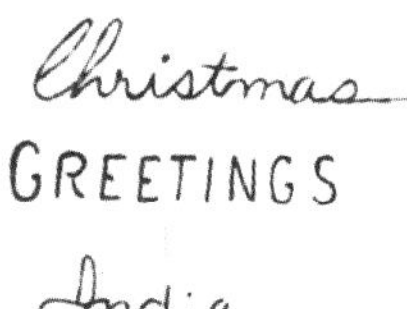

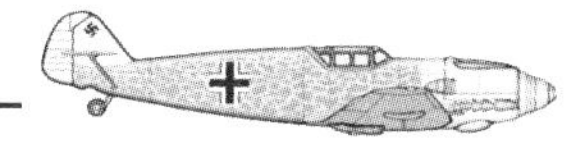

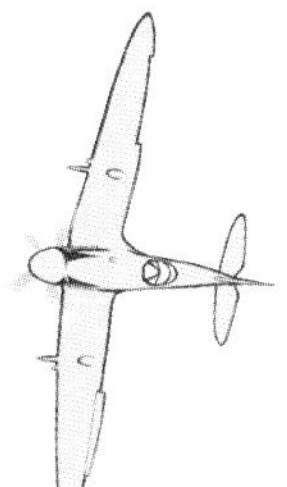

chapter seventeen

HOME

1945 - '46: "PERMANENT COMMISSION AT BAD KNEE"

The entire CBI Theater was winding down rapidly. We were sending our people home as soon as they could be spared. I had one C-54 stashed away for the last of us to use for our getaway. There were efforts made by the Brass to grab it, but with one engine removed and various other parts dangling it was obviously not airworthy. Also, the necessary replacements were 'on back order' and of course didn't arrive until the day we were to depart. I loaded the airplane with all the spare crews we had and blasted off with only the minimum of farewells. We gassed at Karachi, overflew Baghdad, and went direct to Cairo; thence to Tripoli and Casablanca. We were heavily loaded, what with full tanks and all the loot the troops were bringing home. The Ops people at Casablanca had two thousand pounds of mail for the States and wanted to remove some of our people and baggage. Naturally we couldn't have that, so we told them we were light and to just throw the mail aboard, which they did.

We decided that the safest route home was across the South Atlantic, to minimize the likelihood of encountering any Brass that could take our airplane away from us. So the next stop was Dakar on the coast. The ground temperature was so high we knew this would have to be a late night takeoff, what with our overweight and poor old tired engines. We all went swimming and idled around waiting for dark. I tried to sleep, but it was just too hot. We didn't have any trouble getting fuel on the entire trip, thanks to the fine set of orders I had written back at Bharakpore directing me to deliver this airplane, via the most suitable route, to West Palm Beach, Florida.

Fortunately the runway at Dakar ended right at the water's edge, so there were no obstructions to clear on takeoff. This night there was no moon or stars and, of course, no lights. A takeoff under these conditions over water is about the same as a completely blind takeoff. On the roll we checked all instruments and hoped for the best. After liftoff, with the gear coming up, there was not the slightest indication of a climb. I didn't dare raise the flaps, as that would cause us to sink a bit, which would certainly put the prop tips into the water. It seemed like a lot longer than it really was, but we finally got a little extra speed so I could ease the flaps up. At a hundred feet I called for 'climb power' and we were on our way. I leveled off at five hundred and stayed there several hours burning off some of our weight. That was about the hairiest takeoff I've ever made.

We stopped at Belém on the coast of Brazil for fuel and food and were airborne shortly after. The next stop was Ramey on the north coast of Puerto Rico; then on to West Palm Beach. We had a party and a good night's sleep. I tried to get the airplane for delivery to Memphis, but ended up having to ride a train, of all things, the whole rest of the way home.

I stayed around Memphis for a week before I let the folks in Cincinnati know I was back. They told me to report to Cincinnati for further instructions. As this was a quite indefinite assignment, I left Eleanor and Jimmy with her parents and shoved off in my old Ford. My assignment turned out to be Operations for Air Evac. This outfit is charged with moving military patients to and from various hospitals around the country. The boys who were already doing the job knew their business and were doing it well, so I didn't interfere. There was talk about moving the headquarters to Memphis, so there was no point in bringing Eleanor and Jimmy to Cincinnati. I got one little job of

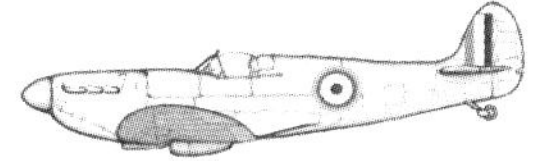

hauling a team of personnel around to all the various detachments to see by just how many people we could reduce the payroll. Most of them wanted to leave anyway, so that was an easy task. Meanwhile I was still trying to figure a way to get a regular commission. I simply had to have a waiver for that left knee, but I knew going through regular channels would be an exercise in futility. A letter would be seen by some clerk and promptly tossed into File 13, so I borrowed an airplane and hied me to Washington.

At the Pentagon I located the head Flight Surgeon's office. As I walked in, the first person I saw was Patterson, my buddy from the 100th Wing! I told him my tale of woe, and – though he was quite sympathetic – he was afraid that nothing could be done. I asked him to take me to the head man, but he said the head man wouldn't see me, and in fact wouldn't see anyone, but, "That's him walking into his office."

So, in for a penny, in for a pound, and I would be fired anyway the next RIF. I walked into the boss's office without knocking. He was a short fat individual, with thick glasses. For some reason he seemed put out at my unannounced entrance: "What do you want?"

"General, I want a Regular Commission. I have been turned down because of injuries to my left knee suffered in an airplane crash in 1935. This knee was good enough for a war and two beachheads – and I figure it's good enough for the peace-time service."

He glowered at me for a while and said, "Oh you do, do you? We'll see. Pull that chair up against my desk. Now climb up on top of the desk. Now jump off and land on that left leg."

I jumped.

"Did that hurt?"

"No Sir," I lied.

"Do it again."

That old man kept me climbing and jumping until sweat was popping out on my brow from the pain. I suppose he finally figured I had been sufficiently punished for my arrogance, because he wrote me a waiver!

"Take this to the Records Section."

I didn't let myself limp leaving the office, but I held onto the wall outside. Patterson was watching, no doubt expecting to see me thrown out on my head. I grinned at him and waved the paper. He shook his head in disbelief as I left.

Down in the basement I found the Records Section, in the charge of an old friend from the 12th Squadron at Fort Knox. Danny got my file and looked through it carefully:

"You need to get someone to write you a glowing ER to replace this one General Sanders gave you."

I got General Tunner to write me one, in which he claimed I could almost walk on water. I was eventually commissioned a Captain in the Regular Service, plus allowed to retain my temporary rank and pay of Lieutenant Colonel. Sometimes that knee gives me a fit, but the pain disappears completely every payday.

We stayed at Cincinnati for about two months and then moved to Memphis. This had been a Ferry Command base for most of the war and there were airplanes of every description on the ramp. So naturally I took full advantage of this opportunity to get myself checked out in anything I had not flown before. I enjoyed flying the B-17. Of course we flew them with only a light load, which made it a sweet airplane. Just a big old tail-dragger and you flew it accordingly. I got a little time in a B-29, but we didn't keep that bird long – as it had a lot of trouble with those Wright engines heating up – and were happy when it was transferred to some bomber base. I was never able to fly the P-38,

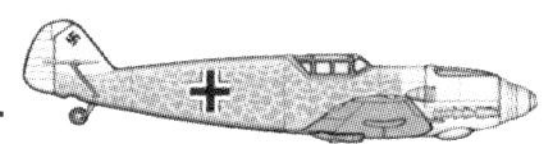

which was the only Air Corps fighter I missed. There were no B-24s around, but the pilots who had flown them said I hadn't missed much.

National Museum of the U.S. Air Force

We had far too many people with not enough work to keep them busy, so the morale on the Base was rather low. I had my usual job as Director of Operations, where I was able to help expedite the departure of those who wanted to get out of the Service. Those that I kept were the eager ones, so I made a practice of putting a Lieutenant into a Captain's job and a Captain into a Major's job, etc. Worked wonders.

I noticed that the mechanics out on the flight line were moving at a snail's pace; that is, when they could be persuaded to come out from the shade of the wings into the summer heat. There was one beautiful gal working in Ops who was a real head-turner. I called her in and told her: "At ten o'clock in the morning I want you to take a letter, or some papers, and walk down to Maintenance, and back, and do the same thing at two o'clock."

She was quite used to getting a lot of attention and obviously enjoyed it. So every day at ten and two she made that journey. Of course everything came to a standstill for a few minutes during the parade, but I made up the lost manhours when the boys returned to their labors with vigor. There may be some old folks who won't understand that bit of applied psychology, poor things.

Quite a number of my former buddies were back. Hook had a job as co-pilot with Delta, Charlie Lewellen was with American, and Red Forman was with General Tunner at HQ. We all got together once a week or so out at a dive known as The Big Apple, each with the intention of coming up with the most outlandish tale of derring-do, which of course must be the absolute truth. Hook had been flying P-47s in China; without blushing he claimed he had killed one thousand three hundred and eighty-seven Japanese by strafing!

Naturally I believed him, but wondered at the system of body-counting behind enemy lines, which must have been a fantastic achievement. Hook had applied for a regular commission as I had. One night his wife, Jewel, called me at home about a telegram from the War Department stating that he had been selected for permanent rank of Captain, provided he wired his acceptance within twenty-four hours. Hook was on a flight, but I was finally able to reach him at Detroit.

At first he thought I was pulling his leg, but I assured him, "Hook, I would kid you about a lot of things – but not about this. Now get that wire off tonight."

I am told by competent authority that he showed up for his Delta flight the next morning, after the passengers had already been loaded, and marched up the aisle with a parachute slung over his shoulder discussing the safety of flight. I don't doubt that happened.

Around the first of December I was called in by General Tunner and given a very hush-hush job. I was to take a group of instructors and set up a training detachment on an abandoned airport at Topeka, Kansas. We were to train five crews of Portuguese pilots and navigators in the gentle art of flying the C-54 and the B-17. I gathered this had to be done in secret because of certain negotiations underway concerning our establishing a base in the Azores for the transatlantic route. This job shouldn't take too long as our students were already pilots but had simply never flown other than single-engine airplanes. So again I left Eleanor and Jimmy in Memphis and headed for Topeka.

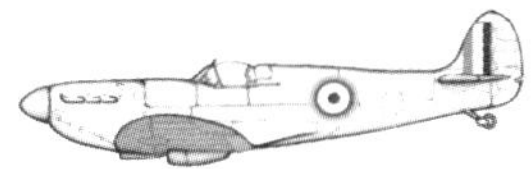

The Base was certainly bleak. There was a small housekeeping detachment that provided us with light and heat in a couple of barracks, plus one hangar for maintenance of our two C-54s and two B-17s. We had the usual GI kitchen and rations.

The language barrier was not too great with the pilots, as some of them could speak a bit of English. Just how the navigators managed I really don't know, but they evidently managed. Our biggest problem was the weather: it snowed and snowed and snowed some more – and man, was it cold! But we progressed.

We had been authorized to wear civilian clothes when off duty and that was a help. If you went out to some bar in uniform, there was usually some drunk who would stagger up loudly proclaiming he had always wanted to kick a Colonel's ass. At that age I didn't really mind, but it gets old after a while. I had bought some civvies, including a heavy overcoat and a fine hat. One night the Base was completely deserted; it was snowing hard with the wind whistling, but I decided to go to town anyway. As I was exiting the barracks, the wind took my brand new hat flying. I tried to run after it but the deep snow held me back. Still I continued the pursuit until I came to a sudden stop in a deep ditch with snow up to my neck. The powdery snow was almost impossible to move in. The harder I tried, the less success I had. I began to sweat from the exertion, and that froze, which made moving even harder. Finally I had a bright idea! Taking a deep breath I went down to the bottom of the ditch and, making like a mole, crawled to the side and pushed up until I could get my arms on top of the bank, where I finally clawed, pushed, and struggled up and out. I was frozen stiff.

Now I had seen all the training films like *Land and Live in the Arctic,* and *Land and Live in the Desert*, and all the others, so I knew what to do. I made my way back to the barracks and started shedding my clothes. Then I got in the shower and turned on the cold water. After a while I started gradually feeding in the warm and finally the hot water until I was steaming and turning red. Back in the room I just happened to have a bottle of new and green whiskey called PM (Post Mortum), which I now sampled freely. I would have gone on to town but all my clothes were too wet.

U.S. Air Force photo

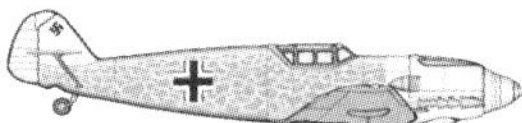

chapter eighteen

WEST PALM

1946: "AIRBORNE SEMI-DRIVER SCHOOL"

When the Portuguese had finished with their training, we all went to the depot at Tulsa and took delivery of three reconditioned B-17s and two C-54s; then everybody headed for the Azores. Everybody except me, as I had to get to Memphis to help with another move, this time to West Palm Beach, Florida, where a new Transport Group was forming. I would be one of the squadron commanders. We had received eight of the new C-74s, heavy-haulers made by Douglas. So now we had two squadrons, each having four C-74s and six C-54s. Housing was going to be a problem at West Palm, so again I left the family at Memphis until I could find a place for us to live. A former student of mine had an automobile agency; through him I was able to buy a new Chevrolet; the very next morning I took off for Florida.

Douglas C-74

U.S. Air Force photo

The C-74 was the first of the really large transports. It had four 4360 Pratt & Whitney engines, known as the corncob engine, as each had four rows of seven cylinders, allowing each individual engine to develop in the neighborhood of three thousand horsepower. The airplane had a new feature that took a while to become used to – an engineer in an adjoining room running your engines! The pilot did have four throttles and a prop control, but everything else was in that back room. You could talk to him by intercom. That was changed in the later model, known as the C-124. In that one you could actually see the guy. There was an elevator in the back for loading the airplane, operated by a crewmember known as the Loadmaster. He was also supposed to be real sharp at figuring weight and balance. The big craft looked a little frog-eyed, as the pilot and co-

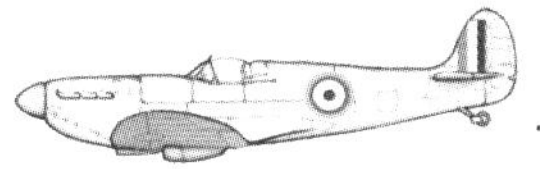

pilot each had his own bubble-canopy – similar to that of a P-51 – which required either of them to duck his head and lean across to do any talking, then stick his head back up in the bubble to see out. Because these canopies were canted to fit the curve of the fuselage, the pilots had a bad habit of landing on the right gear. That feature was soon replaced with a normal cockpit.

About this time I learned that I owed Uncle Sam four years back income taxes. Having just bought a new car, I had to make arrangements to spread the tax payments out a bit. The housing situation in West Palm was worse than we had thought, but the Base was converting the old barracks into four apartments apiece; consequently, Eleanor and Jimmy had to wait a little longer before coming to join me.

When the work on converting barracks to apartments was completed, we furnished ours with GI-Issue furniture, which required some ingenuity to give it a warm, homey, color-coordinated atmosphere. I picked up a few pieces from a salvage place in town and added a small Atwater Kent radio as the finishing touch. Supply donated all the necessary dishes, cups, saucers, and utensils. Having lived in a converted chicken house at Fort Knox, we thought these quarters palatial by comparison.

Eleanor and Jimmy arrived as scheduled, but I kept them waiting in the hot sun for a couple of hours until I discovered there were two train stations in West Palm! We made a comfortable place to live with one exception. We were located so close to the runway that sleep was impossible when night flying was in progress. Other than that it was home, sweet home.

We had three scheduled runs. There was one a day to Ramey in Puerto Rico, another daily to Panama, and a weekly trip down to Rio. The Panama trip always left around midnight, as there were no instrument approach facilities there, so we had to plan our arrival before the daily thunderstorms had time to build up. The airport's being right in town made it strictly a one way approach down the side of the hills, with buildings towering above you on each side. Definitely not a place to be during poor visibility. There were other airports in the area, and why we didn't use them I never knew. Ramey was a beautiful, spacious Base overlooking the ocean – a lushly pleasant place to stop.

I didn't like the Rio run at all, principally because of the weather we had to go through – in particular the Inter-Tropical Front lying across our path with no way of going around it. This weather-wall moves north and south but is always there waiting for you to stick your nose in it, a solid line of thunderstorms reaching up many thousands of feet above where the airplanes of that day could fly; so we had to bore right through it. Someone had decided that the best altitude to penetrate a thunderstorm was at six thousand feet. We normally flew at around eight or nine thousand, so when we approached that wicked looking line, we always descended to six thousand. We had no radar to help us pick out and avoid the worst cells; it was a case of buckling in tight, turning the lights on bright (so the lightning wouldn't blind us) and slowing up to what the manual called 'penetration speed'. There are violent up and down drafts that toss an airplane around like a feather. We learned to ignore the rapid changes in altitude and concentrate entirely on trying to keep the airplane in level flight. Sometimes the rain was so heavy you couldn't see your engines out there on the flopping and bending wings; how they kept running under water is a mystery to me. Of course I always pulled my old sea captain act and sat smoking my pipe, scared half to death. Many airplanes have shed their wings under these conditions.

We stopped at Jamestown, in British Guiana; I always thoroughly enjoyed wandering around that little seaport – it was like stepping back a hundred years. The trading schooners didn't have any auxiliary power but depended entirely on sail. I went aboard one that had a crew of three, two of

whom were escaped convicts; they were certainly a most villainous looking pair. Their bunks were two half-culverts fixed to the deck on either side of the wheel. And the pungent smells in the warehouses! Sacks of fresh coffee beans, tanned hides, tar, and things I couldn't identify. I recall a saw mill, that, instead of a circular saw, had what looked like several regular long crosscut saws mounted vertically, being pumped up and down by a busy little steam engine. I would have liked to have been able to spend more time exploring that place.

Our next stop was Belém for fuel, and then direct over the jungle to Rio. High mountains encircle most of the city, even though a piece of it trickles over to the seashore; the airport is on flat land in Guanabara Bay itself. In bad weather the minimum altitude in approaching the city is eleven thousand feet in order to clear the mountains. At that time there were two radio beacons that we tuned our two radio compasses to, so we could shuttle back and forth between them as we descended, keeping us safely out over the water. I arrived down there one time with only one radio working…that took some rapid re-tuning by the co-pilot!

The first time I was there a big festival was in full swing. The streets were crowded with people gathered in groups, jumping and bouncing around having a high old time. I thought they were all drunk, but it turned out that they got their highs by being squirted in the face with little cans of ether. Let anyone slow down a bit and his buddy immediately gave him a good squirt, and he was off again. They had another custom I found strange. If you ran over someone with your car and could evade capture for twenty-four hours, all was forgiven. Of course you would have to have a car that could climb mountains in order to escape, and there was nowhere else to go. Rio is a beautiful city, but I was just as happy to leave.

I learned that the Army had lost quite a number of airplanes on that route during the War, mostly in unavoidable thunderstorms, as I now understood firsthand. There were still small detachments on many of the islands in the Caribbean that we occasionally visited to deliver supplies or move personnel, but the three routes I've mentioned remained our primary job. We had several Gooney Birds for shorter hauls like Nassau and down the chain, or when we needed to make a whiskey run south to some of those duty-free spots. In fact, whiskey was so cheap and available it became more and more part of all our lives. Naturally it couldn't have any ill effect on my cast iron constitution!

Well, not at first.

Haun family photo

A C-54 arrived on the ramp at West Palm, but only one person climbed out. I was sitting in Operations trying to look busy, when this Sergeant walked in.

"General Tunner wants you on the airplane."

I went out and climbed aboard and heard the door slam shut and we started taxiing. I went forward and found Red Forman at the controls. He waved me to a seat and we took off. Looking around at the passengers I recognized most of General Tunner's staff. Nobody offered any explanation as to our destination, but I saw we were on an east heading and I didn't even have a toothbrush! We landed at Nassau and Tunner finally told me why I was along:

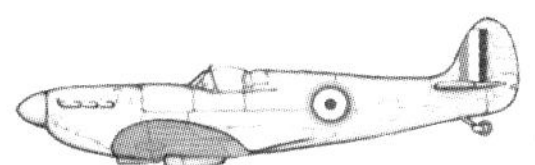

"Take the airplane back to West Palm and come back for us in ten days, and don't tell anyone where we are."

They all got off and left me there by myself.

Yes, Virginia, you can fly the C-54 solo. When I arrived at West Palm I was queried at length about the trip, but I wisely kept my big mouth shut. Ten days later I went back to Nassau; they climbed aboard, dropped me off at West Palm, and departed for their new headquarters at Fort Totten, Long Island.

Shortly thereafter we were told that the Base at West Palm was to close and we were all to be transferred to Mobile, Alabama.

USAF photo

Major General William H. Tunner

"Yes, Virginia, you can fly the C-54 solo."

U.S. Army Air Corps photo

Haun family photo

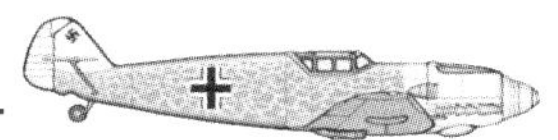

chapter nineteen

MOBILE

1947 – '48: "A PARADISE OF SAILBOATS & C-74s"

So in 1947 I went to Mobile to see what the housing situation was like. I found it really rough; there were several empty barracks available for the single officers and airmen, but married men would have to more or less fend for themselves. I did find a community of deserted houses off Base that had been occupied while the Base was under construction. The houses were in sad shape, but I was able to negotiate a rent that was even lower than I expected. I found a garage apartment that was better than our chicken house and promptly signed up for it. On return I gathered the Squadron and told them what I had found. I explained that the housing was capable of keeping them out of the rain, but would require a lot of elbow grease to make it livable. They all bought in on the idea and the move got under way.

I think I enjoyed Mobile more than any place I've ever been stationed. Far more spacious and livable quarters became available on the Base (Brookley Field) within three or four months. Mobile was a Supply Depot, which meant there was GI furniture available. That's nothing you would write home about, but we at least had a double bed, a full bath, a divan, and two easy chairs. Just like downtown! The Officer's Club was only a stone's throw away and included a nice swimming pool and oyster bar. We kept the bar stocked by our daily runs down to the islands. A Supply Depot always goes first class. This was a close-knit little community of friendly folks, among whom we began making good friends we still cherish – those who are still alive. [1994]

We still had the same routes, but in addition there was the C-74 with its long-haul ability. The Climatic Hangar had not yet been built at Eglin, so we were utilized to test all sorts of new additions to the Air Force, such as new lubricants, hoses, radios, etc. For this purpose we were sent on trips to Saudi Arabia in the summer and Alaska during the winter to see what would stand up under such a wide range of temperatures.

I was fortunate that all the crewmembers in my Squadron had been in the old Ferry Command and were quite used to 'those faraway places with the strange sounding names'. (Remember that song?) Those boys taught me a lot.

Like the first time I landed in soft, powdery snow and made the mistake of reversing the props soon after touchdown – and was instantly blinded by the snowstorm thrown up in front of me. That happened at Great Falls, Montana, on the way to Alaska.

I'll never forget that trip. I had always been taught that you could only pick up wing ice at around freezing temperature. Wrong! Over Whitehorse I asked a lonesome sounding radio operator what the temperature was down there. He came back with, "Fifty-four below."

An hour or so later we were in solid instruments and began to lose speed, a sure indication of icing. The 74 had the new heated-leading-edge wings, which none of us were familiar with. With the old rubber boots, you let the ice build up before knocking it off by inflating the boots, then deflating them and letting it build up again before repeating the process. Not knowing any better, we just turned on the heat and left it on; the searchlight showed the leading edges staying clear of ice. But for some reason the speed continued to fall off. I sent a crewmember down into the belly to see what he could see. He reported that the melted ice from the leading edge flowed back and froze again and had formed a ridge of ice back a foot or so. After some experimenting we found that by

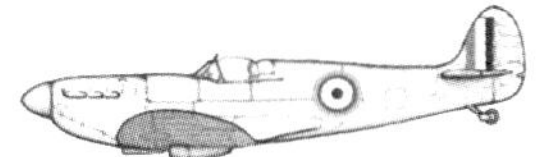

lowering about five degrees of flaps, which changed the wing's angle of attack a bit, we could stay in the air, but still at a very slow speed. On arrival at Anchorage I added about fifty miles an hour to my approach speed and punched it on. There was about three inches of snow on the runway but I didn't reverse the props until I absolutely had to. We found the engine nacelles completely packed with ice, so that not a drop of air could move through, yet the engine cylinder temperatures had read very low. I learned about ice from that!

That night we kept tents with Herman-Nelson heaters on the engines and one hose stuck in the cockpit. The engines started easily the next morning, but we found the controls hard to move, probably from the congealed grease on the pulleys. On the takeoff I learned something else. As usual I pushed the throttles all the way forward, but immediately felt the engineer jerk them back almost half way. It seems that with that extremely cold, heavy air, I was pulling so much power that the cylinders wanted to blow off!

I learned a lot on that trip. We stayed out over the ocean and clear of clouds all the way down to California. The long way around but the sweet way home.

Haun family photo

I've always been the outdoors type, so Mobile was the ideal location for hunting, fishing, swimming and boating. I hadn't taken up golf yet, as in those years I preferred the more strenuous activities. Weather permitting, I usually spent my lunch hour in the Club pool, which kept me slim, trim, and the color of old mahogany.

In the fall and winter there was bird hunting. In Alabama when you say 'bird', you are speaking of quail. I bought a wonderful little pointer from a friend and named her Sis. People say you can't have a bird dog as a house pet, but Sis was different. She was both a house pet and the best bird dog in that part of the country. On one hunt, three or four groups of us converged, and after some conversation decided to join up for a big hunt. With about a dozen hunters and almost twice that many dogs, we set out. Soon one dog froze on a point and all the other dogs instantly also froze in perfect back-up. We walked slowly up behind them, but no birds flushed. Sis was off to the left flank, but I saw her lift her head and search around. She then broke her point and trotted right across the front of the whole pack – to the frantic yells of, "Whoa…Whoa!" All the other dogs turned their heads to follow her as she trotted off to the right, where she froze. We walked up and a covey of maybe fifty birds exploded out of a brush pile! For the rest of the day, whenever a dog pointed, every last one of them would look around to see if Sis agreed. She was the belle of the ball that day. On another day I missed three shots in succession and she left me and went to hunt with someone else, ignoring me completely. I loved that little dog.

Haun family photo

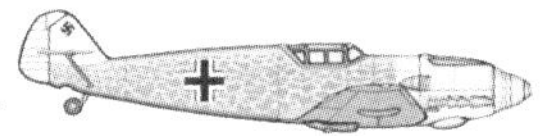

Haun family photo

Being an old seafaring type, and being stationed right there close to the Gulf, naturally I had to have a boat. I found a yawl (two masts) that suited me fine. She was twenty-two feet on the water line and had a deep keel – which incidentally let me locate every sand bar in Mobile Bay. Another minor drawback was that her four-cylinder inboard was maddeningly temperamental. But she had two bunks, which – to quote one of my friends – would sleep "two comfortable or four in love." There was a neat little galley and a head. You couldn't capsize her, what with that deep, heavy keel and a rudder that lost its bite when she heeled way over – the boat would immediately turn into the wind and stop. I tried it.

I kept her across Mobile Bay from Brookley at the Fairhope Yacht Club, a sheltered inlet ten or fifteen miles up from the mouth of the Bay. That location made it a good two hours' sail to the Gulf, if I missed running aground en-route. Out in the Gulf we would troll for King, using a white feather with a touch of red. When someone got a good one hooked, the designated cook got the deep fat boiling. A King, fresh from the water, when steaked and rolled in corn meal, is mighty tasty, especially when washed down with a quart or so of our loot from the Islands. Frequently we would be escorted by a school of porpoise playing alongside. Once they brought along their babies, most about a foot long. These little fellows were learning to jump like their parents, but usually ended with a belly flop. Cutest thing you ever saw. One of our buddies named Smith liked to be towed at the end of about a fifty-foot line, which I thought rather stupid. I would climb high up the mast, from where I could see deep into the water and watch vast schools of some kind of fish rush up from the depths for a look at Smith, presumably to see if he was edible. He was never attacked, but I think he was just lucky.

It was in Mobile we learned that Jimmy needed glasses. We were out in the front yard playing with a ball. I tossed him one, and he held his arms wide as the ball hit him in the chest; he couldn't see it coming. When we got his glasses, he was amazed to learn that those green blobs called trees had leaves you could see from a distance! He was a hardheaded kid. I tried to teach him to swim, but he would have none of my instructing. Later I saw him in the pool learning by himself. I stayed out of sight just in case. Probably got that from his mother.

I decided it would be a smart idea to move the boat around to Perdido Bay, which is along the coast toward Pensacola, and keep it anchored there. Then we'd be able to drive the car to Perdido in an hour or so and be out in the Gulf in a matter of minutes, thus saving that long sail down the Bay. For the move, EP Knox and Pickering decided to go with me, while Eleanor and EP's wife Dotty – affectionately called 'The Old Witch' – would drive around to pick us up. The Saturday of the move, Pickering brought along his latest girl friend. That day there was a strong wind from the south and, as usual, the engine wouldn't start, so we had a long haul beating our way down the Bay. Neither of the guys had ever been in a sailboat before, but with the constant tacking back and forth to stay in the ship channel, they learned a little about handling the jib, while I could handle the main and the tiller. I think the little girl was distracting them, as they didn't learn nearly enough.

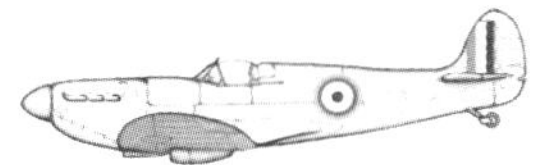

Haun family photo

The weather steadily worsened, with the south wind kicking up waves about three feet high. When we were finally abeam Fort Morgan, I could see the Gulf had turned a solid white with spume from the wave tops. If we left Mobile Bay, there was not another inlet until Perdido, and that offered only a few yards' gap at the entrance. There was no choice but to turn around and go back to Fairhope, so around we went.

With the main swung all the way out and the jib helping, we were barreling along at a fine pace. I'll bet we were making every bit of six or seven knots, which is the top for that hull. Running before the wind is a smooth ride with no pitching or rolling. I was tired from all the beating down the Bay, so I had Pickering relieve me at the tiller. After impressing him with the need to keep the wind directly behind us so as not to let her jibe and maybe dismast us, I stretched out on top of the cabin for a bit.

I must have dozed off, as I was awakened by the boat shivering as the boom swung over my head. For some reason I grabbed the boom and was promptly tossed right out into those three foot waves. I went deep and hit cold water – which made me think about sharks – and I'll bet I came a couple of feet out of the water. There was the boat, drifting backwards away from me with the sails flapping. I started chasing her; but the waves were hard to swim in, and I kept losing the race. I yelled for them to throw me a rope. Pick grabbed a rope by the end and tossed it my way. Of course it went in the opposite direction. We were about six miles from any shore, which meant I had a long swim ahead. I knew I could make it in quiet waters, as I could float and swim indefinitely, but the waves made a different story. Finally, when I had about decided to conserve my strength for a long swim, Pick had the right idea. Having learned that he couldn't throw a rope, he tied it to his belt and swam out to me. Then EP pulled us both in. I had a hard time getting in over the side, as they couldn't understand my calling for the little set of steps provided for that purpose.

I put EP on the tiller, but sat right there beside him. When we arrived off the entrance to the Yacht Club, another problem presented itself. It was now full dark, and the fifty-foot-wide channel was marked by only one light on one end of the jetty and another a hundred and fifty feet away at the other end. With a gale force wind at right angles to me, I can proudly announce that I made it almost halfway through before going hard aground. Did I mention that we couldn't get the engine started? There was evidently a big party the Clubhouse, with the jukebox going full blast and sounds of merriment shattering the night. I blew the fog horn for a while, with no result. So, with a rope tied to my waist, I swam over to the pier and climbed those barnacle-encrusted piles and pulled the boat free.

Pick had his car there, so we had a ride back to the Base. I knew there was no way to get in touch with Eleanor and Dotty, so I made me a healthy shot of 'Old Fearless' and relaxed. The phone rang; it was the Coast Guard calling to see if there was any news of us. They seemed rather upset that they had not been notified of our safe return. I explained that I hadn't been aware that they had dispatched their cutter to scour the area for us, and we hadn't talked to anyone at the Club. He explained that his boys had better things to do on Saturday night than look for would-be sailors.

Eleanor came in a little later on the verge of nervous collapse. After seven hours driving up and down the coast watching the storm develop, she and Dotty had been told by some commercial fisherman that no small sailboat could live out there.

Haun family photo

That poor girl led a hard life, what with my unquenchable thirst for adventure. I doubt if there was another who would have put up with me.

We picked a day with better weather and moved the boat around to anchor at Perdido, which in retrospect was a stupid thing to do. The boat was fairly sheltered in the inlet, though the bilges did need a little pumping every week. Of course I could have tied it up to a dock – except there was no dock there.

As far as I know, I am the only pilot to damage a C-74. A big hurricane had roared through the Gulf Coast area. When it quieted down I was sent to Floyd Bennett Field on Long Island to pick up two Coast Guard helicopters with their crews to help recovery efforts in the New Orleans area. When we got to New Orleans, I found that all communications were out. While banking over the main airport, I saw motorboats cruising the runways, so I decided to look for a more suitable spot to land. Lake Pontchartrain has a nice little airport on a short peninsula sticking out into the bay. It was used by small airplanes only; I'll guess the runway was around three thousand feet long, with the first hundred feet or so covered with water. I shouldn't have even thought about going in there; but with my deep compassion for suffering humanity – plus a small streak of show-off-itis – I decided I could make it.

So with full flaps and power for a carrier-type approach, I came dragging it in. When the water on the end of the runway disappeared, I chopped the throttle and dropped in. With propellers in reverse, plus brakes, I came to a stop with room to spare. Then the crew chief onboard came to the cockpit mad enough to bite nails. The C-74 had dual wheels and tires on the main gears. When I saw the water disappear out my window, I forgot just how far back the gear was, and had dropped the wheels into a foot or so of water, which funneled between the tires to shoot a heavy stream right through the fully extended flaps. *Dahmmy-dahmmy, boy-san!*

We unloaded the Coast Guard and I got a whirlybird ride over the flooded area. I wasn't exactly thrilled by knowing that the rotor blades were held on by one nut, which the crew called the 'Jesus nut'. Helicopters – I never have worked up any enthusiasm for those things. I like my wings tied on a little tighter.

There was no way to repair the flaps where we were, so I decided to take the airplane home with the flaps retracted for takeoff. We were empty and had a light load of fuel, so takeoff was easy. It being Sunday when we got back to Brookley, in time for a little relaxing, I found the area around the swimming pool crowded. I spotted the Group Commander, George Cassidy, lounging at an umbrella table near the diving boards; so I marched up to him to get my sad tale told.

After I finished, he glowered a bit and said, very sarcastically, "Well, Jim, I know that you CAN fly."

I suppose I deserved it. Of course Cass never liked me much anyway. I was known as one of Tunner's Boys, and he wasn't.

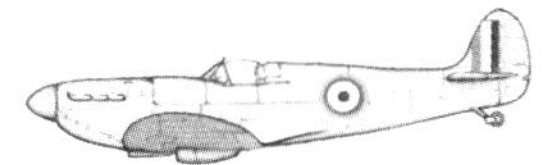

"I enjoyed Mobile more than any place I've ever been stationed."

U.S. Army Air Corps photo

Haun family photo

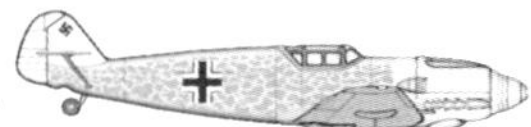

chapter twenty

BERLIN AIR LIFT

1948: "ROUGH DUTY BUT LOADS OF LOOT"

Two or three weeks after moving the boat over to Perdido Bay, some of us planned on a deep sea fishing trip. It was a bright sunny Saturday morning with a gentle breeze, promising a fine day. As we were going through the main gate, I was stopped by the sentry on duty and told to call our headquarters. Colonel Cassidy wanted to see me; so like the cops say, I responded immediately to the HQ building.

There was a big flap on, about some trouble with the Russians in Berlin. I was told to gather double crews for three C-54s and prepare for thirty days temporary duty at Rhein Main Airport near Frankfurt, Germany. I was also told there would be three more airplanes from Great Falls, Montana, and three from Fairfield-Suisun, California. At this, I suggested that we ask MATS to form a Squadron of these nine airplanes, so as to have better control of the effort, whatever it was to be. After a call to Fort Totten, this was agreed to, and I was told I would be the Squadron Commander, with departure time as soon as we could get loaded. A call was sent out for all available pilots and mechanics, plus three navigators, to pack their bags and handtools.

On a bright Saturday morning a lot of people had already left the Base, but we were able to round up a sizeable number; I took my fishing gear home and grabbed a bag. Eleanor was terribly torn up, although it was to be for only thirty days. I left her in tears.

We took off shortly after noon, en-route for our first stop at Westover, where we gathered the three ships from Great Falls, together with a copy of their orders, complete with a roster of their personnel. I had set up a 'day room' in my airplane and appointed a First Sergeant to commence the business of forming a Squadron. The next stop was Stephenville, Newfoundland, where we landed only long enough to take on fuel and food for the next leg to the Azores. The navigator had to go right to work on that 1400-mile leg.

At Lages, the American base in the Azores, I learned more about why we were being sent to Germany. The Russians had stopped all ground traffic in and out of Berlin in an effort to force the Allies out of the city, which, though deep inside Russian occupied territory, had by treaty been placed under the control of the Americans, British, French, and Russians – each with a sector amounting to roughly a fourth of the city. It looked very much like we were heading into a war. We stayed at Lages long enough for a decent meal and then departed for Rhein-Main, arriving there in daylight – for which I was thankful – knowing that air traffic control would probably be less than desirable.

We were met by a Lieutenant, who directed us to a shabby brick building, where he briefed us on what was happening. This was on July 11, 1948, when the airlift operation was in its first throes of getting organized. The Russians had not bothered trying to restrict access to Berlin by air, as they assumed there was no way to feed two million people except with rail and road transportation. They were wrong!

My first duty of course was to feed and house my troops. The Base was already filled to capacity, so I was offered a compound off-Base currently housing DPs (Displaced Persons). I was shown this area, a mile or so away, and wasn't exactly pleased with it, but as that was the only

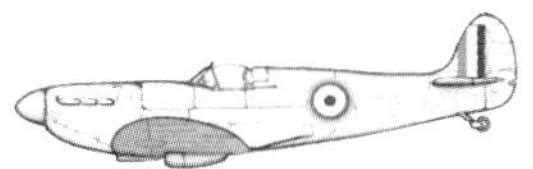

Col. Haun photo

space available, it would have to do. The DPs were a sad looking bunch, mostly from Eastern European nations, all former slave laborers who had no desire to return to their old homes, now under Communism. They were somewhat better fed than most prisoners I had seen but were dressed much the same. I agreed to take the area, provided all bunks and cots were replaced with clean, louse-free ones, and the entire place fumigated. While this was being done, the troops stretched out on the ground, anywhere they could find a dry spot, and went to sleep; I couldn't afford that luxury with all that had to be done. Our airplanes were already on their way to Berlin, loaded with sacks of flour or coal, and being flown by some very tired crews.

I had put Captain 'Pappy' DeWitt in charge of Operations and Lieutenant Sid Parks over Maintenance. Sid turned out to be the best scrounger I've ever been able to find; in short order he had secured our maintenance area and had a materials shelter organized. We would have been painfully hard pressed without his talent at thievery.

Haun family photo

The polite term for this activity is 'Midnight Requisition'. I had told the Base Commander we were the 17th Squadron from Mobile. That was fine until we tried to draw supplies and it was discovered no such Squadron existed! Supply people are, and always have been, sticklers for having their paperwork in order at all times – the idea of issuing parts and equipment to a non-existent Squadron was wholly beyond their comprehension. So we just plain stole what we wanted! Sid soon had two trucks and a Jeep; I certainly didn't ask where they came from. Shortly thereafter he had three nose docks built, which greatly aided in keeping our engines in good shape.

The Base had a compound with all sorts of goodies we needed, but it was under armed guard. Top get around this obstacle, I came up with a bright idea. Taking Sid and some help in one of our new trucks, we drove up to the compound's gate. Skidding to a stop in front of the guard, we jumped out, and in a towering rage I gave Sid the chewing out of his life; man, I out-Pattoned Patton:

"And when I tell you to go get something, I don't mean tomorrow; DO you understand?"

Sid was saluting like mad and Yes-Sirring like the good little soldier he was. The guard just stood there at port arms grinning from ear to ear.

Sid ran the truck through the gate while I strode up and down giving the guard a most profane lecture on what a man has to do to get anything done in this Army! Sid came out with several compressors and ground power units we needed. I think he must have gone back several times after that, as our supply of ground equipment steadily increased. At future bases, the first man I would always try to have assigned was Sid Parks.

Now that most of the housekeeping jobs were well in hand, I could take my first trip to Berlin. I picked a clear day for this first flight so as to get the whole route well in mind. After entering

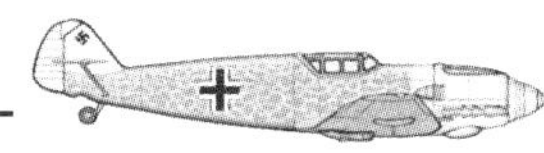

Russian territory, we were restricted to a corridor twenty miles wide; should we stray out of that space, the Yak fighters would appear on our wingtip making threatening gestures. We must maintain our assigned altitude, which this day was 6000 feet; then when we reached the beacon at Fulda we reported our time-over and altitude. We had heard the ship ahead of us report three minutes before, he being at 5000 feet. Three minutes after we passed the beacon, another ship reported over Fulda at 7000 feet. By all keeping our speeds at exactly 170 mph we were supposed to maintain separation. This became vital when the weather closed down. Fulda was the last fix we had outbound that could enable us, hopefully, to determine our wind drift angle and so maintain our course along the centerline of the corridor. There were no further radio aids for the next two hundred miles, until we could hear the range station at Berlin. One leg of that range was beamed down the centerline of the corridor, which enabled us to correct our course if necessary. Given the inevitable variation in air-speed-instrument readings, our spacing on arrival at Berlin could and would be off from the desired three minutes, but not much. We then followed the tower's directions for landing.

Col. Haun photo

I had seen a considerable part of the destruction of Germany during the war – but from 100 feet or less – so had never been able to appreciate what might have befallen an entire city. Flying over it now, there must have been some two million people living in that pile of rubble, but how they managed to even stay dry was hard to imagine! Ironically, about the only undamaged structures seemed to be the apartment buildings we had to come over or between on our final approach to Templehoff.

Col. Haun photo

This is, or was, a rather small airport, never intended for use by large aircraft. I don't remember the exact length of the east-west runway, but it behooved us to come in low and slow so as to drop the bird in just past the edge of the approach end. The runway was covered with PSP (Pierced Steel Plank) which always became slick when wet. Still, I don't recall but one airplane that slid off the far end and got considerably bent.

All traffic – in, out, and on the ground – was one way. We rolled in under the long curving portico that made up the entire length of what had been the terminal building. As soon as the engines stopped turning, someone was beating on the cargo door. We opened up, and in came the unloading crew from a flatbed truck backed up to the door. The men looked much like the DPs we had seen, but these were German civilians. They were

U.S. Army Air Corps photo

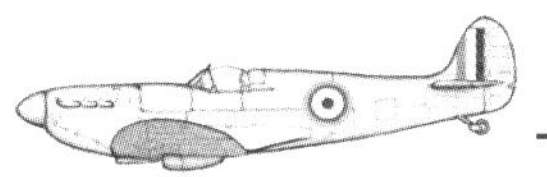

obviously happy to greet us, with the usual handshaking all around. Germans are great for handshaking, but such was not to distract them for more than a few seconds from their rush to get the airplane unloaded. We, meanwhile, had about twenty minutes to grab a hot dog and cup of coffee from some nice ladies, then be given a slip of paper with the latest weather, our assigned altitude, and call sign for the return trip.

Col. Haun photo

We followed the standard departure pattern to keep clear of the unrelenting three-minute rhythm of incoming traffic and so went back to Rhein-Main. The total flight time was right at five hours. All crews made two trips a day, which – after adding the time of loading and unloading – made for quite a tiring stint.

It was quickly obvious that I must find more crews to handle a seven-day-a-week, twenty-four-hour-a-day job. In and around Frankfurt there were numerous military air organizations, including a P-47 Group with pilots assigned to various administrative duties who would like to get back in the cockpit. I found a number who could be spared from their jobs for a day or two a week, especially on the weekend. Promptly thereafter I upgraded all my regular co-pilots to Captain, thereby gaining these spares available to fill that right seat. That helped some. Now the problem was maintenance. The woefully limited number of mechanics we had been able to round up on that Saturday morning wasn't nearly enough to handle this heavy workload. I got lucky.

While hanging out in one of our favorite watering holes in Frankfurt, I had become acquainted with a former German fighter pilot, a rather likeable fellow who spoke good English. After finishing all the war talk, we got around to the Air Lift. I told him about my overworked maintenance and finally asked him what had become of all the Luftwaffe's mechanics. He said there were thousands of them around with nothing to do, besides pick bricks. He told me I could get all I wanted who would be happy to work for one carton of cigarettes a week – a carton that sold for ninety marks on the black market. Lights began to flash, and the next day I got Sid and his troops together for a little session. How many of them would like to have a helper for one carton a week? Every last one of them! As we could each buy two cartons a week – and the PX didn't ask if they were solely for your own consumption – why not?

U.S. Army Air Corps photo

DeWitt, Haun, Parks, and two unidentified Captains with "Shmoos"

Shortly thereafter we got a most satisfying number of recruits. Of course they didn't speak English, but after you showed them how to remove the engine cowling, or take out and replace a spark plug, or fill a hydraulic reservoir, you could be sure they would do it properly the next time. With this increase of strength, I naturally needed an increase in food rations; quite a bit of it I'm sure was taken home. All this was likely a shade illegal, but my airplanes were running. The Base Commander was quite upset at me and claimed to be worried

about sabotage. I just laughed at that. With just the eight men running the radio beacon at Fulda being the only troops between us and the Russians, I figured the Germans would be more than helpful to us. Which of course turned out to be the case.

General Tunner came over to take command of the Lift and brought his staff from the Hump operation with him. Red Forman was there as the head of the Operations Planning Office, a job in which he excelled. More and more Groups of C-54s were arriving to replace all the Gooney Birds whose slower speed made them incompatible with the separation requirements. We picked up a few pilots from them.

It had become evident that this was not going to be a thirty-day job, so we started making ourselves as comfortable as possible. We were learning all the tricks of dealing in the black market and, in the process, collecting some fantastic loot. I got a new little one-cylinder motorcycle for a few cartons of cigarettes and some Hershey bars. We didn't ever dicker about the price, being filthy rich compared with these folks. Those that were mobile usually had bicycles with tiny gasoline engines attached to the rear wheels. Before the Air Lift was over, there were swarms of those little motorized bikes cluttering up the streets. The resilience of these people was a marvelous thing to watch; when the war was over they crawled out from the wreckage and immediately went to work at whatever they could lay their hands on. I never saw one begging.

General Tunner came by one day to inspect us. He asked me what I was doing that gave our Squadron the highest in-commission rate on the Lift. There was no point in hiding it.

"General, I've hired a number of German mechanics, paid for with cigarettes donated by the men. I have further falsified my strength returns so as to give them a hot meal a day."

He thought about that a minute and then asked, "Can you get any more? I can't pay them with cigarettes, but I can get the money."

I told him there were thousands and was promptly given the job of getting them. That was easy; I just turned the assignment over to my ex-fighter friend, and I'll bet he made a bundle out of that deal. Before the Lift was over there were thousands of Germans working for us, leaving our rations to use for our own avaricious ends. You should see some of the stuff I brought home!

One of our civilian employees at Rhein Main told me he owned a Fiat that was in a garage in West Berlin, and that if I could figure some way to get it out, I could use it as long as I wanted. One of our C-74s had come with spare engines. Its pilot was a fishing buddy. I asked him if there was some way he could devise to land at the British base, Gatow, in the Berlin area, with some minor emergency. Of course you can always find something wrong with an airplane, so I rode to Berlin as a passenger and, by various means, found the Fiat. The 74 was waiting at Gatow with the elevator already lowered. We pitched the little Fiat aboard and went back to Rhein-Main at night. No one questioned me as to where I had acquired the car, as such activity on my part seemed to be accepted as the norm. It was a little two-seater with a sliding roof. The thing had so little power that it would hardly carry two people – until Sid sawed off the clogged exhaust pipe; then it ran fine, though rather noisily. I can't swear to it, but I think seven of us went to town in it one night.

Col. Haun photo

Being worried about my boat anchored out in the slip at Perdido, I wrote another close buddy, Shubrick, requesting that he see if he could get it moved back to Fairhope before the hurricane season arrived. In due course I received a letter from him with the sad story…seems he and another

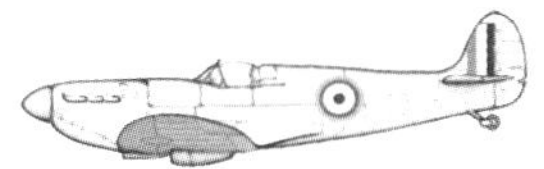

Brookley AFB photo

fellow and their wives got the boat out of Perdido and had a very pleasant sail until reaching the mouth of the Bay near Fort Morgan. There, one of the usual summer s qualls came up that put them promptly in trouble. They tried to shorten sail but their lines refused to come untied, the engine wouldn't start, the boat weathervaned into the wind, and they could only make headway backwards, if you can follow that. As the wind was from the south, they ended up on the beach, including some rocks. Fortunately the Coast Guard happened to be right there and succeeded in pulling them off. Shubrick said they were towed to a boat dock, not specified, for repairs, with the pumps working. I sent Shubrick a blank check for repairs. After several months the check hadn't cleared. Then Shubrick came over with a load of engines and I got on him about the check. He said that he brought it with him, but the night before he had gotten drunk down in Frankfurt and was rolled for his wallet, which had the check in it. He was sure sorry about that. I cabled the bank to stop payment, but nothing further was ever heard. Just plain lucky.

A GCA (Ground Controlled Approach) system had been installed at Templehoff. I had never flown a GCA and very much wanted to see how it worked. I was surprised with the accuracy of the directions we were given on the approach down between two apartment buildings. We had an extra pilot aboard, so I got off and went to the shack housing the GCA unit. As the weather was appropriately bad, the operators were glad to let me observe while they explained just how the thing worked. There were three screens, or scopes. One looked down the approach corridor for quite a few miles. This screen showed like a single blob on or near the centerline. The operator started calling two planes by number:

"Big Easy 123, turn right five degrees. Big Easy 124, turn five degrees left." Apparently they were getting a little jammed up out there. The big blob separated into two little ones. The operator played with them until they were in proper position.

As a ship arrived over the range station the pilot would call, "Big Easy 123 over the station," and immediately turn left to a new heading, slow up, and put down some flaps. (It's been so long ago that I've forgotten such details as headings and speeds.) The approach controller would guide you around to where the final controller picked you up. He used the other two scopes, the first to show any deviation from the center, or course line. Monitoring this scope he would call for gentle little turns that would keep that tiny blip coming right down the center; meanwhile the other scope showed the descending glide slope that ended at the end of the runway.

It was most comforting, on solid instruments, to hear that calm voice: "You are on the centerline, on the glide slope. You are going slightly high on the glide slope, bring it down a bit. Back on the glide slope. Approaching minimums, take over visually."

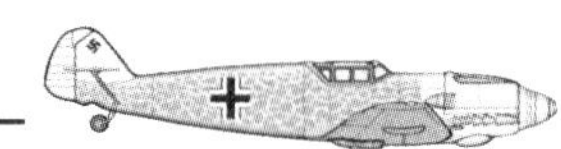

As the controllers got better and we learned to trust them implicitly, our minimums became lower and lower, until we were crawling there on our hands and knees. Eventually, there were no minimums, if you had the guts.

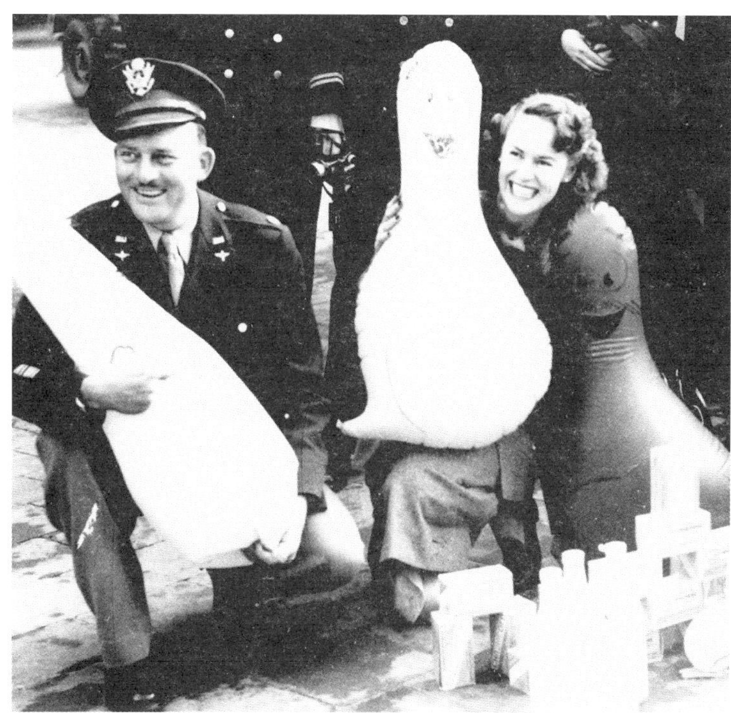
U.S. Army Air Corps photo

Coming out of Berlin after delivering a load of flour, I was nearing the boundary of the Russian zone. We were in solid cloud, with the autopilot doing the work; so with the seat slid back and my feet propped up on the dash, I was regaling my new co-pilot with some tall tale, when about five hundred feet above through a momentary gap in the wispy clouds, I spotted the dim shape of another airplane. He was a bit faster than us and quickly disappeared, along with the last of the fading daylight. I made some comment about people that didn't maintain their proper speed and altitude, and at that exact instant there was a terrific explosion right on our nose, accompanied by the strong smell of smoke. I took it off the autopilot and tested the controls. Everything worked fine. All instruments showed normal, but there was a lingering smell. I figured it must have been some sort of noisemaker the Russians had dropped from that airplane I had glimpsed. Exactly three minutes later the same thing happened again. I started taking evasive action by diving and turning, which is about all you can do in a C-54. I didn't want people to think old Jim had just spun in, so I picked up the mike and told the world in general that I was being fired on in the corridor! My co-pilot was staring straight ahead and didn't open his mouth the rest of the way home.

As I throttled the ship into my parking spot, several staff cars came roaring up. The Base Commander was visibly quite upset and demanded if I had ever seen any flack. I advised him that I had seen a lot more than I had wanted to. I walked around to the nose and my flashlight showed a number of holes, about the size you would expect double-ought-buck to make. He told me General Tunner wanted to see me immediately in his quarters at Wiesbaden, about a thirty-minute drive away. The driver already had the engine running.

I was ushered in to see the General. The entire staff was there, mostly in pajamas and robes, with the appearance of men recently aroused from their slumbers. There wasn't a friendly face in the crowd as I told my story.

"General, I know it wasn't high explosive…"

"How do you know?"

"Because it was right on me, and when you can see it, hear it, and smell it, that's too damn close."

"What do you think it was, then?"

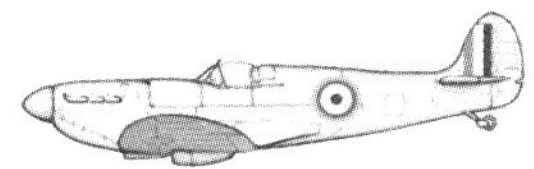

"I suppose it was some sort of noisemaker to scare us, except for those holes in the nose." Out of the corner of my eye I saw a Navy Captain watching me with a grin on his face, and I wondered, *what does this guy know that I don't?*

He spoke up: "General, what happened here was a static discharge. I've experienced it many times in the Pacific."

I bristled. "What about the holes in the nose?"

He said, "Did you check the tail cone for holes?"

Of course I hadn't.

"When you get back, check the cone and you will find the same number of holes where the charge came out."

The General shook his finger in my face. "That was a static discharge, do you understand?"

I allowed as how I did and got out of there. When I got back to the Base I went around to the rear of the airplane and, sure enough, there were a bunch of holes in the tail cone!

A Jeep rolled up with the Captain in it. He said he was sorry that he had to embarrass me, but, as we were hanging on the verge of an international incident, he had to do it. Captain D. W. Tomlinson III and I became fast friends. We've hunted together out in Arkansas many times. He was the first man to fly an OX5 Jenny from the East Coast to the West Coast, collecting sagebrush in the gear en-route. He knew Lindbergh and Howard Hughes, and was known as the Navy's Bad Boy prior to WW II. He pioneered Carrier Operations on the old Langley, our first carrier. I no longer receive his usual "Christmas Log," so I assume he is dead.

U.S. Army Air Corps photo

With winter coming on we began to get some dense fogs. On final approach at Rhein-Main one time there was a solid white bank approaching past one edge of the airport. After landing I was able to taxi about halfway to parking before it closed down completely. It was so thick we had to get out and leave the airplane sitting on the taxiway. Later these fogs would become ice fogs, which covered everything with a solid sheet. We continued to fly, while our weather minimums went lower and lower. The approach at Templehoff crossed a cemetery at the edge of the field, where some powerful neon lights had been installed that turned the fog a comforting red glow and reaffirmed our faith in the controllers:

"On the centerline, on the glide slope."

I missed one approach, but that occurred when I reported over the range station and hit a strong prop-wash from another airplane. When the controller asked me if I was the aircraft over the station or the one that had just passed, I replied that I was the one climbing to the west! With maybe five hundred aircraft funneling into the Berlin airspace, it is understandable how one little blip could be

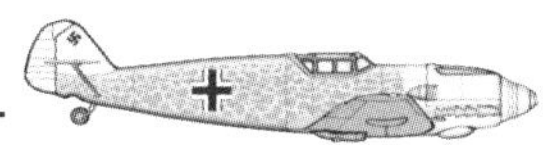

missed on the scopes. Red Foreman had done a fantastic job in setting up the approach and departure corridors, which were so successful in handling that volume of traffic.

At the departure end of the runways there were always two tankers that sprayed de-icer over each aircraft just before takeoff, so we had no trouble that way. Of course we had the standard rubber boots should we encounter icing while in the air. The Berlin Airlift was undoubtedly the best-organized and performed operation in our history. Today, of course, a Squadron of C-5s could do what it took our entire fleet to do.

One of the pilots in our Squadron started his own operation. Shortly after we arrived in Germany he commenced dropping candy bars, attached to little parachutes, to the kids gathered near the approach end of the runway. Gail Halvorsen has written a most interesting book entitled *The Berlin Candy Bomber*, which gives a far better picture of the entire Airlift than I have here. His "Operation Little Vittles" attracted attention all over the States, so that he began to receive large cartons of candy bars, with each bar tied to a parachute. The quantity of candy grew until Halvorsen required the help of the other Squadron members in making his almost daily delivery to literally thousands of those little German kids. He was honored by the German people and by the Air Force. I last saw him at the Airlift Reunion in Las Vegas.

The Berlin Candy Bomber

by permission of Col. Halvorsen

Flying wasn't the only thing we found to do in Germany. I met an old German named Schumann, a gunsmith. He and his wife lived in two rooms of what had been their nice home. He had a shop in the basement where he and his helper turned out beautiful hunting rifles. I found an old 30.06, scoped, with a carved and inlaid stock – a finely hand-tooled work of art. I also bought a little .22 Hornet made in Czechoslovakia and smuggled into the country through channels best known to him; he did an equally beautiful job on that. As usual, I paid with cigarettes and candy.

The Germans were not allowed to own guns or hunt, but old Schumann knew where all the best hunting was in the Black Forest, and was on intimate terms with the Foresters who controlled the area. They knew every roebuck and wild boar practically by name and address. I went hunting with them several times. The *yeagers* (hunters) would gather enough pals to act as drivers, who herded the game past my stand. I was only to take one roebuck, but Schumann made it plain that if I should accidentally get one or two more, it would be appreciated. At times I accidentally did that, and the *yeagers* never did turn me in. John Kelly had hunted a lot back in Alabama, so naturally he went with me once or twice. One day I heard his rifle fire several times; when I came up to him, he explained that a whole herd had flushed and that gun of his just kept firing in spite of all he could do to stop it! The whole Squadron had meat that night.

Haun family photo

The Germans had one custom I didn't take to very well. We passed an inn out in the country that had a veritable stack of game of all sorts lying in a pile in the front yard; in addition, hanging by their necks from rafters, were ducks and geese. I was told that when the hanging game fell from its own weight,

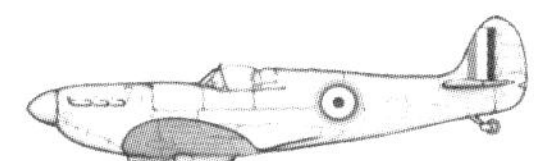

it was ready to clean and cook. I understand this treatment makes the meat mighty tender and savory, but I passed on verifying that.

Another thing we missed was good drinking whiskey. They had some rather bad champagne and all sorts of liquors and beer, but we missed Old Grandad. A C-74 crew brought me a case one day, which attracted quite a crowd to gather in my quarters. In a matter of thirty minutes or so, all I had left was twelve empty bottles. So much for Rhein-Main, sometimes known as Rain-Mud!

The Squadron was ordered to move to Wiesbaden, which had much better facilities. When we drove out the gate, we took all our scrounged equipment, which included a flat bed, two trucks, and masses of ground power units. The Base Commander watched us go and must have wondered at such a well-equipped unit, having lately arrived with only hand tools. We moved into a nice hotel which had been completely renovated, but I think we all rather missed our old Zepplenheim compound, where we were not constantly under the watchful eye of all the Brass as we would be at Wiesbaden.

Shortly thereafter I was moved over to Headquarters and given a job that had something to do with hiring German civilians. Sitting at a desk shuffling papers has never been my strong point. General Tunner got tired of my constantly bugging him about wanting to get out of there and gave me a set of orders directing me to return to Brookley!

Now *that* perked up my spirits.

Haun family photo

Mobile Saturday Night

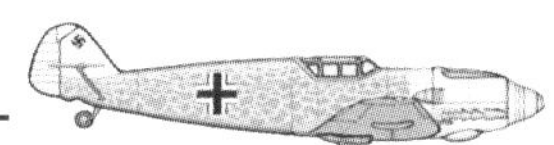

chapter twenty one

BACK TO BROOKLEY

1949 – '50: "A BIG HAIRY BIRD COLONEL"

A C-74 was reported inbound, so I started gathering my loot. I had my little motorcycle, two rifles, a complete set of Dresden china, a lot of cut crystal glassware, and various figurines. At the last moment I also bought an accordion, which I learned to play walking back and forth in the empty cargo space on the ride home. It sounded fine when accompanied by the roar of the engines, but lost all its charm on the ground. Like singing in the shower! We landed at Brookley at night and taxied to the Squadron parking area, so I didn't have to fool around with customs. Eleanor and Jimmy greeted me with open arms. I had been gone almost a year.

It was good to be home! I gradually got back in the regular routine of life on the Base, with the usual work at the office, which took very little time…meeting newly assigned people, scrounging parts and supplies, and spending a lot of time in the swimming pool. I met the man who had the ham radio station that kept us in weekly voice contact with our families.

During this time, the Air Force was separated from the Army, so we bought all new uniforms and traded our brown shoes for black. The new Air Force decided to raise the educational level of its officers and decreed that all Regular Officers must have at least two years of college. That meant that I, with only a high school diploma, must get some 'larnin'. The University of Alabama had a night school there at Mobile, so I approached them. After they had evaluated my military record, they decided I needed just two more courses to meet the requirements for two years' credit. I enrolled in American History, which I knew as well or better than the professor – although I didn't tell him that; and Sociology, which I slid through by pretending I agreed with everything the teacher said. I worked my flying schedule around to fit. Naturally I made straight A's.

The troops came back from Germany, and we settled down to the old routine. Eleanor had made some close friends, especially while we had been gone. There was Frankie, Shubrick's wife, Dotty Knox (The Old Witch) and Sid's wife, Thelma. We all knew how to grill steaks just to the others' tastes.

Then out of the blue I received orders to the Command and Staff School at Montgomery, Alabama. I hated that, but there was no way out. We put our goods in storage and departed Mobile. I was able to find a furnished apartment near the Base and we moved in. What a drag!

There is something about male teachers that gets under my skin. I suppose it's because I can't stand to be talked down to, but obviously you are in need of instruction or you wouldn't be in school in the first place! We had one speaker who was loudly advocating that we should immediately go blow Russia off the face of the earth. He was forced to retire the next week. We had a session on how best to refuel a hundred fighter planes with only ten tankers. Real deep stuff.

North Korea invaded South Korea, and President Truman called on the UN to resist with force! **War!**

And here I sat in school, no less, with all this going on. I took the family and drove to Mobile. Glen Birchard was now Group Commander; I went directly to him. I explained why we couldn't possibly win a war without me in it and asked him to see what could be done about that. He

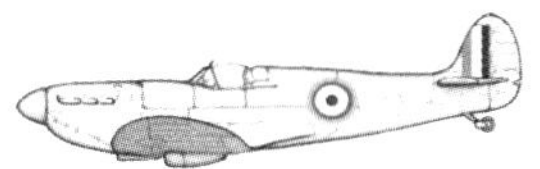

promised, and I went back to school. I sat there on pins and needles for another week before I was called out of class with the news that General Tunner had asked that I be reassigned to Mobile. We left Maxwell Field that same day. We had given up our quarters on the Base when we left Mobile, but the set right next door was available so we moved in.

Birchard had flown B-17s in Europe; the experience had sort of dampened his enthusiasm for flying, so he made me Deputy Group Commander to handle that end, while he shuffled the papers – which arrangement satisfied us both. Mobile was under the Continental Division, MATS, with General Jim Stowell commanding. Headquarters was at San Antonio, Texas. We received a telephone call from San Antonio to the effect that General Stowell wanted to see Birchard and me immediately.

The weather was absolute zero-zero, but the Man had said 'immediately'; I told the boys to gas a Gooney Bird for us. I could tell Birchard was a bit apprehensive about the weather, but he crawled in and got in the right seat. We found our way out to the end of the taxiway, and the bird checked out perfectly, so I pulled out on the runway. It was night, but I could only see the nearest runway light. Birchard told me to stop, so we sat there while I convinced him this was no big deal, that I had taken off in such conditions numerous times before. He finally agreed, and we left. It was nice and smooth on top; we had a quiet ride to Texas. When we landed, a car was waiting for us which took us directly to the General's quarters. He explained that General Tunner had been selected to command the Air Transport operation in Korea and was assembling a staff to go over there. Birchard was to be a member of that staff while I was to stay at Mobile and assume Birchard's job as Group Commander. I was happy about that, as I had already spent about five years overseas. We returned to Mobile the next day.

As the Korean War progressed, there arose a mounting need for air lift to bring the wounded back to the States for hospitalization. At certain times of the year the easterly winds between the West Coast and Hawaii increase in strength to the point that the C-54s have trouble making that long haul with a heavy load of fuel and patients. Our C-74, with its ability to carry seventy-four litter patients, plus its higher speed and longer legs, was needed; so we were put to work on this route. The hospitals on the West Coast were soon filling to capacity, so sometimes we had to continue on to hospitals further and further inland. One time I had to go all the way to Mobile to find a hospital with sufficient beds to handle our load. Whenever we approached the Coast, we would be advised where to go; that's when the very long range of the C-74 paid off.

I had a new experience on that run. All multiengine aircraft of that day had some way to synchronize the RPM of the engines, otherwise the propellers made an aggravating rumbling sound like Ruhr-Rhur-Ruhr. To stop this pulsation, the propeller control knobs could be adjusted slightly to bring the props all to the same speed and eliminate this noise. The Gooney Bird, having only two engines, allowed you to do this by ear. The C-54 had an instrument on the panel with four little propellers that would start turning slowly left or right to show which engine was out of sync with the others; there were four propeller controls, one for each engine, to correct this. When I checked out in the C-74, I noticed there was only one prop control for the four engines. On inquiry I was told that, by some means completely beyond my comprehension, engines numbers two, three, and four were slaved to number one. As this was a built-in feature, and there was nothing either the pilot or the engineer could do about it, I gave it no further thought. The engines always hummed along in perfect harmony, unless one of them became a bit sick. Then you feathered the thing and continued merrily on your way.

I had left Travis Air Force Base for Hawaii with a full load of passengers and some freight, plus full tanks of fuel. We had more fuel than we needed, plus several hundred gallons the engineers

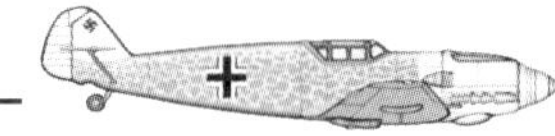

U.S. Air Force photo

always added for what they called 'home owner's insurance'. The entire West Coast was covered with that famous California fog. We broke out in the clear at around two thousand and continued our climb to nine thousand, our cruising altitude. I leveled off and called for 'cruise power' – and all hell broke loose! All four engines let out the most terrifying scream as the props went into low pitch and the tachometer needles went right past the red line and off the gauge. We jerked the throttles closed and things quieted down.

I asked the engineer what he had done; he denied doing anything unusual and confirmed that the tachs had gone right off the gauges, which have a red line that marks the limit of safe prop speed. I did know what can happen when an engine is oversped: the piston rising in the cylinder may slap the valves before they can close; then all sorts of damage can occur.

I certainly wasn't going to head out over the Pacific with four probably damaged engines, so I turned around to return to Travis. We had left Travis that morning under zero-zero conditions, although I had been able to see maybe a hundred feet down the runway – which is OK for take-off but way below minimums for landing. I asked Control if there was anything open in the Valley, but they came back with the report that the nearest open airport was Reno! To get there would mean using a lot of power to climb to eleven thousand to clear the mountains, and I wasn't about to put any power on those engines over what was required to just barely hold our altitude. So we went back over the Travis beacon and floated around there for around two hours. It was a beautiful, sunny day on top, so I knew the heat would lift the fog before too long. The C-74 had no way of dumping fuel, so we would be landing heavy and I wanted enough visibility to help me make a grease job on the landing. Control called with the welcome news they had minimums, so in we went.

I called Mobile with the news and asked that they send me another airplane. Naturally Maintenance screamed to high heaven and demanded that I take the airplane on to Hawaii; but I refused, and a replacement arrived the next day. I told the crew to fly it slow on the way home, in daylight, and suggested it be kept around the airport for awhile to see what happened to the engines. It turned out that all four engines failed after around twelve hours. They were removed and replaced. I couldn't refrain from telling Maintenance, "See, I told you so."

On the return trip we had seventy-four litter patients in tiers of stretchers, plus some nurses and corpsmen to help. I'll never forget one young fellow. He seemed to be in high spirits, laughing and joking. I asked him where he had been hit, and he pulled up his pajama tops to show me. There were seven little purple holes across his stomach. He told me, "That Gook stood right over me and pumped seven rounds in me with a submachine gun." How he survived that, I can't imagine.

People have asked me how the responsibility for the lives of all those people riding back there affected me. I'll let you in on a secret, just between us. I've always heard that the Pilot was the first

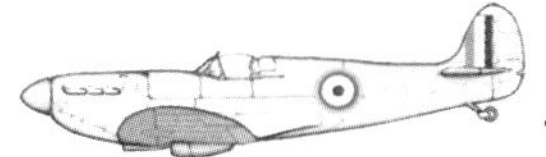

person to arrive at the scene of an accident. To that end I have always carried with me into the cockpit a firm commitment to exercise every bit of experience, training and skill that I possess to insure that my own warm and tender body will arrive at the intended destination unscarred and entirely functional. Whether there are two or two hundred back there in the cabin, they each and every one will be the beneficiary of my unwavering dedication to this commitment. Amen, Brother!

U.S. Air Force photo

I've gotten way ahead with the chronology of this log. Back a year or more, the Air Force had ordered us to send one of our 74's back to the Douglas plant for modification. We had one old hangar queen that was always giving trouble, so naturally we sent that one. The factory had designed a new model that would greatly increase the bulk that could be carried, plus simplifying the task of loading and unloading. This model was designated the C-124. Our old 74 was used for everything except the fuselage, which was a large, slab-sided thing, more than twice the height of the old one. It had a folding upper deck that, when in place, doubled the number of passengers that could be carried, to around two hundred. The old elevator had been eliminated by using a chin ramp that unfolded – allowing trucks, tanks and whatnot to drive right up into the cargo area. The crew could find their way up a ladder to the cockpit, perched some twenty-five or thirty feet above the ground. It was a big bird!

These aircraft had started rolling out of the factory and most were sent to the Pacific. Our old 74's were put back on their former routes. But now, in addition, a new Base had been opened on the north coast of Africa at Tripoli. Some of the people assigned there were from Mobile; in that part of the world it was difficult for these people to get all those little things that we consider necessities in everyday life, such as baby formula, mosquito nets, fresh eggs – you name it. We at Mobile received weekly mail asking that we bring along a large list of these various items, which we gladly did. Naturally none of this ever appeared on our cargo manifest. Sometimes we carried household furniture, tricycles, spare tires. (You never know when *you* might end up stranded in a place like that!) We made a practice of free delivery everywhere we went, but were careful that there was no official record kept in case Drew Pearson found out about it. (For you young folks, Drew Pearson was a Washington columnist who loved to dig up dirt on the Military.)

Our route extended on to Dahrain, Saudi Arabia, where we never left the Base. The Saudis had their own ideas about drinking, law and order, and various behavior, with a code that, if violated, could get your body mutilated beyond recognition. On the way out we sometimes chased camels! Whole herds of them!

On this trip I found another item that needed correcting. When leaving Europe we had the choice of two routes. One was to Keflavik in Iceland, while the other was to the Azores, thence either to Stephenville, Newfoundland, and home, or through Bermuda. This trip I chose Bermuda. For several hours after crossing Gibraltar we were cruising peacefully along in solid cloud, letting the autopilot do all the work. Wright Field, in its wisdom, had decided that we had no use for an

old-fashioned magnetic compass, since now we had a gyro-stabilized compass buried somewhere back in the wing, thence remoted to an instrument on the panel that looked like a compass and was tied into the autopilot as well. So we could just select our course and then sit back with this 'latest development in the state of the art' taking us exactly where we wanted to go. No sweat.

It was a quiet night. I had my seat slid all the way back, with my feet propped up on the panel, smoking my pipe and thinking beautiful thoughts, when we ran out of the clouds into a lovely starlit night. Looking up at the glittering constellations I suddenly recognized the Big Dipper, pointing at the North Star, directly on my nose! The compass repeater indicated we were on the proper course for Bermuda, on a heading of perhaps 250 degrees – decidedly not north! Now, as I watched, that star that insisted we were flying due north was moving slowly around to our left, which indicated to me we were easing in a big circle out there in the middle of the Ocean, while the compass still read a steady 250 degrees! I woke the navigator from a sound sleep and told him to break out his mysterious tools and see if he might give us some idea where we were. Meanwhile I had disconnected the autopilot and headed for a brilliant star that I knew was in the approximate direction of Bermuda. (I think it was Venus, but I wouldn't swear to that.) We had the early Loran that was housed in a cabinet about four or five feet long that at times worked fairly well, if you had plenty of time to fiddle with it. While playing around with his tools, the navigator told me to just follow that bright star. Then I remembered I had an old Boy Scout compass in my bag that I always carried for emergencies. With that in my hot little hand and the North Star a little behind my right shoulder, we proceeded on our way. After a few hours we picked up the Bermuda beacon and used the radio compass for the rest of the trip. At Mobile we scrounged some compasses originally intended for Gooney Birds and installed them in all our airplanes. For some reason we never had that malfunction again, nor have I heard of another case. I still have the little compass.

I'll get back to the right time frame. With Korea hot, the Reserves were being called up in large numbers for duty wherever they were needed. Birchard had left and I was now the Group Commander at Mobile. We set up a reception center for the arriving Reserves. As soon as they reported we screened their records to see where their former service might best fit them into the Group. Some we put directly into flight refresher training on Gooney Birds, and the rest into classes to acquaint them with the changes that had come about when the Air Force separated from the Army; but all of them were put to work. I used my old theory that putting a Lieutenant in a Captain's job, with the prospect of promotion, always got fine results. I had the reputation, probably deserved, of being somewhat of a Cowboy, so I knew I must mend my ways. With my first staff meeting I laid out my policies:

"A man's judgement is no better than his information. I expect reports that you can back up with facts, not opinions. If you don't know, say 'I don't know.' The most dangerous person a commander can have around him is a 'Yes Man.' Now I will listen to everything you have to say; but after I've come to a decision, that's it – period."

I replaced a couple of them and after that things went along smoothly.

General Stowell was scheduled to pay us a visit, which gave me an excuse to get the Base manicured, shampooed, and polished. I met him at his airplane, ready to show off our preparations. Instead, he climbed down the steps and greeted me with:

"Let's go to town, I want some oysters."

We spent the afternoon at the oyster bar and headed back to the Base. He directed me to take him straight to his airplane.

"General, don't you want to look us over?"

"Hell, I know what you are doing," and left.

My duties rather restricted my flying to the short Stateside trips. Fred Hook was now Air Advisor to the Air National Guard at Memphis. They were equipped with P-51s, and he offered to let me keep one at Mobile. When it was due for maintenance, I would take it to Memphis and swap it for another. I enjoyed flying a fighter again; but, as I wouldn't let anyone else fly it, there was a certain amount of animosity created among the Base personnel. Mobile was a Materiel Command Base with a General Martinstein commanding. His Flying Safety Officer decided the P-51 wasn't getting the proper maintenance it required. The General then told me to get the thing off the Base before it fell on someone, so I had to give it back to Hook. So I had to let my play-pretty go. Hook delighted in calling me a truck driver. "Get your ice cold beer, right off the Hump. Five bucks a can!"

U.S. Air Force photo

There were recurring rumors about one of the pilots that indicated he had a tendency to panic in any emergency. His Squadron CO hinted at it, but seemed reluctant to do anything about it. A Sergeant who flew with him often helped me work on my boat's cranky engine, so one day after we had finished tinkering with the engine I cracked open a bottle of 'Old Fearless', and the story all came out. The latest episode was a missed approach in Portugal where the co-pilot had to take over to prevent their hitting a mountain. I grounded the pilot and put him in a desk job. Months later he was sent to Korea and was the co-pilot on a 124 that set the record for the greatest number of people ever killed in an airplane to that date. Their problem? They had to feather one engine shortly after takeoff! The other pilot was the only one I had had to send home from the Air Lift, for much the same reason. Today's screening process seems to have eliminated most of these erratic characters, but some will inevitably slip through the net.

The next time General Stowell came to Mobile, I again tried to get him to inspect our operation, with the same negative results:

"Jim, you work too hard. Do you know how I got to be a General? I could make the best chicken salad sandwiches in North Africa!"

I had him and a large crowd over to the quarters for grilled steaks that night. I had been tipped off as to his favorite whiskey, so naturally I had a jug of it on hand. We had a fine party until Birchard's wife, who still lived on Base, came in uninvited. She hated my guts for taking her husband's job; she even made a practice of walking in on my staff meetings so as to let everyone know who the REAL commander was. We shared a mutual admiration!

General Stowell was obviously pleased with my work; nevertheless I was surprised when he called me at home one night.

"Well Jim, it looks like those damn fools in the machine records section have screwed up again. They promoted you!"

So now I was a big hairy Bird Colonel. We had a giant party over at the Club after the word got out. I overdid it a bit. Eleanor danced until her feet gave out. I learned later that General Stowell had gone to the Pentagon and practically forced my promotion, over the heads of several thousand eligibles. That one bottle of his favorite whiskey was probably the best investment I've ever made!

Brookley was a happy Base, at least as far as our Group was concerned. Our airplanes were flying on schedule, with the best in-commission rate in the Continental Division. We had most of the bugs worked out of the old 74's, and with the Douglas factory turning out the new 124, there were sufficient parts common to both types to keep us well supplied. I had delegated as much authority as possible to the unit commanders, which they appreciated, so that I rarely had to interfere. Our social life was more or less confined to the families of those who had been on the Air Lift, so I suppose there was a clique there. A commanding officer is usually subjected to a certain amount of flattery, praise, and admiration, especially from wives whose husbands are overdue for promotion! Human nature being what it is, this ego massage is hard to keep in perspective. Fortunately, I had the experience of the old 12th Squadron behind me, so I knew that within a week of my departure, these same people would hardly remember my name.

And so it turned out.

U.S. Air Force photo

"Being known as a somewhat controversial character..."

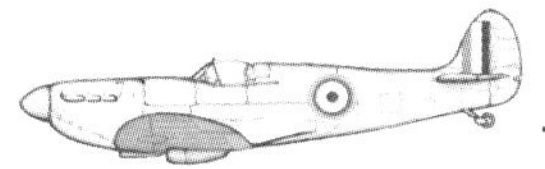

U.S. Air Force photo

Truman's *Independence*

The Flying White House

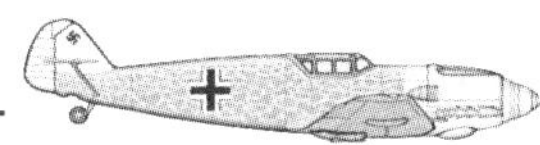

chapter twenty two

WASHINGTON NATIONAL

1950: "TRUMAN'S MUSTACHE CUP HAS DISAPPEARED!"

Time went on, as time will. I now had more freedom for hunting, fishing, and sailing my boat. Then one day I received orders transferring me to the 1254th Squadron at Washington National Airport, Washington, D.C. This Squadron was the home of Air Force One, President Truman's airplane, the *Independence*, as well as President Roosevelt's old airplane, the *Sacred Cow,* and a fleet of Constellations. The job was to provide transportation worldwide for government and military officials with high enough rank to warrant red carpet treatment. I was crushed. I simply could not imagine myself operating in that rarefied atmosphere. I did everything I could trying to get out of it, including turning in to the hospital for a minor operation to stall a while. Nothing worked; so we packed up.

My little bird dog Sis had just delivered a litter of pups that would present a problem if we had to drive to Washington with them in the car, so I cranked up a Gooney Bird and took them to a vet up there. Nobody caught me doing that, so it appeared my luck hadn't evaporated completely! I also took that opportunity to rent a house in Arlington from an officer who was being transferred. We called the movers, who packed our loot, then headed north.

The 1254th was directly under command of MATS Headquarters, so that was where I was to report. I was taken in to see the Commander, Lieutenant General Kuter. If you have seen a picture of the "Big Three" at Yalta, that is General Kuter standing behind Roosevelt, Churchill, and Stalin. I don't think General Kuter has smiled in all his life. He briefed me:

"You will be living in a goldfish bowl over there, under constant scrutiny. My advice is that you don't fly the same VIP twice and avoid having your name connected with any political figure."

End of briefing.

I was beginning to realize under what conditions I'd be working. I had never been accused of having the slightest trace of the diplomat in my make-up – the exact opposite would be more fitting. Well, PRESS ON!

I called the 1254th and told them I would be there the following morning. When I arrived, the entire Squadron was lined up for a "Change-of-Command" ceremony. Colonel Chet Moomaw introduced me with a most flattering speech; we saluted, and that was that. My new office was about thirty or forty feet long, facing the ramp through a wall of windows. There was one desk, mine, and a comfortable reclining chair. I sat down and started to put my feet up on the desk but in time remembered where I was …mustn't do that any more! No telling who might walk in.

U.S. Air Force photo

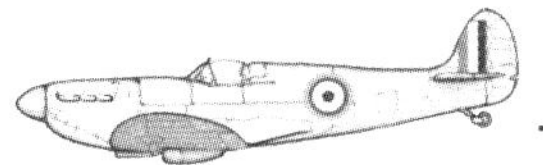

U.S. Air Force photo

The Operations Officer, Major Peaty, walked in from the next room and introduced himself. He had some important information for me: *THE MOUSTACHE CUP was gone!* I requested some background.

It appears that when Truman and Dewey were the opposing candidates in the last presidential election, the Air Force had been so certain Dewey would win that they bought a brand new Lockeed Constellation to be the new Air Force One. The interior was plushed out with the finest available furnishings, including bunks, galley, and all sorts of the latest electronics. It was one fancy bird! The name *Dew Drop*, the state flower of New York, Dewey's home, was beautifully painted along the nose. When the votes were counted, Drew Pearson laughed about it in every newspaper in the country; the paint was hurriedly removed, and old 608 became Air Force Two by default.

President Truman also read the newspapers, so one day he evaded the Secret Service and searched the antique shops in Georgetown until he found and bought an old moustache cup. (Dewey had a little Hitler-like moustache.) This he presented to the Squadron with the admonishment that it be carried in 608 at all times as a reminder that "The best laid plans of mice and men…"

Well, the moustache cup was gone. Of course I had a pretty good idea where it was, but that was really none of my business. Whenever the President was departing in the *Independence* we always had a back-up airplane parked right behind him with a crew aboard, just in case. One day Frenchy Williams, Truman's pilot, couldn't get number three started. He cranked and cranked but the thing wouldn't hit a lick, so the President and all his party got off the *Independence* and boarded the back-up airplane, which just happened to be old 608, formerly the *Dew Drop*. They were gone about four hours.

I was in my office when the group returned. Truman's aide, a big, bulldog-faced Major General, whose name escapes me, stomped into the office with the look of a man that had just been thoroughly chewed out by the President.

"Where's the goddamn moustache cup?"

"Moustache cup, General? I'm new here…"

"I know exactly when you reported. Now you find that cup, and if you can't, I can!" And stalked out.

I called Peaty in again and asked what more he knew about the cup. He denied any further knowledge, so I put in a call for the former commander, who was in school down at Maxwell Field, Montgomery. They got him out of class and put him on the phone.

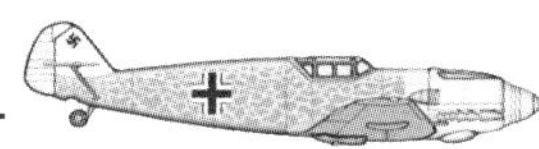

"Chet, there's a big investigation going on up here. Matter of a moustache cup. If you can tell me what desk drawer it's in, how about sending it back and I'll find it."

"Well, it could have possibly gotten mixed up in my stuff; I'll look."

Several hours later Peaty came in all upset:

"There's a C-45 inbound from Montgomery with the highest rank aboard a Captain. He can't land here." (To keep the riff-raff out, only Major Generals or above could land at Washington National.)

I told Peaty to take the rest of the day off and I would tend to it. I left for an hour or so. When I returned, there, right in the middle of my desk, was a moustache cup! I had never seen it before, but I instinctively knew it was the long lost article.

I called over to the White House:

"General, I've found it!"

"I thought you would. Now I want you to have a very nice case built for it and then mount it permanently in the rear cabin of 608."

I found an excellent cabinetmaker who made me a beautiful solid mahogany case. I figured there should be some inscription on it, which led to some heated discussion. I decided to keep it simple and plain. It was a little brass strip engraved with, "Presented by Harry S. Truman."

There is a sequel to this. When Eisenhower was elected, Peaty came in again:

"What are you going to do about the moustache cup?"

"What about it?"

"Look, Eisenhower is a Republican; we could get in a lot of trouble. You sure better clear this with General Smith." (General Smith was the new commander of MATS.)

"Naw, that's too heavy a burden to put on The Old Man. I'll think of something."

I well knew I was treading where angels fear to venture, dealing with some of the most inflated egos in captivity, as well as a few of the most fragile. This must be done on tiptoes. So I called the number-three man in the Air Force, General 'Bozo' McKee. He was the man who told us who could fly in these airplanes, when to go and where.

"General, I've been thinking about the moustache cup in 608, whether to leave it or take it out?"

He thought about that a minute…"Well, uh, um, uh…I'll think about that and call you back."

Just like I thought. This is really high level stuff! I had a friendly spy over in the good General's office. You just can't operate at these altitudes without a spy to alert you to things to be prepared for. So I called and told this fellow the story, then asked him to follow it and see who finally makes this momentous decision.

He called me three days later: "Well, General McKee took it to General White; then General White took it in to General Vandenberg; then I lost it."

I told him not to worry, as I figured it would have to go all the way up to the top. About a week later General McKee called me back:

"I've been thinking it over. You can leave it in 608."

I said, "Thank you, General." I'll bet I know who made that decision. Do you? Everyone concerned in this drama is now dead, so I won't be court martialed for telling tales out of school. We have a saying in the Air Force: "Arlington Cemetery is full of indispensable men." That's a good thing to remember.

***

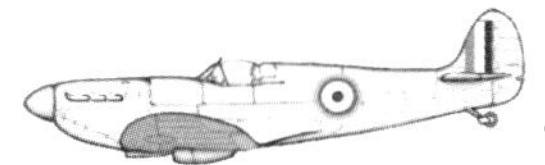

U.S. Air Force photo

The Lockeed Constellation was one fine airplane [brainchild of Howard Hughes], the first in its class to have pressurization, which allowed us to climb above most of the weather, insuring a smooth ride. The controls were all hydraulically boosted, making it light to handle. We had radar for avoiding the worst of thunderstorms; and even when we had to drive through one, it was comforting to see how little bend and flex there was to those sturdy wings. I was told that the wings had the same design as the P-38, but of course much larger. The only objection I could find was that it was powered by Wright engines instead of my old favorite Pratt & Whitneys. I found the Connie extremely easy to land by using full flaps, approaching safely above stall speed with some power on. The Squadron pilots called this a 'carrier landing', in contrast with their preference for burning them in like they'd been taught in school. Of course I was a 'seat of the pants' pilot, which gave me an advantage. People say there is no 'feel' to a large airplane, but they are wrong.

On my final checkout in the airplane, I had to make a landing with all the 'Boost' shut off, simulating a failure of that system. In this condition the flight controls become so heavy they cannot be moved by human hands. Directional control is maintained by varying power on the two outboard engines. There is a trim tab control on the yoke under your left thumb. With this little button the nose can be gently raised or lowered. I made my turn somewhere over Virginia and landed at Friendship Airport in Baltimore!

My first overseas flight was to England. We climbed out to twenty thousand; I leveled off and called for 'Cruise Power'. Nothing happened. I turned to the engineer and repeated the order.

He replied, pointing to the panel, "That ***is*** cruise power."

The check pilot sitting in the right seat confirmed it. "That is how we operate. Our passengers are all on important government business, so we must get them there as fast as possible."

That didn't sound like much of a reason for heading out over the Atlantic pulling so much power out of those engines.

I was further informed that, "Eastern Airlines runs these same engines wide open from New York to Miami every day."

I had to think on that a while.

The chief of the Air Force Flight Safety Office, a Major General, was visiting us. I asked him how he supposed Eastern could get away with running their engines so hard.

He laughed and said, "They don't. The Wright Company, in order to sell the engines to Eastern, gave them a guarantee that they could operate at this very high power. Now they keep a freight train load of spares en-route to Miami almost daily. Of course, given that back-up, Eastern can and does run the same airplane from Miami to New York and return the same day. They make money."

I passed a law. In the future we will split our climb. We will stop at ten thousand and stay there for several hours until enough fuel has been burned to allow us to climb to twenty and then use cruise power.

On my next trip we had two airplanes depart at about the same time. The other crew beat me to Germany by over an hour. They admitted to having been at twenty all the way. I brought that pilot home as my co-pilot. The next day I called MATS Personnel and asked them to find that boy

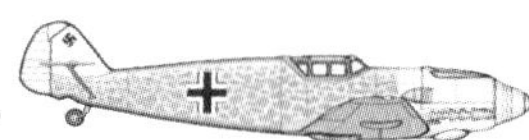

another home. After that I had no further trouble; our turn-around maintenance dropped drastically, and the passengers bought the story about strong headwinds!

One of the first things I did after arriving in Washington was to request Sid Parks for Maintenance. As the Squadron had such a high priority we could get just about anyone, by name, we wanted. I didn't need Sid for his famous scrounging ability, but rather I wanted someone who wouldn't hesitate to tell me if he saw me going on the wrong tack – something I wasn't getting from the Squadron.

He, Thelma, and two kids arrived at the office one rainy night after a hard day's drive. Thelma had her hair in curlers and the kids were worn out. It just so happened that out on the ramp, four platoons – Army, Navy, Air Force, and Marines – plus a battery of saluting cannon were formed up waiting for the arrival of a foreign diplomat (I think it was Adenhaur from Germany) to be welcomed by President Truman. Now our man Harry wasn't so red hot about all this protocol business, and never was. Adenhaur's airplane got hung up in traffic, and it started raining harder. Truman left the ramp and suddenly appeared in the office, which was no surprise to me but shook Thelma a little more than somewhat! The office had three doors; Truman came in the one at the far end; Thelma squealed and made a run for another door, but was halted by a menacing figure in a trench coat, with both hands stuck deep in his coat pockets. Another Secret Service man materialized in the door behind me, which blocked Thelma's last remaining escape route. Truman stood there grinning, while I, grinning, escorted the four past the guards.

Those boys led a hard life trying to keep Truman covered, as he would sometimes suddenly take off for parts unknown. I think he rather enjoyed the game. He and Eisenhower were the exact opposites.

Haun family photo

We had made friends with another couple, Herm and Dinky Sales. He was the Lockeed Tech Rep. Herm knew the Connie inside and out, which proved a big asset to me when I had to know something about the various systems. I made a habit of taking Herm along whenever I was flying. He was the man who found the problem when Lockeed's new Electra propjet started having engines come loose from the mounts and depart the airplane.

We bought a new house in a crowded subdivision out on Fenwick Drive in Falls Church, still smelling of uncured pine, for the outlandishly high price of $13,000. It was here that we brought our brand new son David home from the Leesburg Hospital. He was a perfect baby, and has continued to bring much joy into our lives. Jimmy was then twelve years old and became a fine baby sitter. Our cup runneth over!

The Pentagon ordered us to set up a trip out to Indian Flats, in Nevada. Two aircraft would be needed. As there were only two available – the rest being away on other trips – the choice was obvious: one Connie and the old *Sacred Cow*. For sentimental reasons there were a rather large number of people in Washington who wanted to ride in the old *Cow* so they could sit in Roosevelt's chair! I would fly the trip in the Connie. The passengers were mostly Senators and Congressmen. The purpose of the trip was to let the lawmakers observe an atomic explosion first hand.

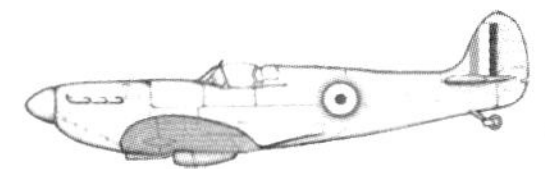

National Museum of the U.S. Air Force

At the appointed time the lobby filled with eager passengers while both ships were towed into position. The Connie had no sooner been brought to a stop, than, with an audible sigh, she expelled the gas from her left landing gear strut, causing that wing to sink half way to the ground!

Sid Parks, who was on the scene, made a quick assessment of the time needed for repairs. He reported, counting on his fingers, "Time to tow to the hangar, get it on jacks, remove the strut and replace the O-rings, fill with gas, and tow: Six hours."

I went back to the lobby and delivered the bad news: "There will be a six hour delay on the Connie, but the *Sacred Cow* will depart immediately" – then fled to the security of my office.

There was to be no escape, however, from the wrath of the Distinguished Senator from South Carolina, Mendel Rivers – who, by the way, was also Chairman of the Armed Forces Committee, a power on the Hill!

"Roll out another Connie!"

"Senator, there are no other airplanes on the field."

"Nonsense, you've got fifteen of them, roll one out!"

"Well, Senator, there is one, the President's airplane, but I doubt if we could get that one."

He got the message. After he left, I called over to the Pentagon and talked to some General in the Legislative and Liaison Branch about my irate passenger.

"Don't worry about that. Old Mendel is trying to get Charleston opened up again; he's giving everybody a hard time."

After exactly six hours the Connie was rolled up, the passengers loaded, and off we go. An hour or so later I went back to the cabin for a quick look-around. The good Senator was still all in a huff and not talking to anyone. Returning to the cockpit I asked for the passenger manifest, to see if there was anyone I knew. There was a *Mason – Rep., D. of Tennessee, hometown Jackson.* I went back to the cabin and found him. Naturally one old Tennessee boy would ask another old Tennessee boy if he would like to come sit in the front seat a while. He certainly would. We sat around talking about folks we both knew in West Tennessee, and he asked if my father's name happened to be Yandell? I assured him that was my Dad, a lawyer in Memphis.

"I thought I saw the resemblance. I've known Yandell all my life; sorry to have learned of his death. He was highly regarded in the legal profession."

I told him I was a bit worried about the incident back at National and explained what had happened. He laughed and went back to the cabin. Five minutes later Senator Rivers came to the cockpit, bubbling good cheer and insisting that I come back and meet every one of the passengers. There were some very famous names in that bunch.

We landed at Las Vegas so all the troops could have a night on the town. I went with a crowd of them to one of the shows on the Strip, and because of all the VIPs we were seated right down in front. Celeste Holme was on stage doing her thing and recognized me. I had ferried the *Oklahoma* troupe to Berlin earlier when she was the star of that show. She stopped long enough to introduce me to the audience and made some very complimentary remarks. My stock really went up in Congress. In the morning I was finally able to round up all of my little lost sheep, and we went to Indian Flats, out in the desert.

There were several hundred spectators seated in the bleachers. We were briefed that the bomb would be dropped from a B-36 from (I believe) around ten thousand feet. Could have been more. The bomb would explode high enough so that the resulting column of dust would chase but not catch the fireball, to prevent the dust from becoming contaminated, and spreading radiation downwind. We were given hoods and warned we mustn't look at the fireball until we were told it was safe, else severe damage to the eyes would result. A large body of Infantry was marched rather close to 'ground zero'. We saw the B-36 approaching – I believe it was more like fifteen thousand or even twenty, in that clear sky.

The emcee called over the loudspeaker, "Lower your hoods!"

I also shut my eyes! Even with my eyes tightly closed, I saw a bright flash and started counting; one tomato, two tomatoes…so I could estimate the distance we were from the explosion. Then we were hit by a rather solid 'Thump' and heard a single 'Crack'. There seemed to be no echo, but there wouldn't be out in a flat desert. The emcee said we could look, so I took a peek before raising my hood. There was a brilliant fireball several thousand feet up, with a huge column of dust trying to reach it. I'm going to guess our slant range was six or seven miles. Finally there was the familiar mushroom cloud drifting slowly toward the east. The Infantry came out of their trench and marched past us, all seeming in good health and spirits. Some of those men have since claimed to have experienced various maladies caused by their exposure that day. I got a nice sunburn.

As I watched, small fires sprang up. First, fence posts began to smoke before bursting into flames. Soon there were small fires all over the area. I was glad to leave.

Several days later, prior to departure for a repeat demonstration, another crowd gathered in our lobby. Senator Rivers was also there. Although he didn't go on that trip, he introduced me to every one of the passengers with the pronouncement, "We've got to get these boys some new airplanes. These Connies are old, and there are not enough of them. You help me, you hear?"

Sure enough, within a year the Squadron, now a Group, was re-equipped with new C-118s, the military version of the civilian DC-6. I had left by then.

I know I did a good public relations job there by the results. Drew Pearson had one of his spies staked out with us looking for any item he might find to harass the Military or Government with. One cold, rainy night I spotted this character wandering around outside the office. I went out and invited him in for some hot coffee and told him he was always welcome to stay in the lobby and that we had nothing to hide, so just ask. We also built a platform on top of the office with numerous electrical outlets for the radio and TV people; there was never anything said about that, but a case of fine Scotch appeared in the office, donor unknown. I didn't like Scotch much, so I kept one bottle in the desk, for snakebite, and passed the rest out to my troops.

I did have to deal with some massive egos in that job. General Mark Clark stormed in one day with the demand that I roll out a Connie to take him someplace, and then swarmed all over me when I advised him that he would have to get authorization for the flight from General McKee over at the Pentagon. I thought he was going to blow a gasket.

I took another trip to Indian Flats with a full load of military people. There was no flight servicing out there in the desert, so I sent the airplane over to McCarren for fuel and food for the return trip, which had been set for 1400 Hrs, allowing plenty of time for the crowd to wander around assessing damage, etc.

The blast went off around 10:00 AM, but around 11:00, the Chief of the Army, a Four Star General, walked in to announce he wanted to return to Washington immediately, if not sooner. The

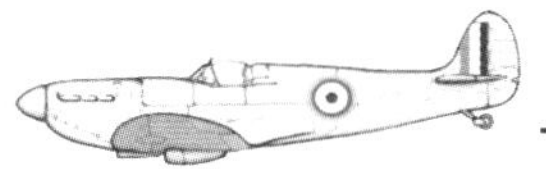

mere fact that the airplane hadn't returned from McCarren, and that there were some seventy-three other officers wandering around in the desert, didn't matter in the least. I was ordered to produce the airplane. Of course I wouldn't, whereupon he advised me that he would "speak to Van about this." (Van being General Vandenberg, Chief of the Air Force.) There was a young Major General from the L&L Branch acting as shepherd on this trip, so I dropped the hot potato in his lap. I got pretty good at that!

Then there was the time I had to roll out two Connies to take two men to New York to speak somewhere! The next time General Vandenberg wandered through the office unannounced, he gave me a broad grin and kept walking. Which I translated to, "Now you know what it's like in the big city," or words to that effect.

I took a load of Congressmen to Paris once; we were scheduled to depart at 9:00 the next morning. A few showed up around 10:00, but as there wasn't a quorum present, someone suggested we adjourn until after brunch. We got off around 3:00. People have asked me why I haven't flown corporate aircraft. That's why!

We were notified that Winston Churchill was due to arrive, so preparations were made to greet him on the ramp as he deplaned. About an hour before his ETA, the weather turned foul: rain and high wind, coupled with panic and near hysteria. I was finally able to attract the attention of the Chief Protocol Official and suggested that he set up in my office, which was certainly large enough to handle a moderate size crowd, plus the TV equipment. With the aircraft pulled close to the front door, there would be only a few steps to cover. He mulled this suggestion over for a moment and then came up with a brilliant solution to the problem:

"We will commandeer the front office of this building!" There was a mad rush into the office, cables were laid, and wires strung. I cleaned off my desk, put my nameplate in a drawer, and left an ashtray handy – which, incidentally, was not used. The lobby was rapidly filled with the see-and-be-seeners.

President Eisenhower was not much into the 'meeting and greeting' business, so for this Churchill arrival, Vice President Nixon would, as usual, handle protocol. Pushing through the waiting crowd, I felt a tap on my shoulder. It was the VP. He had a Fedora pulled well down over his eyes and looked quite inconspicuous. He asked if there was a desk he could use to scribble out a welcoming address. In a small office adjoining mine I rousted out the Executive Officer, who was much displeased at losing his vantage-point, and got Mr. Nixon settled. Before I left, two self-important reporters walked in. I'm sure they recognized the VP, but one of them walked over and tapped him on the shoulder:

U.S. Air Force photo

"Hey Bud, we're looking for Nixon. Know where we can find him?" Nixon tipped his hat back and looked up with only a trace of a grin: "That's me."

In my humble opinion Winston Churchill was the greatest statesman of this Twentieth Century. With his mastery of the English language he mobilized an entire Empire to perform miracles in the defense of their homeland, against fantastic odds. Even today I have shivers run up my spine when I listen to recordings of that bulldog-like growl:

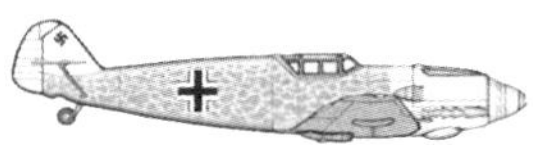

"We will fight on the beaches…their finest hour…Now the Battle of Britain is about to begin…Never…have so many owed so much to so few."

The old man arrived, walking slow, and was seated at the desk. He spoke rather slowly and the old growl was not there. His complexion was a pinkish white, with the tiny capillaries quite visible under very smooth skin. I don't remember what he said.

My next trip was to Eglin Air Force Base, near Pensacola, to watch a firepower demonstration. I had a full load of Pentagon Brass. A very nice General, probably of WW I vintage, asked if he might ride in the right seat and do a little flying. I couldn't object to such a nice fellow, so we left. By this time I had mastered the technique of landing the Connie to the extent that sometimes I was surprised to feel that the wheels were actually running down the runway. I mean real paint jobs! Well, I pulled off one like that at Eglin and again back at National. If I had to do it over, I would insist on a bounce of at least twenty feet in the air!

"He sure broke up my playhouse!"

U.S. Air Force photo *National Museum of the U.S. Air Force*

You see, this nice General was at a party with my boss, General Smith, and filled his ears with tales about "That Colonel over there – the one with the thick southern accent – can land a Connie slower and smoother than any other pilot in captivity."

Of course he was right, and I'll be the first to admit it, in all modesty, but he sure broke up my playhouse!

National Museum of the U.S. Air Force

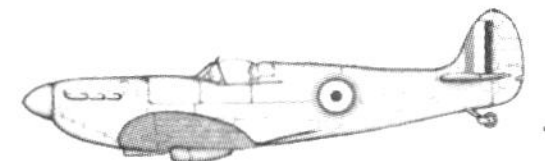

U.S. Air Force photo

Truman's pilot, Col. "Frenchy" Williams

(an important friend further down the road in Japan)

Haun family photo

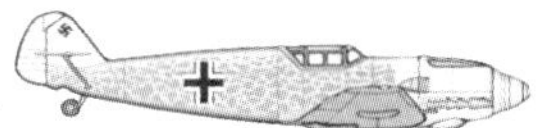

chapter twenty three

MATS HEADQUARTERS

1951 – '54: "ILLUSIONS OF GRANDEUR IN D.C."

A week or so later Red Forman dropped over for a visit.

"I've got bad news for you. The Old Man is going to reassign you to MATS HQ as Chief Pilot. I've told him you would be the worst Chief Pilot we've ever had, but he insists; so there's not a lot of use arguing. Don't let anyone know I tipped you off."

Sure enough, in about a week I got my orders to report for duty over at Andrews AFB, across the river in Maryland. Thus I entered on the worst assignment I had in the Air Force. My only talent was the ability to get men to fix and fly airplanes. True, I had read a regulation or two, but one of my earliest commanders had explained to me that regulations were written for those people who, when they had no idea what to do about a particular problem, could find the answer to their dilemma in the Book. Now I was supposed to go over there and help WRITE the Book! I was devastated.

On reporting to MATS HQ, I was ushered in to see the Deputy Commander, General Allen, a charming fellow. We had coffee brought in by his secretary and spent some time on idle chitchat. He finally, and rather apologetically, got around to the subject at hand. You see, at that time, I was handled more or less with kid gloves because nobody knew for sure who or what VIP I might have become buddies with during those last two years over at National. General Allen, apparently a bit confused at my seeming indifference to the bad news, asked if I had been tipped off beforehand. Naturally I assured him I hadn't been. He didn't believe me for a minute!

There was an Officers Call and everyone gathered in the main auditorium. As is customary at such gatherings when The General enters at the rear, someone calls "Attention" and everybody jumps to their feet, while The General marches down the aisle to the front – this time with his arm around my shoulders! A chill ran up and down my spine as I thought I could hear the knives being loosened in their scabbards! And I was right, too. Red picked up on it immediately.

After we broke he came up to me with, "What was that all about?"

"What do you mean?"

"I mean The General walking in here with his arm around your shoulder!"

"Damifino!"

Of course I did, in spades! I was now a threat to all the Colonels in the Command, and it behooved me to grow eyes in the back of my head. After a fairly miserable drive home through D.C. rush hour traffic, I got a tad drunk that night.

MATS was having a rash of accidents due to pilots landing short of runways – hitting ditches, fences, or sea walls. General Smith told me this was to be my first task: How do we stop this loss? Well, there wasn't any secret why accidents were happening. The Army, and then the Air Force flight schools, had taught pilots to approach the runway at a speed well above the stall speed so as to prevent falling out of the sky. The Navy, on the other hand, had to teach a somewhat slower approach to permit carrier landings, and had set definite speeds for each type airplane. The Air Force pilots prided themselves on coming in low and fast, putting the wheels right on the runway

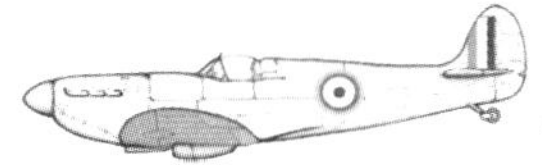

end, or 'on the numbers' as it was called. Their excess speed then had to be dissipated with a long rollout down the runway, sometimes clear off the far end!

Obviously, there was a happy medium between the two systems. I had always come in a little high and a little slower than most for these very reasons; but I would have to get some exact data before I could sell the idea to the pilots, most of whom relied on the airspeed indicator entirely to set up their final approach.

First I visited the aircraft factories of Douglas, Lockheed, Boeing, Convair, et al. There I talked with the company test pilots about the way these airplanes were designed to be flown. I wanted to know what speeds would allow an approach at fifty feet high over the fence, and then float gently to a spot some five hundred down the runway for touchdown, followed by reasonably short rollout. Every one of the factories said that was exactly the way the aircraft had been designed, and even had all the figures readily available. When I tried these numbers in all the different types we flew, they worked out perfectly. After forty years, don't ask me to remember just what they were, except that they were considerably slower than Air Force practice.

General Frederick H. Smith *U.S. Air Force photo*

I reported to General Smith what I had found. Naturally his first question was:

"How will you enforce it?"

"Well, General, you will just have to pass a law setting forth how these airplanes will be flown."

Every Squadron, Group, Wing, and Division had a Chief Pilot whose duties covered this sort of thing. The General sent out a message to every base in the world announcing there would be a meeting at West Palm Beach on such and such a date and that all of the above named people would attend. We had quite a gathering of the troops. I made my short pitch, explaining what had been determined and how the program was to be implemented. Then General Smith took over. His went something like this:

"In the future, all MATS airplanes will make their approach using full flaps fifty feet over the fence, with the power required to maintain the approved speeds, and a touchdown five hundred feet from the threshold. Anyone landing short will be court-martialed. Anyone sliding off the far end of the runway will be automatically forgiven. Anyone that has an accident and survives will report to my office within twenty-four hours. Meeting adjourned."

After that I had to visit all the bases and fly with some of the chief pilots. You can imagine the chilly reception I received! Those guys hated my guts! Here I was telling pilots with ten, fifteen thousand hours how to fly! But you know what? If there was ever another landing-short accident, I never heard about it! General LeMay came over to find out how we managed to have such a good safety record, and promptly put SAC on the same program.

I had a pet project of my own – instrumentation. When airplanes started adding new instruments to the panel, they were placed just about anywhere they would fit or where some individual wanted his favorite one located. When you climbed into any airplane, it was important to

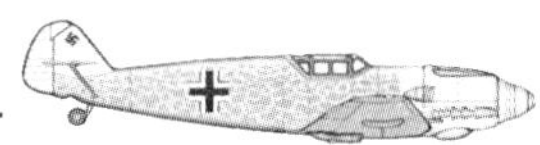

take time to study the layout carefully before take-off in case you suddenly needed to find a particular one. Obviously some standardization was needed. We worked with Wright Field on this one. With a camera mounted on top of the panel and focused on the pilot's eyes, a movie was made in numerous aircraft while flying under solid instrument conditions. The number of eye movements and direction was carefully studied and plotted. We finally arrived at what is known as the 'standard T pattern', which proved to take a great load off the pilot and is in almost universal use today. We had all the MATS airplanes reconfigured.

The Strategic Air Command (SAC) was making large demands on the available supply of the more experienced pilots to man their fleet of new, very high performance bombers. We in turn were notified that we would be receiving brand new Second Lieutenants right out of school as replacements for those we were losing. When this was announced in staff meeting, there arose an anguished howl, especially from the Flying Safety people. Dire predictions of mass slaughter of passengers! After thinking about this for a while, I dared to remind the staff that we had, in the recent past, won a tough war using mainly very young, inexperienced pilots, who seem to learn with commendable speed, when properly trained and led. Then everybody piled on me.

Well, we were going to have to do it, so "Press On!"

We already had a MATS manual that outlined in general our operating practices and procedures. This would have to be expanded to cover any conceivable situation or emergency, and all terminology used between crew members must be standardized so as to prevent any misunderstanding. As a for-instance: on one occasion a pilot had called, "Take-off power," and the engineer did exactly that – he took off all power. Now he would have to call "Max power," or "Climb power," or "Cruise power" – standard commands for standard responses. After a while it worked fine and everybody knew what was expected of him under any circumstance. As to the actual flying, that was the easy part; a pilot who can fly one airplane well can, with the proper training, fly any other type. Now-days, with the advent of computerized simulators, a pilot can become quite proficient in a new type before he ever sits down in a real one. Of course a few take-offs and landings in the genuine article helps a lot!

On re-reading the preceding section, I can readily see where it might appear that I was capable of performing great feats of policy-making single-handedly. Not so. In my Office there were five other pilots, a navigator, and three busy secretaries. These pilots were all old experienced line pilots; two were Navy. None of that crowd showed the least reticence in expressing their opinions and convictions, which I not only welcomed but demanded. Likewise, we made a practice of soliciting comments from the field on any new or revised regulations/proposals – and invariably received a flood of mail in response. Besides, I was a great one for delegating. For example, Tom Collins was the prime mover on the instrument location project.

So by this time my formerly held high esteem for my own brilliant ideas had been eroded to a more realistic level. I had learned that I must listen to all sides of any question before making my own decision.

I recall one instance that helped get my head on straight. I was a member of an accident review board. We sat around for a week arguing what this unfortunate pilot had done or should have done before arriving at the foregone conclusion, 'Pilot Error'. We called the young fellow in to hear his fate…his response has stuck with me:

"Gentlemen, I'm sure your findings are right. You have had a week to examine and weigh all the circumstances. I had ten seconds."

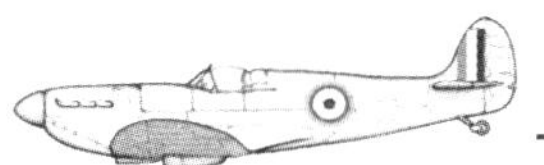

U.S. Air Force photo

We received notice that out at Travis AFB in California a C-124 had been bent a little bit more than somewhat. The pilot, in conformity with General Smith's edict, was en-route to our HQ. He appeared in my office bright and early the next morning, visibly all stressed out. I sat him down and got him calmed to where he could tell me the story. He was a nice looking young kid, recently promoted to Captain, and this had been his first trip as Aircraft Commander. I was quite familiar with the runway at Travis. It is roughly twice the width of the average runway, putting the border lights extra wide apart. The night was dark and stormy with heavy rain and high gusty winds. He made a normal approach, with windshield wipers whipping at full throttle. Those widely spaced runway lights, coupled with the rain-covered windshield, fooled him into believing he was considerably lower than he actually was. When he flared out for his landing he was really still twenty feet too high. He continued to hold it off until the old bird simply couldn't stay in the air any longer and returned to earth with a resounding crunch. It hit so hard that all four engines came partially loose and were hanging down at a most unusual angle. His statement coincided exactly with the one we had already received.

I sat quietly thinking, *There but for the grace of God go I.* And just what would I do if I was in his shoes? I came up with one of my brighter ideas:

"The Old Man knows you are in the building, so he will call for you after-while. Here's what I want you to do. When you walk into his office you will see a mean looking old man sitting behind a very long, wide desk. He wears half glasses down on the end of his nose and will be glaring at you over the tops. I want you to march smartly up to him, salute, and say…'Sir, I screwed up!'"

This shook the boy no end. "I can't do a thing like that!"

I told him, "You had better do that, and do it exactly like I've told you, you understand?"

Shortly afterwards he left. When he returned, he flopped down in a chair, as limp and wrung out as a wet dishrag. I asked him what happened.

"I did exactly like you told me. He looked at me for a minute and then said, 'Well, you won't do it again, will you?' I said, 'NO Sir!' and left."

At lunch The General was regaling the Staff with the story: "This kid came in and saluted and said, 'General, I fu…uh, fu…uh, I screwed uhup!'" After everybody finished laughing, the Old Man turned to me… "Did you put him up to that?"

I solemnly denied.

Douglas was producing a new airplane, the DC-7C, some of which MATS was considering getting. American and United both had them, so I was sent to see what I could find out about this new bird. From New York I took one of American's that was non-stop to Los Angeles. The pilot was their Chief Pilot, named Red Clark, a wholly likeable fellow who had no objections to my riding the jump seat. This airplane had the new Wright Compound Engines that had three turbo recovery units on each engine. These little turbos were driven by the exhaust gases and supplied power to turn all the accessory section, thereby adding some three or four hundred horsepower to the engine's output…which sounded like a fine idea, if it worked.

Leaving New York we climbed directly to altitude. After we leveled off, the throttles stayed in the wide-open position and the engines pounded away flat out.

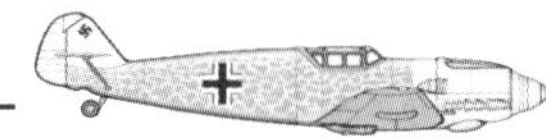

After a while I asked Red, "How do you feel about running your engines like that?"

He came back, "It scares the hell out of me, but United runs them that way, so we have to. Our schedule has to be at least as fast as theirs."

Where had I heard that song before? I caught United for the eastbound trip. Their pilot was 'Dusty' Rhodes. I asked him the same question about all the power they were pulling, and his answer was exactly the same as I got from Clark:

"It scares me, but that's the way American runs them, so we have to keep up."

I suggested he and Red Clark ought to have lunch sometime.

The airlines didn't keep those airplanes long. The engines, especially the little turbos, gave a lot of trouble, and before long the DC-7C could be bought for a song, and you sing the song yourself. The drug smugglers bought a lot of them and smashed them up trying to land in unlighted hay fields around the South. The Navy had very good luck with their Super Connies, but then the Navy doesn't rawhide their engines.

All in all, and against expectations, I rather enjoyed my first year there at MATS HQ. I had a boss I liked and we had a team that worked well together. I was getting a lot of flying, under the guise of giving route and line checks, which took me to Europe or the Pacific. But my hunting had slowed down considerably since leaving National. There I had taken my famous bird dog Sis with me to work one day, and while I was up in a local test hop, she got out of the office and picked up some rat poison. After she died at the vet's, I drove out to Rock Creek Park where no one could see me and cried like a baby.

Nat'l Museum of the USAF

Every Air Force base keeps a few airplanes around for the rated pilots to fly in order to maintain their proficiency; they also draw extra pay for 'Hazardous Duty' if they fly as much as four hours a month! For years the Gooney Bird and the smaller C-45 were used for this purpose. The C-45, known today as the Beech 18, was a lovely little twin-engined tail dragger that required a slightly different technique to handle during take-off and landing that many of the 'Chairborne' lads didn't master, with the result that the supply of aircraft diminished rapidly to the point where they were removed from the inventory and sold. They were replaced with the jet trainer, the T-33. Since few of us older pilots had any experience in single engine jet aircraft, we had to go to school before being qualified to fly this radically different bird. I went to the field near Selma, Alabama.

Nat'l Museum of the USAF

We learned how a jet engine works, fuel management, the control system, and especially the EJECTION system. This bird had dynamite under the seat that could blow you right through the canopy unless you blew the canopy first! When you sat down, the first thing you did was raise the armrests. This cocked the explosives. There was a handle under each armrest that acted as the trigger. Squeeze the right one first and the canopy disappeared. Squeeze the left one and you – still strapped in the seat – would depart the aircraft, being sure your feet were tucked well under the seat or else you would leave your feet behind. Afterwards, in case you forgot how to open your parachute, another little firecracker would explode, unbuckle the seat belts, and pull the ripcord for you. I always raised those armrests like a good little boy, but I did it very slowly and carefully!

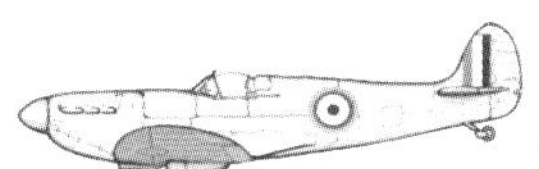

My instructor took me up high and let me play around a bit. It was a sweet flying bird with the most sensitive controls I had ever felt. You didn't actually move the stick, you just thought about what you wanted to do and it was done. The instructor showed me how to make a 360 degree overhead approach, leaving on 55% power all the way down. Then, just as I figured, he slammed it on the runway so hard I thought the wheels would punch up through the wing! I asked if I might try a slightly different touchdown. Either he was a very brave lad or because I was a Colonel and he was a Lieutenant, he sat quietly while I made a half dozen paint jobs simply by holding it off until it settled gently to the runway. Sure enough, it was just another airplane that wanted to fly like an airplane should.

There were only two things I didn't like about that T-33. First, with that early model, you had to wait until you had 200 knots on the airspeed before starting to climb. I felt like I wasn't the boss when I had to hold it a few feet off the ground letting the speed build up while the far end of the runway and the trees were rushing up…too fast to stop and not yet fast enough to climb! And second, the fuel totalizer would spin so fast I just knew I wouldn't have enough left to get there.

Fred Hook ("Call me Supersonic Fred") was still in the fighter business, stationed at Suffolk County, Long Island. He persisted in calling me "Truck Driver Haun," so after I had about 80 hours in the T-Bird, I dropped in on him for a visit. I convinced him that there was no instructor hidden in the back seat and that I had indeed made this perilous flight unaided. Upon returning to Andrews, I turned in my hard hat, parachute, and other equipment. That was my last flight in a T-Bird.

I gave Chuck Yeager a ride to the Pentagon on my way home. Asked about his recent scrape with death, he said, "The aircraft became unstable about all axes, and knocked the padding out of my helmet." Then promptly changed the subject.

General Smith had a new C-118 for the Staff airplane, somewhat plushed up. He got a party together to go fishing in Alaska. We went non-stop. A new invention called anti-skid brakes had been installed recently. When we arrived at Anchorage, there was the usual three inches of snow on the runway, which is the way the Air Force has learned to do: the three inches prevented ice from forming as it would if scraped clean. In addition to runway lights there were small fir trees planted along the edges so you could see where the runway was. On approach, General Smith was standing between me and the co-pilot:

"When we touch down I want you to slam on the brakes, hard. I want to see how these new brakes work."

Well, it was his airplane, so on touchdown, I began to ease the brakes on…

"SLAM THEM ON, I SAID."

So I did just that. Incredibly, nothing extraordinary happened. I could feel the brakes grabbing and turning loose while we came safely to a stop – much to my surprise!

We went way up some river in a floatplane and really hauled in the salmon. The river had large numbers of bright red fish floating down stream. I learned that this was spawning season, and that after the female laid her eggs, she died. I guess all the fish we caught were males! It was right about in this area that Glen Birchard was drowned a couple of years later. He slipped and fell off a pontoon dressed in heavy clothes. I always liked Glen, even when he got to be a Major General.

That trip took us along the entire length of the Aleutian chain, a most beautiful string of mountains, completely snow covered, and the most forbidding landscape I've ever seen, including the Hump. They have fierce storms, winds, and sudden dense fogs. Pity the poor airman that gets stationed there. We landed at Tokyo for a short visit, then to Midway, Hawaii, Travis, and home.

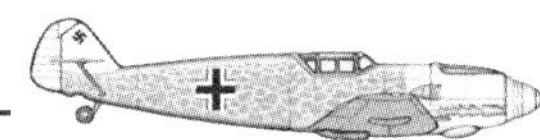

All in all a most enjoyable trip. I slammed the brakes on at every stop and they worked fine, much to the delight of the good General, and much relief to me! My good times at MATS were about over.

Upon our return to Andrews, I discovered I had acquired a new boss. Brigadier General Al Wilson was now the Operations Officer for MATS, and my immediate superior. He had been in SAC for many years, so was thoroughly indoctrinated with their practices and procedures. He was a West Pointer like his father before him and completely military in his thoughts, bearing, and actions. He described the changes he wanted to see made. First, the term 'chief pilot' smacked of the civilian airlines – which of course was where MATS was born. He much preferred we be called a Standardization Board like SAC. That's fine, what's in a name? But then he didn't like our practice of downgrading an aircraft commander should he not measure up to the standards required on the annual instrument and line checks. He considered it demeaning and bad for morale. That's when I bristled. We had an outstanding safety record and operated more airplanes over more routes than any number of the other airlines combined.

I don't have a poker face. I have been told that when I dislike someone, that person knows it immediately because it shows. In the Military you are allowed to express your disagreement with your superior in a respectful way, but after the decision is announced, you either comply or ask to be relieved or transferred. I knew all that, but maybe I had, as they say, gotten too big for my britches, what with my successful tour over at National, and now being General Smith's fair-haired boy. I well knew I brought all my troubles on myself, but having started a fight I just couldn't knuckle under. My friends in the HQ, not wanting to get tarred with my brush, dropped me like a hot potato. My every suggestion or project was promptly attacked with alternate suggestions. Where once I could do no wrong, now I could do no right. I kept a fifth of whiskey and a canteen of water under the seat of my car and staggered home at night to make my wonderful little family utterly miserable. I went over to General Tunner in Germany to see about coming to work for him. I was met with stony silence.

It didn't come as a great surprise when one day in staff meeting General Wilson announced, "Old Jim is going to the 315th Air Division, 5th Air Force, in Japan to be their new Inspector General."

U.S. Air Force photo

The idea of me being an IG was so ridiculous I almost laughed. I could count on the fingers of one hand all the regulations I had ever read!

"Well, General, I'm going to Japan because I've got a set of orders that says I'm going. But I won't be an IG!"

"Oh you won't? Well, you go over there and just take command of all the transport business they have."

You know what? That's exactly what I did!

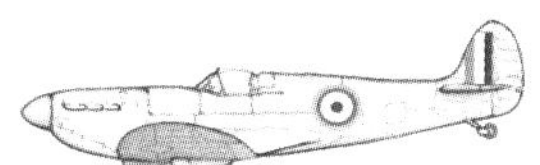

USAF photo

Haun family photo

August 1955 - Hauns Take C-97 to Japan

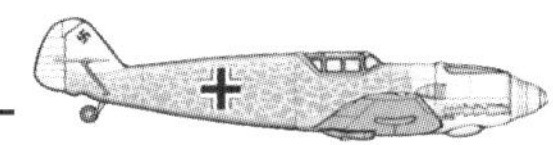

chapter twenty four

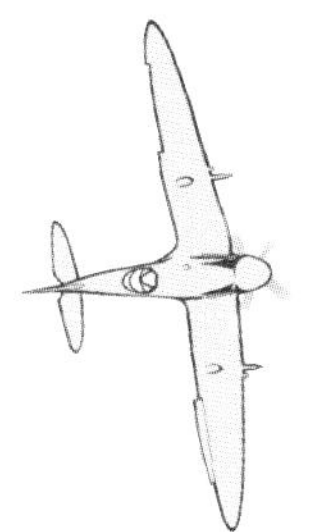

TO JAPAN

1955: "THE KOMAKI CALL-GIRL CRISIS"

When suddenly faced with a move from Washington D.C. to Japan there are an awful lot of details that must be taken care of. First, I accepted a friend's offer to fly Eleanor, the kids, and me to Memphis in his Beech 18. Then I returned to sell the house, call the movers, and decide what to take and what to put in storage. There were also two dogs left from Sissy's last litter: one named Sally and the other later named Po Devil by my sister Julia. He was a sad, mournful looking mutt, while Sally was only minus the tip of her tail where David had slammed a door on it. It took two weeks to sell the house. Then I drove our two-tone tomato-red Mercury with the white top to Memphis, where, after a short visit, we all piled into the car and left for Travis AFB in California. I had already dropped Po Devil off with Julia and shipped Sally.

I was feeling as low as a whale's belly. I had been with MATS ever since the end of the War and had risen to positions of some prominence, only to be now cast into, what was to me, outer darkness! All on account of my big mouth! So I wallowed in self-pity and kept a fifth under the seat. It's a wonder we arrived in California all in one piece. We took the southern route through Albuquerque. We could have used air conditioning crossing the desert, but that hadn't been invented yet, at least not for automobiles. We checked into Transient Quarters, meanwhile making arrangements for our car and Sally to be delivered overseas. Sally went by Pan Am, in the baggage hold, and was a nervous wreck when she arrived in Japan. She was never any good for hunting after that, but there was no other way to ship her.

I had written the Travis Chief Pilot and asked him to see if he could arrange to be our pilot leaving Travis. He met us at the terminal with his boss, the Group Commander, one of my former cohorts at MATS. This worthy was happy to advise me that, while he couldn't spare Willie at the moment, he had selected a nice young crew whose Aircraft Commander had just that week been up-graded to that position – so have a nice flight!

But the boy did a fine job with the C-97, and we had a smooth flight to Hickam, where we spent the night. I was asked to visit some of my former acquaintances at a small party and was there subjected to some not too subtle sarcasm about having been fired – called the Former Great Chief Pilot by Cassady, etc. I stayed about ten minutes before deciding I needed some exercise, like a long walk.

We left the next day. I was standing behind the pilot on take-off. Shortly after becoming airborne, one engine developed trouble and had to be feathered. After landing I called the Group Commander and complimented the crew on the smooth, professional manner in which they had handled the emergency. Eleanor remained wide-eyed but courageous. We transferred to another C-97 and proceeded on our way. We had a short stop at Wake Island and then on to Japan.

MATS had a detachment at Haneda, the main Tokyo airport, on the waterfront. Their only duty was handling passengers and freight into and out of Japan. I don't know why it was called a 'Wing', unless it was some place to stash a Colonel. We were met by my old buddy Tom Collins, who had left Andrews a few months before. He was embarrassed and rather hesitant to give me what he probably thought was bad news. My orders had been changed, and I wasn't going to the

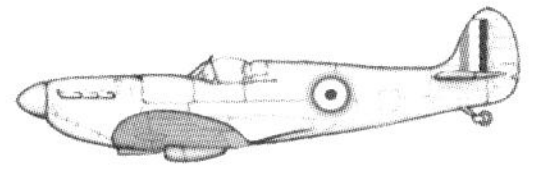

Haun family photo

315th Air Division at Tachikawa, but was re-assigned to the 5th Air Force at Nagoya! News travels fast nowadays with all the new electronic devices! At least that saved me one problem; I wasn't going to be an IG after all!

We spent the night with Tom and his wife. They had a nice little Japanese-type house alongside a canal. I woke up the next morning to the distinctive sound of a single-cylinder engine pushing a fishing boat down the canal. I stepped outdoors, and the smell of Japan hit me. You finally get used to it.

Tom had secured a Gooney Bird to take us to our destination, which turned out to be a place named Gifu, about ten miles north of Komaki airport, which lay midway between Gifu and the large city of Nagoya. Gifu was a former Japanese airbase that was now used entirely as housing for American personnel working in that area. Our crew arrived, obviously miffed at having to fly before noon, if then. The pilot waddled up, most of him hanging over his belt. One look at his bloodshot eyes convinced me that I had better fly this trip, so he could catch up on his sleep en-route.

The old Gooney chugged along quite faithfully, as Gooneys do, under a rather low overcast sky that dripped constantly. From what I could see of it, the country appeared rather rugged, but pretty. My co-pilot didn't know exactly where Gifu was, but the beacon at Komaki was working, so I found that, and about ten miles north found the strip. It looked usable, though quite unused, but then a Gooney never worries about things like that! There was no one around what I figured was once the terminal, so we unloaded our bags and sought shelter from the drizzle. Shortly thereafter a blue GI ambulance showed up, driven by a long, tall, broadly grinning Lieutenant who welcomed us to Gifu. He apologized for having to meet us with the ambulance, but that was the only piece of government transportation on the Base! Made us feel right at home.

He then insisted on giving us a tour of the Base, with which we were quite impressed, except for David. En-route in the air, Eleanor had taken him to the john, back in the rear of the cabin, three times without success, but once on the ground the trouble was, shall we say, quickly eliminated. We were shown the Club, with its nice swimming pool, the Theatre, and the PX. We went in there and were suitably impressed with the quality and quantity of the merchandise. I noticed haircuts were available next door for 25 cents, while a movie ticket would cost us a dime more than that. I bought a little statuette of the most forlorn holy man I had ever seen, which I promptly named 'Po Devil'. I still have it.

We were finally taken to our new quarters and discovered the reason for the extended tour. Quite a crowd had gathered to greet us. A most bountiful meal had been spread, including some excellent steaks, from Kobe, no less. I had started getting mellowed up immediately after landing and could now join the merriment with gusto. Apparently the news of my downfall hadn't reached this far out in the boonies, or perhaps they figured this guy may turn out to be our new boss, so – bottoms up! And Press On!

I thumbed a ride in to the Komaki airport and from there the additional fifteen miles to the city of Nagoya, where the Headquarters of the 5th Air Force was located. The narrow two-lane highway

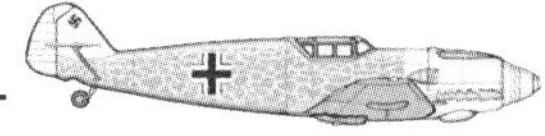

trip from Gifu had been a study in how to play 'chicken' with extra-wide blunt-nosed hauling trucks. All the native vehicles had these 8-inch orange plastic flippers on the sides for turn signals; passing tolerances were so close in the little villages on the way that you'd best hope the oncoming monster didn't have his nearer flipper deployed as he went by. But everybody seemed comfortable in knowing that last possible instant to swerve aside. Fifteen-year-old Jimmy was going to be riding a Japanese bus, complete with little uniformed stewardess, along this route to school every day with twenty other military dependants. *Chotamate, boy-san!*

When I got to Headquarters, I just went into the lobby downstairs to sit around for a while. The place was full of officers similarly just sitting there. Most of them looked like I felt…lost. I could tell they were all new arrivals, dropped out there at the end of the world wondering what fate awaited them. A short, fat officer walked by, stopped, and came back to me with a bright smile…Major Davis, who had been with me at Mobile. After some enthusiastic hugging and backslapping I asked him what he was doing out here.

"I'm Chief of Personnel for 5th Air Force!" Small world!

He thought for a second – then said, "Say, I've got a job you might like. We need a Base Commander out at Komaki. Also the General has a C-54 out there and no one to fly it. Think you would like that?"

Is the Pope Catholic? So again I come out smelling like a rose!

I felt like a piano had been lifted off my shoulders! Another chance! *And this time I won't screw it up.* Riding out to Komaki that morning I had time to make a critical analysis of my many weaknesses, faults, and shortcomings, as opposed to certain abilities that I'm afraid I had imagined greater than reality warranted. (Of course I had actually been going through this self-analysis for the past month. Everyone should try this exercise once in a while. If done objectively it can be rather humbling to the ego, but most beneficial to your well-being among your contemporaries!)

There was no MP on the gate at Komaki. The sides of the streets were strewn with trash of various description. Sheets, towels, and clothing hung from windows in the barracks. Japanese, both male and female, wandered in and out of the buildings. There were a few Americans visible, barely distinguishable by their dress, or lack of it, from the civilians. There was a bare flagpole in front of the Headquarters building. Major Davis had said Komaki needed a Base Commander, and that was quite obvious – as were my duties. Now I had a job I knew how to do!

The Base staff was gathered in the CO's office to greet me. What a crew! The man I was replacing was to move out to Gifu, and I could see several others who would shortly go out there to join him, or go elsewhere. The Exec was a jolly fellow that I thought I could use, until later that afternoon I told him I wanted to have a stand-by inspection in the barracks at 0800 the following morning.

He was aghast. "You can't do that! The houseboys don't get here until eight!"

"Well, I want to see what the troops remember from boot camp, so pass the word."

At 0800 sharp the next morning I entered the first barracks, followed by an apprehensive Exec and someone he had found to act as First Sergeant. The houseboys had obviously not arrived, and I saw a couple of the maids scuttle out the back. I found the barracks chief:

"Have the troops fall-in on the street for thirty minutes close order drill." The old Sergeant had forgotten all he may have known, but I was pretty good at it, after four years ROTC. This gave the other barracks time to clean things up a bit, but not well enough to escape the drill session.

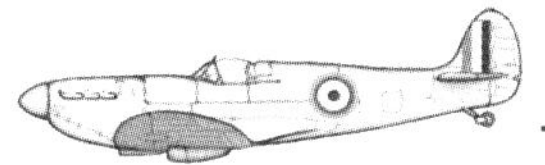

I then marched the troops to the front gate and we had a fine session picking up trash throughout the area. Of course there was moaning and groaning and dark glances thrown, but I detected a lot of sly grins of approval among the older men.

There were eleven or twelve separate units on this Base, including two fighter Squadrons: one F-86D and one F-84. The F-84 Squadron was the atomic delivery bunch, if you can imagine that, trained in what was called toss bombing'. The idea was to dive at very high speed to the target, pull up in the start of a loop, release the bomb, then at the top of the loop, roll out and head for home! No one likes the idea of being ordered to commit suicide, so this was the most uneager bunch of jocks I've ever seen. We had the bombs in storage, minus the cores, which were kept somewhere outside Japan, by treaty.

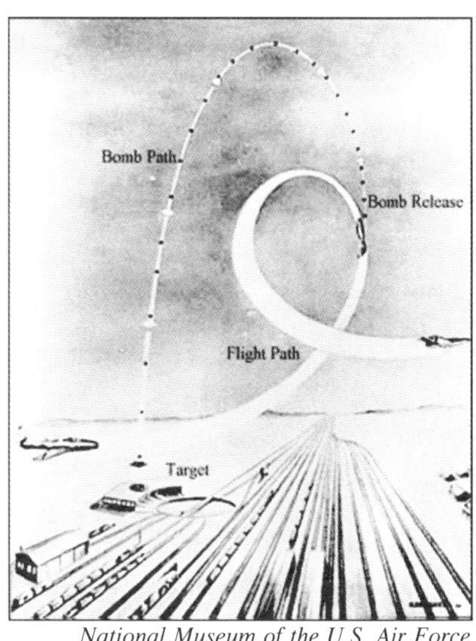

National Museum of the U.S. Air Force

We had an anti-aircraft battalion whose CO was an enthusiastic partner in my clean-up campaign. I had secured a large American flag for the HQ flagpole; plus we had a loudspeaker system that could be heard over most of the Base. Armed with a rather scratchy record of all the bugle calls, the AA boys asked to provide details for the flag ceremonies. Soon we had the troops looking and acting like they were back at old Fort Knox! I sent the Exec and several others packing and asked Major Davis to look for some replacements who would fit in with my ideas; he sent me several fine people, each of them one grade lower than the T.O. called for!

We still had two problems that required fixing. First was the runway. I forget the length, but it was barely long enough for the fighters to take off, especially if they were heavily loaded. We had chain barriers to catch the airplanes if they were about to run off the end into a ditch. Land is the most precious thing the Japanese have, so extending the runway wasn't worth discussing.

Col. Haun photo

The other problem was our very high VD rate. Fifth Air Force wrote numerous letters bemoaning this situation and making all sorts of suggestions about giving lectures, etc. I talked it over with all the unit commanders and they agreed to furnish patrols of their oldest Non Coms to help patrol Komaki City. This was a town of some three hundred houses, most of which had at least two or more quite pretty Japanese girls eager for our boys to teach them to read, write, and speak the English language.

Without asking permission from 5th AF, thus saving them any possible repercussions from the Japanese, I placed Komaki City 'Off Limits' to all American personnel, with the MPs, augmented by the other units, set to patrol the place and arrest anyone found there. The first night our jail was packed. This establishment was a thing of beauty. The Base Chaplain, may his tribe increase, had scrounged some fine furniture for a large day room. There were comfortable bunks, ping pong tables, radios, and something that looked like a Japanese TV set. In fact, with smuggled beer, my prisoners had a ball.

So let's try another approach. I ordered the Sheriff to remove all the beds and ping pong tables forthwith.

He screamed bloody murder. "They will riot. They will tear the place down!"

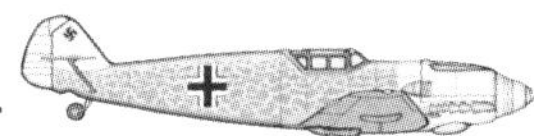

I pointed out the number of fire hoses located at strategic spots that would cool down any such disturbance. I looked in on the operation that night around eleven o'clock. Everything was peaceful. There seems to be something about a big, ugly MP with a high pressure fire hose in his hands, grinning at you through the bars, that induces slumber, even on bare concrete floors! Perhaps our Sheriff here in Nashville might try that trick.

The next night we had three customers at our inn, and after that, none. I saw pretty little flowerbeds and other improvements springing up all over the Base, with our former inmates hard at work – well supervised, of course. The repercussions were not long in coming. First, the Mayor of Komaki City came over with a bevy of his beauties in tow, each with an armful of flowers for my desk. We all grinned, bowed and hissed at each other while I learned that I was wrecking the local economy. I was deeply grieved at being unable to relieve their distress, but after all, that is – as we say in American – the way fortune cookie crumble! In a few days we had another visitor, the Governor of the Prefecture (roughly a county). He spoke some English and was a former Colonel of infantry; as such he could know how I felt about my responsibilities to the folks back home to protect our boys from all sorts of bad things. We did more of the hissing and bowing, and he left.

U.S. Air Force photo

Fifth Air Force was staying carefully on the sidelines in this, but did keep me informed. A delegation of six members of the Japanese Diet – that's sort of like our Congress – wanted to come for a discussion. I further learned that all six owned property in Komaki City! *Aahh sooo, boy-san!*

I had two papers drawn up, one lifting the off-limits subject to certain actions by the Mayor, and one specifying that a strip one thousand feet long and one hundred feet wide be turned over to the Air Force for an extension of the south end of the runway. When they arrived, I had an interpreter handy while we went into some deep Hissing...

In the end, I signed one paper, they signed the other; the runway was extended, the boys and girls became friends again, and peace reigned. Fifth AF sighed a deep sigh of relief.

My tomato-red '54 Merc had arrived from the States, and we were comfortably settled in our quarters. Gifu was a beautiful Base, surrounded by rolling hills covered with pine or fir forest. The Base had everything we needed and more. The Japanese are artists at sculpting trees, bushes, and shrubs into amazing figures and patterns. This Base was landscaped to perfection. I mean, it was not unusual to see a gardener trimming the grass in front of the PX with scissors! We had inherited a live-in maid named Kimiko, who was a jewel. Eleanor didn't have to lift a hand if she didn't want

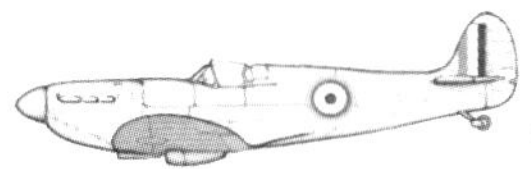

to, and Kimiko wouldn't let little Dave out of her sight. I had to give Dave a little paddling once and Kimiko cried for hours. Apparently the spanking of small boys is unknown in Japan.

I was flying the Staff C-54 around to various 5th AF bases, but mainly it was used to haul the General's wife and party on shopping trips. We went to Seoul, Korea, to Tokyo and nearby Tachikawa. There I discovered my old cohort from National, Frenchy Williams, President Truman's well-chosen pilot! He was now the 374th Wing's Commander at Tachi. This was a Troop Carrier Wing, with two squadrons of C-124s, a squadron of C-54s for Air Evac, plus numerous Gooneys and whatnot. In fact, he commanded about all the long-range airlift in the Far East! Wheels began to spin in my head. FRIENDS and peace reigned.

The Commanding General of the 5th Air Force was scheduled to return to the States and be replaced by a new man, General Freddie Smith, who had been a fighter pilot in the Pacific during WW II. We took the Staff C-54 to pick him up, heading home by the usual route: Midway, Hawaii, Travis, and on to Bolling Field across the river from National. General Smith wasn't quite ready to leave Washington just yet, so I lived in the transient barracks there at Bolling for about two weeks. There was no point in visiting either MATS HQ, or National. It was summertime and Bolling had a nice pool at the Club. The General's aide was a young fellow named Davis, who had been with me at Mobile. We spent the time on the trip back to Japan recalling the good times we had back in the old 17th Squadron. The General did a lot of the flying, so the entire trip was most enjoyable.

Meanwhile I was increasingly pleased with the improved conditions at Komaki. The Base was finally neat and clean, with all the appearances of a well run military post. Personally, I had cut way down on my drinking and now spent lunch hour in the gym playing handball and doing sit-ups – actually working up to a daily hundred. Twenty-five pounds of flab disappeared. I tried golf for the first time, but for some reason my drives always took a ninety-degree curve to the right!

Every chance I got, I managed to stop in at Tachi to visit with Frenchy; I wanted to get back into the Transport business, and I knew this would be my only chance ever.

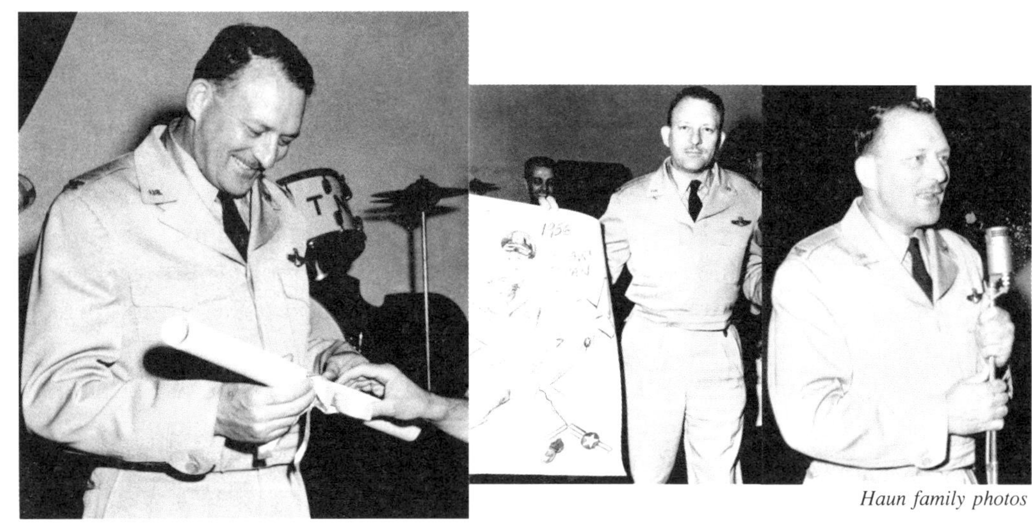

Haun family photos

Bye-bye Komaki

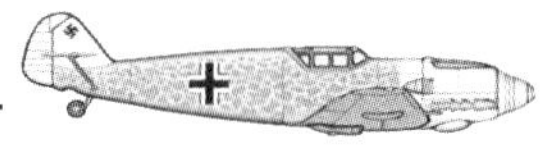

chapter twenty five

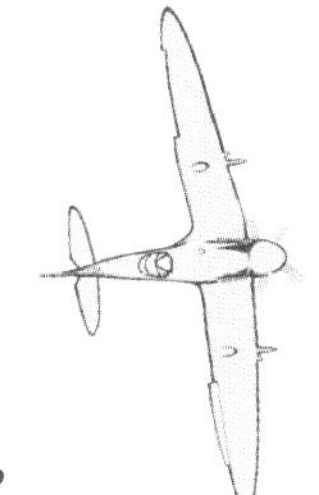

TO TACHIKAWA

1956: "COMMANDER, 374th TROOP CARRIER WING"

Frenchy finally called to offer me the job of Maintenance Group Commander if I could get relieved from Komaki. I was flattered that 5th AF didn't want me to leave, but when I explained to General Smith how much I loved those big airplanes, he let me go. Again we called the packers and movers to get us to Tachi. All our household goods were GI-issue, so that didn't take long. We took our maid Kimiko along with us and drove the two hundred fifty miles to Tachi.

That was one weird ride. The roads, such as they were, had been so wrinkled up by recurrent earthquakes as to make many places almost impassible. There were no road signs to help us find our way, while Kimiko, being a Korean, had trouble translating the constantly changing dialects we encountered. No one along the entire way had ever seen a Mercury of any color, let alone a tomato-red one with a racy white top! The trip took us all day long.

Haun family photo

We had been assigned a very nice set of quarters that had already been furnished with all the necessities, even groceries, plus we found the beds already made up with brand new sheets! Just like moving into a nice hotel! We were to live on the west side of the Base, known as Tachi West, home of the 315th Air Division Headquarters and the Troop Carrier wing, while Tachi East was a Materiel Depot where we got all our goodies and was also the site of a large hospital. As having been originally slated to be their Inspector General, perhaps I should have dropped by the 315th HQ to pay my respects, but somehow neglected to do that!

The 374th Troop Carrier Wing, Colonel Frenchy Williams commanding, provided most of the freight and troop transport to and from Korea. We had a one-a-day flight to Seoul as well as trips to any other bases that required our services. We went to Okinawa, Iwo Jima, and you name it. I was assigned to the 6th Troop Carrier Squadron for flying. I preferred the run to Seoul, as that was over and back the same day, and I could get back to my other duties. I managed to get in twenty-five or thirty hours a month, which is enough to keep your hand in. We had a five thousand foot runway at Tachi, with obstructions at both ends. I tried to convince the pilots that there was a much better way to land an airplane rather than slamming it in like they did, but got few takers; so I requisitioned additional tires, wheels, and brakes, letting Frenchy worry about the flying end.

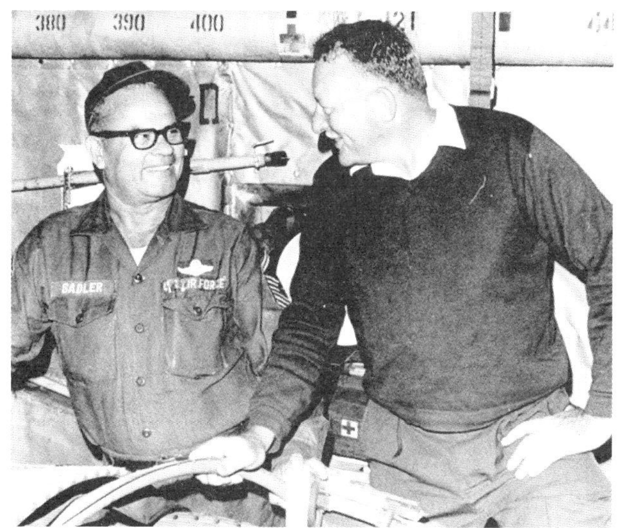

U.S. Air Force photo

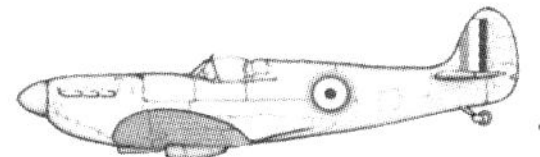

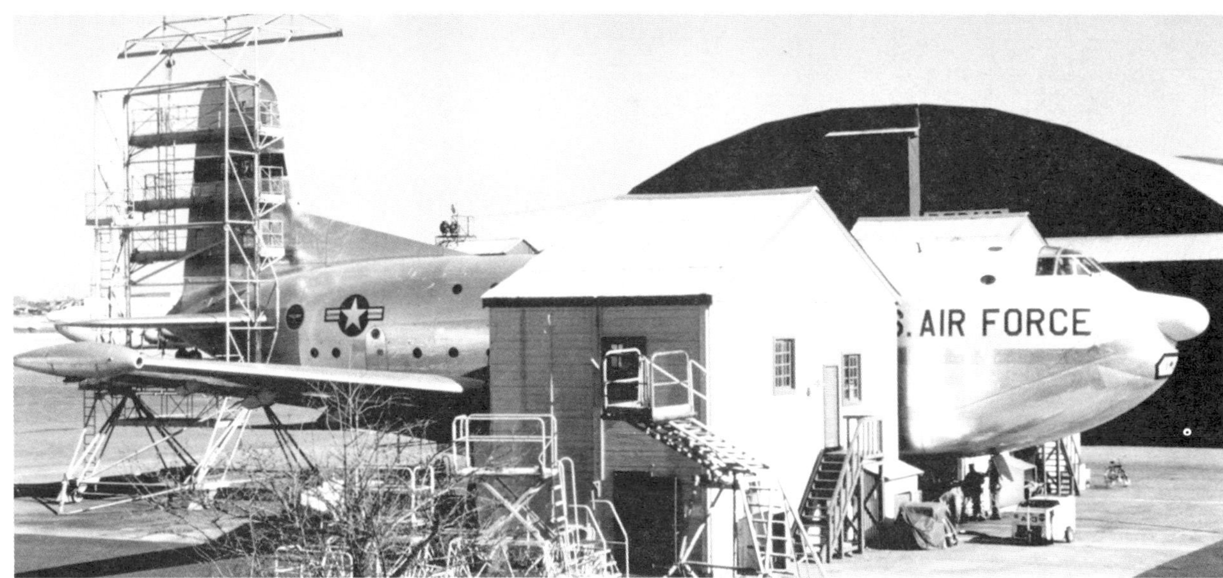

U.S. Air Force photo

I had never actually been a Maintenance Officer, but my experience with MATS had given me some definite ideas as to how the Group should be organized and run. Naturally the first thing I did was request the assignment of Sid Parks from wherever he was at that time. He arrived several months later. The Wing maintenance was being performed by the old crew-chief system, time-honored since the beginning. With this system, a sergeant was given one airplane plus a crew of men to take charge of that one airplane. Most men respond well when trusted with responsibility to do a given job. When I was a Squadron CO, I never once made a walkaround inspection of an airplane. It was always, "Is she ready, Chief?" and jump in. And it always was ready. The fallacy of this system is that it allows a man to inspect his own work – while at the same time he is expected to be an expert in all the different systems on a very large airplane…an expectation to which very few men can measure up. So I opted for consolidated maintenance, as I'll explain.

Frenchy agreed with me, and it was set up – amid much moaning and groaning from the old crew chiefs. But they came around. We built a number of nose docks where the men could work inside, out of the weather, with platforms built to fit around the engines, and all the special tools and equipment fixed close at hand. The supply of parts was consolidated. Now, when a man needed a part, he no longer had to go to the Supply Hangar to get it; he merely placed a little marker in front of the nose wheel, whereupon the 'ramp expediter', seeing it, would drive up in his Jeep, find out what was needed, run to Supply, secure and deliver it to the airplane. Walky-talkies would have been nice, but we didn't have them in 1956. We left a crew chief on each airplane. He soon saw the advantages. Someone else did all the wrenching while all he had to do was inspect the finished job and have his helper do all the paper work!

The new system paid off at once. For example, the 124 had five johns and urinals in the very rear of the cabin. These leaked on the cables mounted directly beneath the floor. As a result of the better overall exchange of information, we found that almost every control cable in the fleet was rusted and frayed very close to the failure point. I had to start grounding airplanes to replace cables, much to the horror and disbelief of the Air Division HQ, so I took a bundle of the cables and plopped them on the General's desk. End of problem!

***

Styrons, Hauns, Cooks
Haun family photo

We made some good and lasting friends at Tachi. We still hear from Woody Styron and his wife Mary Alice; Guy Cook's widow Mary, and many others. Guy was a jack-of-all-trades and master of every one of them! I bought a Heath Kit from the hobby shop, which Guy turned into a hi-fi set second to none. A Japanese shop made me a beautiful speaker cabinet and another to hold the record turntable and tuner. Stereo wasn't invented yet but our system could still shake the house with *Rhapsody in Blue*. (Thirty-eight years later, I still have them in my living room.) Woody, Guy, and I took up golf, and with the help of the club pro, I showed some improvement. In fact, I once broke a hundred!

We drove around the country quite a bit, but usually stayed close enough to get back to the Base at night. I had a 16mm movie camera that we used to record most of the places we went and the strange things we saw. We got into Tokyo for a few of their theatres, but I frankly lacked the imagination required to translate their symbolic acting into what the play was really all about. I liked to wander around the side streets and watch those people in their little shops making all sorts of things entirely by hand, or foot. Frenchy was having a rather large cabin cruiser built, beautifully appointed with much brass and teakwood. He was transferred before it was finished, and I had the job of finally having it deck-loaded on a freighter bound for New York via the Panama Canal. It arrived in good shape.

with Major R. L. Nixon
U.S. Air Force photo

When Frenchy first received his orders transferring him back stateside, there was much speculation as to who would be the new Wing Commander. I asked Frenchy who he thought it would be and he hadn't any idea. I asked him if he might put in a good word for me. He looked surprised, as I'm sure he hadn't thought about that, and jumped up and left the office. A week or so later, General Waldron, Commander of the 315th Air Division, had all the Wing Staff over to his office for the big announcement.

Guy Cook and I were sitting together. He whispered in my ear, "Who do you guess it will be?"

I whispered back, "Me."

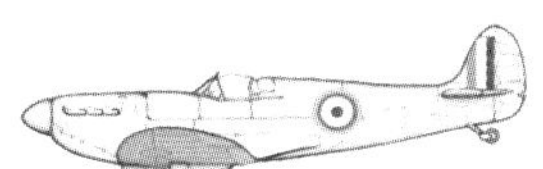

U.S. Air Force photo

He laughed out loud at this joke. Then General Waldron spoke: "I have a message from the Headquarters Far East Air Forces. The following officer is hereby appointed Commander, 374th Troop Carrier Wing, Tachikawa, Japan. Colonel James R. Haun, 5415A. By order of…"

You should have seen Guy's face! I slapped him on the back and asked him what job he wanted. He wanted Operations.

"Sorry about that, you'll have to take over Maintenance for awhile." Which he did, and did well. Guy was killed in Hawaii when he dived into the surf and broke his neck.

When we had sent that old C-74 to the factory from Brookley, Colonel Cassady had made a number of suggestions for improvements, every one of which had been rejected by Wright Field as "not invented here." The 28 cylinder Pratt & Whitney engines were wonderful powerplants, but on the 124 we were down continually due to pulled exhaust ports. This problem could not be repaired in the field, so the cylinder had to be removed and returned to the Depot for repair. The cause was simple. Each row of four cylinders was fitted with one exhaust pipe, which was then bolted firmly to the engine mount and again at the firewall. There was a balljoint provided to allow the stack to move a bit when the engine had cause to twist or shake for any reason. Trouble was, those balljoints would get carboned-up and freeze tight, so when the engine twisted around a bit, like when it backfired, we had what amounted to a crowbar prying out the exhaust valve ports.

One of the old crew chiefs and I were studying the problem. He pointed to the balljoint:

"If we could keep those joints from freezing up, the trouble would be over."

I told him to get some little springs and put them under the tiedown brackets so that the stack would jiggle, only on this one bank of four cylinders. If it cured that one bank, try it on all seven banks, but for Heaven's sake don't let anyone know what we're doing, else we could end up in Leavenworth!

Meanwhile we had four new engines in the shop that had been completely robbed of cylinders, worked over by a half dozen Japanese cylinder-change-crews that could whip off a cylinder and pop on a new one in under three hours. Those little fellows really worked. As they should! We were paying them thirty American dollars (in script) per month, which by Japanese law was all we were allowed to pay them.

Our test engine stopped losing cylinders, so we fixed all four with those little springs. The airplane stopped losing cylinders. At about this time, having decided I needed to go pheasant hunting in Korea, I had the morning flight drop me off at Seoul to let me wander off across the hills. It was biting cold and I couldn't stir up a pheasant, so I gave up and went back to the airport. A 124 was due in within the hour, and I planned on taking that home. But it so happened that there was an Air Evac 54 on the ramp loading a few litter patients, so I decided to ride home with them. As we taxied out the incoming 124 landed, and I read the number on the tail. *No, that ship's not my secret weapon.*

When we arrived at Tachi we received the news. That 124 on takeoff had number three engine drop a master rod, which froze the engine while pulling full power. The propeller sheared off and

U.S. Air Force photo

went through the fuselage, killing a number of people and cutting the control cables. Out of control, the airplane went into the river. The nose was split open and the two pilots were thrown out, still in their seats. The pilot landed headfirst and drowned, the co-pilot landed right side up and wasn't hurt. I had just missed a really rough ride.

General Waldron called for me to come to his quarters. "Was your secret invention on that airplane?"

"No Sir."

Those little springs allowing the exhaust stacks to jiggle continued to do their job so well that we soon had all twenty-four airplanes equipped with them. Our maintenance record improved dramatically.

We still had a few problems at Tachi, however. The Base was surrounded by Communist sympathizers who would call a strike and set up picket lines outside all the gates. We had about two hundred Japanese working on the flight line. Their head honcho would always let me know when something like this was slated to begin, so we could get in a supply of rice and stuff to feed our workers, who would bed down in one of our hangars. They had no intention of losing their well-paying jobs; after all, thirty bucks a month would buy an awful lot of rice and fish heads!

These Commies had another annoying little habit of erecting tall bamboo flagpoles directly off the end of the runway. Of course a heavy C-124 wasn't much bothered by the tip of a light bamboo pole, so we took them down as fast as they could erect new ones!

I recall one other minor headache. Our parking ramp was really packed with airplanes. There was so little room we had to have men walking beside the wing tips, universally known as 'wingwalkers', to help prevent taxi accidents. I came in one really bad night – heavy rain, just barely GCA minimums – and after landing turned off onto the entrance to the ramp. I waited for the wingwalkers to appear, but none showed. There were lights in the windows of the Alert Shack, so I knew there were men on duty. We shut down the engines and I climbed out.

When I walked through the door of the Shack, there were some twenty or thirty men sitting there, glaring at me like, "Well, what are you going to do about it?"

I thought, *Now I'm going to have to do this just right.* I spoke in a conversational tone of voice, but everyone heard me:

"Normally, when a Colonel walks into a place like this, the room comes to attention." They all popped-to.

Turning to the Chief, I added, "Most Master Sergeants know that. Get a tug and go park that aircraft, then be in my office at 0800 in the morning." And left.

The next morning the adjutant came into the office. "What did you do to Sergeant Jones last night? He's out there shaking like a leaf. He says you never raised your voice but tore great strips off his back."

I explained to the Sergeant about accident investigation boards, and who always gets the blame, etc. After that the Alert Crew shaped up nicely.

With so many new things to see and do, we thoroughly enjoyed our stay at Tachi. Already down in Gifu we'd become accustomed to the smell of their fields, well fertilized from the contents

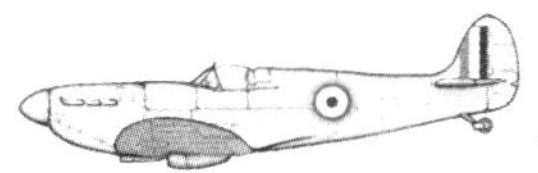

of the ‘honey buckets’ collected daily throughout Japan. They grew fabulous crops from the stuff. Did you ever see a carrot three feet long? All our food came from a huge hydroponics farm, so we seldom ate off-Base, unless it was seafood. On our trips to the northern-most islands, we often returned with delicious king crab and lobsters – fresh from icy ocean waters. I’m drooling!

We had an Aero Club off the Base with some Aeroncas and Pipers available. Unknown to his mother, I was giving my son Jimmy flying lessons in the Aeronca. He learned fast, but I didn’t let him solo until he got mad at me for just sitting in the back only riding! That told me he was ready and I let him go. He flew for around twenty hours and then just lost interest. Years later he confided that he didn’t like being so high off the ground and preferred the sensation of speed close to earth. He chose the safety of motorcycles over airplanes!

Haun family photo

We almost went broke from bargains. I think there are still a couple of barrels of glassware and hand made knicknacks in the attic, still packed. Rattan living room furniture covered with raw silk. A solid mahogany dining room from the Philippines – that sort of thing.

The bandleader at the Officer’s Club, known as Smiley’, was a regular visitor at our house. He would sit for hours listening to my records; then shortly thereafter the same music would reappear in his orchestra. It made no difference if it was Guy Lombardo, Benny Goodman, or Spike Jones – he could imitate them perfectly. When Eleanor and I walked into the dining room, Smiley would stop the music and break in with *The Tennessee Waltz* until we were seated. As I was the Boss, everybody smiled politely!

Haun family photos

Tennessee Waltz

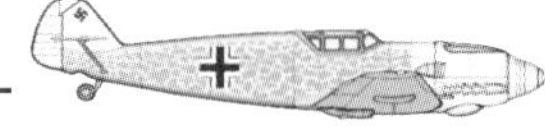

chapter twenty six

BACK IN MATS

1957 – '58: "WRIGHT FIELD RETALIATES, BUT WE'RE U.S. BOUND"

The Japanese were putting pressure on our government to move the MATS operation out of Haneda Airport. At that time there wasn't anywhere else except Tachi available, a fact generating much talk about breaking up the Wing or dividing the assets. General Joe Smith was still the MATS Commander, so I wrote him a long letter advising him that we had an efficient, smooth running operation, and it would be money in the bank if he took over the entire Wing – lock, stock, and barrel.

In the end that was what happened. The 1503rd MATS Wing moved to Tachi and combined with the 374th, whose name was dropped so we all became the 1503rd Wing, MATS. Herm Rumsey came with the move, but I ranked him by one day, and the law says: "A day of rank equals another grade," so again, I and my fate lay in the loving hands of the MATS Staff. For the present, at least, I was in command of all the heavy air transportation in the Far East.

Meanwhile, at this juncture I learned that General Al Wilson, my old nemesis at Andrews, had been transferred to Korea as a member of the hapless group that sat out in that tent arguing with the North Koreans year in and year out. What was the name of that place? Panmunjom? Al was a great golfer – and there were no golf courses in Korea! Sour grapes? Sure. I never said I could walk on water!

My problems started right off. I had to take my Staff to Travis to explain why I had resisted the move from Haneda. Of course the only problem was actual space to handle the extra traffic, which now included finding a passenger terminal and freight warehousing. While there, I was allowed to see some letters Rumsey had written claiming that the solutions to all these problems were to him 'crystal clear', and how much better he could run the operation, etc. After I cooled down a bit, I remembered I had done practically the same to General Wilson back at MATS HQ, so I never let Herm know I was reading his mail, but I certainly kept my back covered. I decided to turn those very problems over to Herm, and he in fact did a creditable job; he became Wing CO after I left and was promoted to Brigadier General.

The 1503rd Wing's area of responsibility now extended from Tachi down through Iwo Jima, Clark Field near Manila, across to Saigon, Bangkok, Calcutta and Karachi. We had detachments at all these places, so naturally I had to visit all of them on a regular basis. Tough duty! I had a fine C-54, all plushed up with bunks, a galley, and comfortable airline-type seats. On these trips I would take about half of my Staff, plus at least one member from the Base Hospital, and one from the Depot. On the first trip I also took Herm along – just to get him familiar with the route, of course. On the return trip we stopped at New Delhi. That's where we could buy those heavy brass coffee tables everybody wanted. So we were taking on ballast.

U.S. Air Force photo

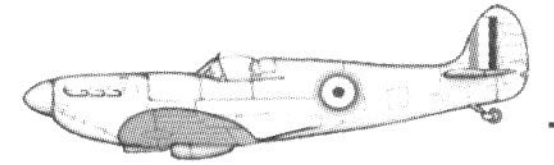

Then to Hong Kong. I had been there before while stationed at Komaki, so I knew how to navigate the approach up the fjord leading in. The Chinese were not at all friendly, so we were not permitted to fly over land, but must stay over water and below five hundred feet all the way in from the sea. Well inside the border, you come to a fork in the fjord where there is a sheer bluff painted white to identify it. You must take the left fork to reach Hong Kong. The right fork narrows rapidly to where there's no room to turn around and you die. Our navigator had never been over this route. When I approached the white bluff and turned left, the poor guy went ballistic and prepared for death! I, calmly, and with masterly skill, lowered the gear and flaps, completed the turn around the mountain and landed straight ahead.

Before anyone could deplane, I made a speech:

"Now you guys look around. We've already got quite a load. We'll be taking full tanks of fuel, so don't lose your heads and buy out the town or you might have to walk home."

The next morning after stopping by the weather office, I went out to the airplane. There were two trucks backed up to the rear door; those guys were throwing masses of stuff aboard! Some were trying on new suits or shoes, while a horde of salesmen were taking orders for further shipments. My fine Chinese friend from my own shopping spree of the day before had my three Italian silk suits as well as two pair of alligator hide shoes. So what could I say? When everybody was aboard, there wasn't a place to sit left in the cabin.

There is (or was) only one direction to take off from Hong Kong, and that's the way we came in. I made a running take-off from the run-up area and we actually became airborne before the wheels could get wet. A very gentle turn around the mountain at around a hundred feet and we were gone. I had planned on stopping at Okinawa, but having been successful in coaxing this load off the ground once, I had better just stay aloft. I've searched my logbook but am unable to positively determine the length of time those guys had to stand up on the way to Tachi. I think it was around eight or nine hours.

When General Smith came over to inspect his new Command, the first thing he wanted to know was how we were able to get such a high in-commission rate with our 124s. I showed him the little springs we had installed in the exhaust system. He was so favorably impressed that then and there he put in a call to Wright Field demanding that a team be sent to Tachi. He insisted that the entire fleet of MATS 124s be so modified. The team arrived in due course and was most unhappy with us. You see, any piece of equipment installed on an Air Force aircraft must have been invented or approved by Wright's own shops; anything else is obviously not airworthy. We had infringed on their prerogatives; some way must be found to slap our wrists.

U.S. Air Force photo

They found it. The T.O. [Tech Order] sent to the field showed some neat little brackets and springs, but they added a torque value to the tie-down bolts that mashed the little springs flat, completely destroying their usefulness. Years later I was in Nashville, where the National Guard was at that time equipped with the 124s. They were having the same old cylinder trouble. I asked them if they had loosened up the tension on the bolts so the stacks could jiggle a bit. Of course not, the T.O. called for a certain torque value, and like good little soldiers, they must comply. So they continued to lose cylinders like popcorn out of a popper.

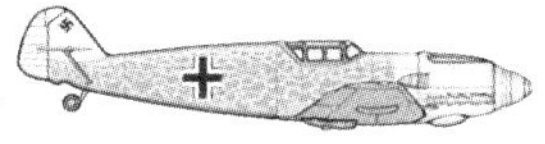

Haun family photo

MATS was great for having frequent gatherings of their unit commanders. I didn't mind going, as about all we did was listen to speeches and play golf. (As previously noted, I had found a pro who helped me with my game to where I once actually broke a hundred!) I would always load the C-54 with passengers and make a leisure-trip to Hawaii or Travis or wherever the meeting was to be held. On my last meeting I really screwed up. This time we were going to a firepower demonstration down at Eglin AFB in Florida. We were all invited to go. Well, I had seen a number of these demonstrations and wasn't really interested in seeing a lot of bombs dropped from a B-36 onto the peaceful Florida landscape, although it is quite a sight. I had been overseas for two years and would much rather go see the homefolks at Memphis.

I approached the WESTAF Chief of Staff with this idea. He allowed as how he couldn't see any trouble with that, but suggested it might be a good idea to clear it with the Admiral, who commanded WESTAF. (MATS had some Navy units, thus the Admiral.) The only way to see the Admiral is through his Aide. To this day I can't believe I was so dim-witted. I should have seen the trap. I got in touch with the Aide. He, likewise, couldn't see any problem with the idea, and said he would talk with the Admiral; he added that if I didn't hear from him, I could consider myself cleared for the trip. Having heard nothing further from the Aide, I cranked up the C-54 early next morning and hied me to Memphis. I was at supper with the Welches (Eleanor's folks) when I received a frantic telephone call from my 'old buddy', the Chief of Staff. That worthy said he was dumbfounded to find me in Memphis, using a government airplane for personal transportation, completely without proper authorization, etc., etc. He stated that the Admiral had ordered me to appear in his office – in the San Francisco area – at precisely 0800 in the morning.

Fortunately I was able to locate the rest of my crew. We had to fly all night, but I did report to the Admiral at exactly 0800 the next morning. I told my story, and the Admiral, being a savvy old coot, seemed to understand what had transpired. He said I had been doing a fairly good job at Tachi but now was starting over from scratch. Thus chastened, I returned to Tachi.

Some years later I had occasion to look at my Efficiency Report covering that period. About all it said was, "He makes a good speech." Period. You will note that I have carefully avoided mentioning the names of the individuals involved, nor have I discussed their character, legality of birth, or ancestry. Both the Chief of Staff and the Aide attained high rank.

The Air Force was becoming increasingly worried about the number of heart attacks suffered by the more senior officers, so a program was set up for all officers in the grade of Colonel and above to have an extensive physical exam each year. It also specified that their wives should have the same checkup. When the time came for my annual physical, Eleanor and I reported to the Tachi Hospital for this work. We were given a nice private room. Each morning we received a stack of little pink slips indicating where we were to report and at what time.

We had been in the hospital for three days and had one last stop to make. This was to see Doctor 'Hemorrhoid' Henry. I went in first, and got the full treatment. They have a chair that you kneel in; then, with a crank, they tilt you into a heads-down position with your rear end pointing in the general direction of the ceiling. They have a cute hollow metal tube about a foot long and an

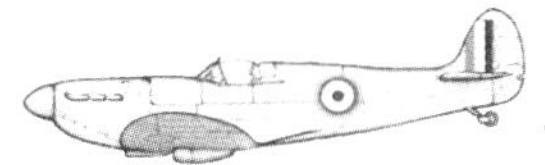

inch in diameter known as the 'Silver Stallion'. With this thing properly greased and inserted, there follows some internal clanking noises as the good Doctor uses a slender telescope to peer about in your insides. With much glee the Doc announced he had found a little polyp, which he could forthwith excise. As there is no feeling at all in this area, he proceeded to burn the thing out, using some sort of hot wire device.

While I was thanking my lucky stars that my chances of dying from cancer had been greatly reduced, in walks a pretty little nurse, chattering to herself about her various problems. Her tirade is cut off in mid-sentence with:

"Geez, look at the blue smoke coming outta that guy's ass!"

I twisted around to where I could look upwards, and sure enough, there was a little puff of blue smoke rising! I didn't tell Eleanor what to expect.

When we were returned to our room and started packing to leave, I noticed a little silver tray with a card in it.

It read, "Cocktails – six to eight, Dr. Henry's quarters."

Eleanor bristled, "Must I meet him socially?"

Things were changing around Tachi. General Waldron was transferred to Travis, replacing the Admiral. There he cleaned out the Staff and replaced them with his own people, as was expected. I breathed a sigh of relief. Right after Jimmy graduated from High School in Tokyo, I received orders transferring me to a base near Seattle, the name of which I've forgotten. We enrolled Jimmy in a college near there and started packing. I sold my '54 Merc to someone on the Base. I could have gotten three or four times as much for it if I sold it to the eager Japanese, but Sid Parks had just escaped the firing squad for trying something like that. (We later heard that the car did in fact end up in the hands of a Japanese Samurai movie star.)

U.S. Air Force photo

We had wanted to go home by sea, but we had been outranked on that, so I requested permission to use the C-54 for the trip to the States. General Waldron approved, also advising me that my orders had been changed, assigning me to Travis. Seems Travis was getting the new C-133s; he wanted me on that project. So we gathered five families of our friends, with all their kids, which made a full load for the old bird. [*Editor Jim Junior notes:* My Dad here politely fails to mention that one of those families was that of Lt. Col. Ray S. Brill – which meant that their lovely sixteen-year-old daughter, Patsy, my steady girlfriend for the past year, was seated beside me on this memorable flight. My father's usual comment on this facet of the episode, which he opted not to include in his official history, was, "Us four parents were a little worried about Jimmy and Patsy sharing a seat for two whole nights – since we already knew from the time they boarded the plane they were back there swabbing each others' tonsils!" Well, as to

Haun family photo

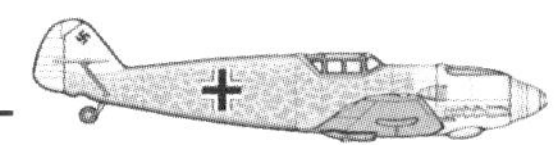

'swabbing' – guilty as charged, but he was way overestimating the danger of premature grandchildren!]

Haun family photo

Our first stop was Midway Island, where five-year-old David got pecked by a giant gooney bird that had made her nest right beside the sidewalk to the mess hall. When you make a nighttime approach to the runway at Midway, your landing lights flush them up so bad it looks like it's snowing. We always hit a few, but they don't hurt an airplane much unless you get one through the windshield. It's a different story if a jet inhales one into the engine. Efforts have been made to get rid of those birds, but the Animal Rights people have stopped those, as it is well known that the birds are far more valuable than the lives of people on airplanes!

Our next layover was Hickham Field in Hawaii, where we stayed for three days waiting for the winds to subside. At that time of year, the easterly winds can be so strong as to make the trip to California in a C-54 a bit iffy. So in the meantime we rented a car and toured that beautiful island – at least it was then, before it became a tourist trap. Each day I spent an hour or two in the weather office checking the winds. On the third day, we came up with a thirteen and a half hour flight plan, so I decided to go.

We left in the afternoon, as I wanted the navigator to have some stars to shoot at. We might as well have started earlier since we didn't see many stars for most of the trip. As daylight faded, the last I saw of the Pacific was a solid sheet of white where the surface winds were tearing the wave tops to shreds. I, for once, thought about what awaited anyone who had to ditch in that weather; when you have your own family riding with you, it does make a difference.

The trip wasn't as rough as I thought it might be. At least not at first. We were in and out of cloud most of the time, but the navigator was able to get a shot once in a while. He came up with an estimate, saying that, timewise, we were at about the half-way point. The kids were all asleep. When we passed the Ocean Station ship, they gave us the best information they had, which was thirty-foot waves and a full gale. *Don't even think about ditching tonight.* I noticed a movement of the oil pressure needle on number three engine. It was reading eighty pounds, temperature normal. Then the oil pressure dropped to twenty pounds. Why must it always be number three? All of mine have been. All I could do was just sit there. The navigator was insistent that we were about an hour closer to California than to Hickham. So, PRESS ON...what else? That wonderful old Pratt & Whitney engine already had over fourteen hundred hours on it; hopefully it would last at least another six or seven. Of course the other three would get us the rest of the way if necessary. Just before dawn Eleanor came to the cockpit:

"What's wrong?"

"Nothing, why?"

"You haven't been out of that seat all night."

I assured her nothing was wrong, and she went back. Dawn broke nice and clear, but with the Ocean still whipped into whitecaps by the east wind. We picked up the beacon on the Farallon Islands loud and clear. *Now that engine can quit anytime it wants to.* I woke everyone and let them, two at a time, look out at that dark thread on the horizon, the sweet coastline of home. Everybody was singing 'Golden Gate in '58'. As we passed over that bridge, some of them were crying. When I cut the engines in front of the passenger terminal, the clock said we had been airborne fourteen hours and forty-five minutes. I told the alert crew they should check the oil screens on number

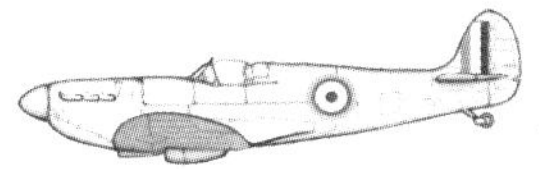

three. I checked back later. They had found a double handful of bearing metal. Those wonderful, tough old Pratt & Whitneys!

We had thirty days leave coming, so naturally we wanted to see the homefolks. A friend was flying that way and offered us a ride, but Eleanor said she had had enough flying to last a lifetime, so we decided to take the train home.

That was a wonderful trip. We went by way of Salt Lake City and through the Utah mountains. I had never seen that part of the country from the ground, and found it to be absolutely beautiful. Later, on the plains, we saw herds of antelope and some deer. It was a novel experience for me to just sit relaxed, and with no effort at all be able to watch the country roll by. At St. Louis we transferred to a very stubby train that reminded me of the comic strip *Toonsville Trolley*. It had one baggage car and one passenger coach; that was all. Rocking and clacking all the way, it wandered down gullies and tight little valleys, making every bit of twenty miles and hour. At noon we stopped at the site of the filming of that old series *Petticoat Junction*. At least it looked identical. Everyone, including the train crew, got off and walked up to this old, rambling former hotel for lunch. On the wide front veranda, five very old men in bib overalls sat on a long bench whittling, with piles of shavings littering the floor at their feet. Their heads turned in unison, watching us as we walked by. Inside was a great round table, piled high with the most nourishing vittles, presided over by a cheery, very buxom lady of indeterminate age. After everyone had eaten their fill, the engineer allowed as how it was time to get back aboard, so we trooped out, followed by the silent stares of the gallery. We made their day. But it did take us all day to get to Memphis.

We were in the market for a new car, but most of the models that year had those high, silly looking fins on the rear fenders. One salesman had the gall to claim those fins gave directional stability! I walked out on that guy. We finally found an Oldsmobile we liked, power everything – plus air-conditioning! A V-8 land yacht grinning with chrome. What sold us, though, was the color – a passionate lavender that Eleanor just had to have. We paid cash; for some reason I hate to pay interest on anything.

U.S. Air Force photo

1503rd Air Transport Wing

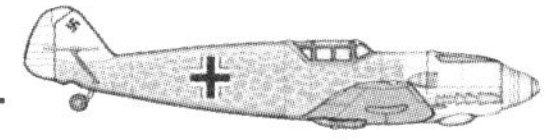

chapter twenty seven

TRAVIS

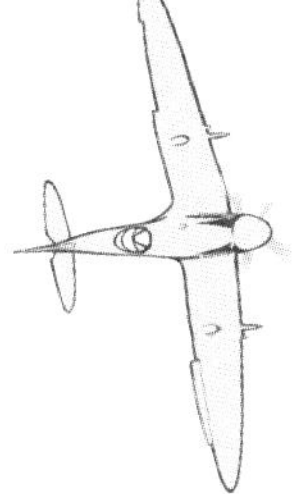

1958 – '59: "THAT DADGUM C-133 DOG OF AN ATLAS HAULER!"

We took the southern route back to Travis. The trip across the desert wasn't half bad, what with the air-conditioner going full blast. The Base quarters assigned to us had been given a fresh coat of paint. Since our furniture had already arrived from Japan, we were soon settled in. I was assigned to the 1503rd Air Transport Wing as the Deputy Wing Commander. I liked the Wing CO, Colonel French. He and I were most compatible: he took care of all the paperwork and I stayed down on the flight line – a most satisfactory arrangement.

The Wing had just started receiving the new C-133s. This was an entirely different bird from anything we had had before: a four-engined turbo-prop with a long, round fuselage that carried its wing about half way back, in the middle. It had eight huge wheels that tucked up into blisters on the sides of the fuselage. Cargo was loaded through a ramp under the tail; in fact, an Atlas missile could be slid right into the cargo bay…it was one more big bird.

Now a turbo-prop engine is a jet turbine with a propeller stuck on the front end. Those on the 133 delivered about 6000 horsepower each. Then, Lord help us, they had electric propellers – eighteen feet in diameter! That's where the trouble started. I already hated electric props, but I was to learn just how much, later. The airplane had been designed by Wright Field – a dead giveaway that we would have trouble. Douglas actually built the giant ship, but they weren't exactly proud of it; their nameplate was on board, but you had to look hard to find it! The thing was fairly fast, yet not nearly as fast as it was supposed to be. The aircraft looked a lot like its older brother, the C-130, only much larger. The engines were excellent; we had no trouble at all with them. They turned at 13,000 revs per minute, while the props were geared down to around seven or eight hundred RPM. (After forty years there are a few details I can't remember.) Actually it was a good airplane and a pleasure to fly – except for those three-bladed, eighteen-foot diameter electric props.

Now a prop tip out on the perimeter of a circle eighteen feet in diameter, whistling around some seven or eight hundred times a minute, is going 'real fast'! So fast, in fact, that those tips will shortly hit MACH 1, the speed of sound, which creates a little sonic boom, which in turn sets up a very high frequency vibration, which naturally travels down the prop blade and into that hub – which is full of electric wiring. The higher we climb, the thinner the air becomes and the more the blade is vibrating… Result? Multiple failures. I guess Wright Field was out of slide rules the day they bought that thing. You couldn't actually feel any vibration, but when you went back into the cargo area and found wiring

U.S. Air Force photo

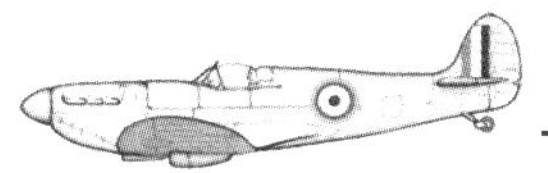

insulation on the floor, or saw the side of the fuselage suddenly split open with a crack maybe eight feet long, you got the idea. The body areas intersected by the extended plane of the propellers had to be reinforced with armor plate to prevent that!

I eventually flew that thing for over five hundred hours, mostly to and from Japan, mostly over water – so we wouldn't fall on anyone. I never once got all the way over and back with the same four propellers I left with! Oh yes, it also had an autopilot; 'the latest development in the state of the art', which wouldn't work – so we had to hand-fly that hulk constantly. That gets old with only a basic crew aboard.

Otherwise the airplane was easy to fly. The engineer and co-pilot did all the work, so about all the pilot had to do was guide it around to the runway, using the little steering wheel down at your left hand, and line up. We always used full throttle on take-off, with the copilot calling out airspeed and distance traveled. When the proper speed was reached, he called, "Rotate" – the nose is lifted, and off we go 'in a cloud of dust and a blaze of glory' as some fellow used to say.

The 133's wings were so far back that the wingtips were not visible from the cockpit. With so little outside reference, we flew instruments all the time, from lift-off to final approach. As I've said, the autopilot simply wouldn't work, but fortunately the airplane was very stable; when once trimmed out for level flight, only an occasional touch of the controls was needed to maintain a steady course. That is, until a propeller decided to malfunction.

This always came without prior warning. The airplane would suddenly yaw violently toward the bad engine. What was happening was: the mechanism that kept the blade angle constant had failed, or shorted out, letting the blade angle shift back and forth from an almost flat angle to a nearly feathered position, the cycle being repeated every few seconds. Whenever the blade went flat, you might as well have a solid disc, eighteen feet in diameter, out there holding you back. A most revolting development! There was only one thing you could do: shut down that engine, punch the feathering button, and pray the other three would behave until you got where you were headed. Once the prop was feathered, you set up a three-engine-cruise and proceeded on your merry way.

On one memorable occasion we had left Hickham, bound for Tachi, with five thoroughly heavy tractors aboard – and no possible way of getting rid of them in the air. It was a beautiful day, gracing us with silky smooth air at twenty-five thousand. The navigator reported that we were at mid-point for Wake Island. At this exact time the old bird yawed violently to the right.

I called, "Shut down number three; feather number three!"

The copilot punched the feathering button, but nothing happened; the violent yawing continued.

I called, "Emergency feather!"

The copilot punched the emergency button, and the prop went into full feather position. We all breathed a sigh of relief, because if it had failed to feather we would have been unable to stay in the air for long. With a ditching no longer imminent, we descended to three-engine altitude, notified Airways of our problem, and – well, "Press On."

By now the entire crew was gathered in a tight knot in the cockpit. You know how fellows act when they have just come through a big scare successfully – lots of horseplay and laughing, letting the adrenaline ease down.

I looked around and thought, *I'll bet I can have some fun out of this crowd*, so I said, real serious: "Fellows, let's unfeather that engine and..."

I reached toward the unfeather control – and my right arm was hit by five karate chops! Every man there gave it his best shot. Stout fellows!

U.S. Air Force photo

"...after finding out what dogs they were..."

I grinned, and they blushed. After all, Lieutenants and Captains are not supposed to beat the hell out of Colonels! At least that's what the Book says.

The Air Force had originally ordered several hundred of the C-133s, but after finding out what dogs they were, the order was cancelled and only about fifty were built. We had half of them at Travis, while the rest were at either Dover or McGuire, I forget which. One of the first was found one morning in a field, on its back, with gear and flaps extended, scattered about in small pieces. Rumor had it that the bird had some very peculiar stall characteristics. The company test pilots, well lubricated with 'Old Fearless', admitted that, yes, with gear and flaps extended, should you move either the rudder or the elevators while in a stalled condition, that control will go hard in the direction of the control movement – and lock!

I had never heard of such a thing. Controls locked by air pressure? I just couldn't believe it. So back at Travis, a couple of us intrepid airmen decided we would just see about that!

We took the bird up to about 16,000 and slowed it down. Gear down, flaps fully extended, and ease the nose up. I took my feet off the rudders, just in case, and when she started to shudder, moved the yoke forward. It jumped out of my hands and locked! The two of us couldn't move it! By this time we were in a mighty steep dive, so I put the flap handle in the up position and had no trouble pulling out, since control was restored as soon as the flaps started up. After further experiment, we found that with only three-fourths flaps extended, the condition was eliminated. The fix was a simple stop-block behind the flap handle so they could not be fully extended. We had no further trouble with stalls, but there were times when we could have used those full flaps, like at Tachi, with its five thousand foot runway!

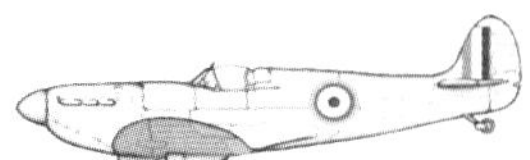

A side effect from flying those airplanes was hearing trouble. My favorite 33-1/3 record was *Nola*, with its high, beautiful bells. I noticed that the bells were growing fainter, and finally, later on, disappeared entirely. I figured the little tweeter on my fabulous hi-fi (as I said, way before stereo) was faulty, but the radio shop said it was OK. Of course I didn't dare speak to the Flight Surgeon about it. But when my next physical came up, he found it:

"You fly those 133's, don't you?"

He told me that everyone in that Squadron was completely deaf in their higher tone ranges, due to the high frequency vibrations we were subjected to. It didn't affect our normal speaking range, so that was that. The other night I was watching some sea story on TV. When they piped the Admiral aboard, the designated whistle-blower made all the right motions, but I didn't hear the whistle. I asked Eleanor if she heard the whistle; she assured me she did. (Since *she* is getting hard of hearing, it must have been a proper blast.) Of course today everyone who flies, or works around jet engines, must wear ear protectors.

On one trip to Tachi there were three airplanes grounded there waiting for propellers. The airplane with our replacements aboard left Hickham and lost a propeller on climb-out. He had reached sixteen thousand when it happened. He tried to feather, but neither the normal nor emergency worked. With full power on the other three he barely made it back to Hickham. Several days later when he made it to Tachi, the rest of us were in the bar meditating on life and stuff. The newly arrived pilot walked in and dumped a bunch of parts on our table. It was the brake that holds the blade at the proper pitch angle; it was made of high quality steel but had split right down the middle into two pieces. I had another double and wired Travis:

"I am grounding these four airplanes until some fix is found for this condition."

The next night around three AM, General Waldron called me by phone to say, "I am releasing those four airplanes for a one-time safe flight to Travis."

We unloaded the birds and left. The Squadron Commander, Tannenbaum, and I took ours all the way home non-stop, by the northern great-circle route, at 33,000 feet. We lost number three prop in the landing pattern. I think that was the first time anyone had made that flight non-stop, but nobody paid any attention to our fantastic feat. That's a long way for two guys to hand-fly an airplane.

The 133 provided another well remembered flight. From the factory we picked up an Atlas missile, complete, for delivery to Cape Canaveral, Florida. As noted, the big ship's rear end opens up for this missile to slide nicely into the cargo compartment. But when we arrived over Cape Canaveral one bright sunny afternoon, we ran into bags of trouble. *Suddenly we had* ***complete electrical failure!*** That was even worse than you might think, because on the 133 the hydraulics are run by a unit that requires electrical power to operate. So – no gear, no flaps, no brakes, no steering, no propeller controls and no power for the boosted controls. Did I mention we had no radios?

I immediately went into my famous 'old sea-captain pipe-smoking act', which succeeded in getting the Crew Chief down off the ceiling. He allowed as how, yes, he did have a crow bar aboard, and given all the muscle available, he could force the gear up-locks and let the gear free-fall. While everybody went back to work on the gear problem, I drifted out over the Atlantic into the most highly Restricted Area on the coast; but it was Sunday, and nobody was shooting any missiles or spacecraft, so we didn't disturb the peace. After a while the copilot returned to report that all the rollers were down and appeared to be locked. I had learned how to fly and land the Connie with the boost cut off, so that should present no new problem. I could make gentle turns using differential

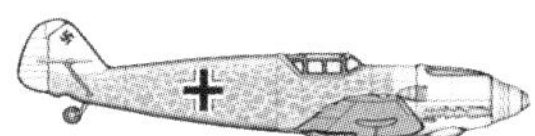

Atlas Missile Loading

U.S. Air Force photo

power on the outboard engines, and the hand operated trim tab could ease the nose up or down. The big problem would come on the runway with no brakes or steering.

You know, I never once thought about the millions of dollars that Atlas missile back there had cost the taxpayers! It would have been wasted energy anyway, because, as it turned out, the big ICBM had already been ruined during the flight by that high-frequency vibration, which effectively destroyed its internal works – so had to be junked. We had a saying in the Air Force: "You will never find out who shot Cock Robin." I'm sure no one ever went to jail for buying those airplanes.

Well, back to this hair-raising narrative. We circled way out over the Ocean, getting the feel of turns – very gentle ones, to be sure. I set up about a fifteen-mile final, during which I descended to low over the water. Having no flaps, I added some twenty or thirty knots to the approach speed and crossed the fence maybe ten feet high, and killed the engines. We didn't float far and settled gently onto the runway. At that point the copilot and I were pulling the yoke back as hard as we could trying to keep the nose wheel off…and the airplane rolled as straight as an arrow right down the middle of the runway, coming finally to a stop at the very far end.

The Crew Chief found the trouble: The main electrical bus is a cable about an inch in diameter; well, right exactly in the plane of the propellers – that area which had to be armor plated – we found this cable cut in two as though someone had cut it with a hacksaw! The next day we got the people on the Base to splice the cable; everything worked fine, so we went home. I'm sure that was the last missile flown aboard a C-133. I suppose the C-5s do that job today.

Travis operated a large fleet of C-97s, carrying most of the military traffic in the Pacific. Personnel traffic, that is. 'Old Shaky', the C-124, hauled the freight. We had a transition school there at Travis to prepare new pilots for their place on the line. There was one Squadron that did nothing but train these new pilots in the gentle art. Now the Air National Guard had for years been flying mostly fighter-type airplanes. Then the decision was made to change most of the Guard squadrons from the fighter role to that of transport.

Of course there arose an anguished howl from the Guard pilots – but there you are! Fred Hook was now the Operations Officer for Guard Headquarters in the Pentagon. He called me:

"Do you think a fighter pilot can become a good transport pilot?"

"Look Hook, a fighter pilot can fly anything with wings; look at me, the world's most greatest!"

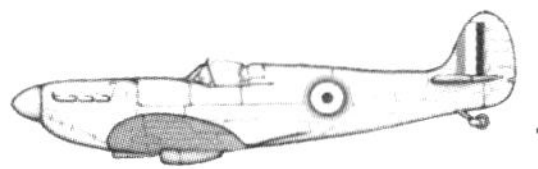

I told him we already had a school for C-97s, the type they would be re-equipped with; and yes, we can check-out some of their crews. MATS was scheduled to get the new Douglas 707s to replace the C-97s.

So it was arranged. We received several crews from five different Guard squadrons; they were unhappy at first, but after listening to our tales of all those exotic 'faraway places with strange-sounding names', they began to see the possibilities. Naturally, they learned fast, and so we produced a fine crop of transport pilots.

Major General 'Wimpy' Wilson was head of the Guard Bureau in Washington. He was a 'Good-ol-boy' from Arkansas that I had met a few times when he was in the Guard back before the War. He and Hook spent a lot of time with us at Travis, where he was most favorably impressed with our training program – especially with the results. When the training period was coming to a close, Wimpy asked me if I would like to come with the Guard program and help out with their transition.

I thought about it a lot. I knew I would never be promoted to General, what with my dismal record on a couple of occasions – plus being what can be charitably called a 'controversial character'. Besides, the Air Force had a policy of 'UP or OUT' after five years in grade, and I had already been a Bird Colonel for ten years! Monetarily this looked like the smart thing to do, so I called Wimpy:

"I will join you guys provided I am stationed east of the Mississippi and south of the Ohio."

Wimpy agreed, and shortly thereafter I received orders to report to the Minnesota Air Guard with duty as Air Advisor. I called Wimpy and screamed bloody murder. MINNESOTA!

After I quieted down, he said, "Look, I got you east of the Mississippi for now. Nashville will be coming open shortly, and you can go down there as soon as it can be arranged. It takes a little doing to get an Advisor assigned to his own home state."

He was right. It took two cold, miserable years!

U.S. Air Force photo

"... being what can be charitably called a 'controversial character'"

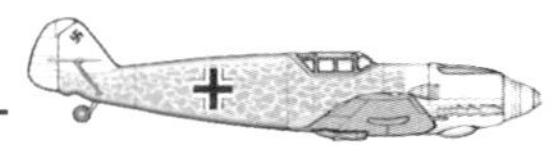

chapter twenty eight

MINNESOTA

1960: "MIGHTY HUNTERS OF THE SUB-ARCTIC"

I had bought a used little Henry-J in California, so was now faced with the problem of moving two automobiles East. It just so happened there was to be an Air Show at Minneapolis, for which a C-133 static display was desired. Naturally I was on the crew! I had hauled all sorts of stuff all over the world for other people, so what could be wrong with tossing my little Henry-J aboard an empty transport? Just in case, I loaded it aboard at night, and we arrived at Minneapolis well after dark. But as I pulled the giant aircraft into the Guard parking area, I spied a large crowd awaiting our arrival! And they all wanted to come aboard for an escorted tour. Problems, problems! I just knew there would be at least one of Drew Pearson's boys on hand.

Solution…we let them come up to the cockpit, but for the life of us, we couldn't get the door to the cargo area open! After the crowd left, we rolled the little thing out and hid it in a hangar.

On the trip back to Travis we faced a line of towering thunderstorms. Even at thirty thousand we couldn't top them. There was a nice clear gap between two of them, so I poked my nose into the clear. Clear hail, that is. Light flack couldn't have done much more. The radome was smashed, the windshield grazed, the leading edges of the wings battered, and I think they scrapped the airplane.

A few months later I learned there was a big I.G. investigation out at WESTAF – which was still my boss – but there wasn't a single one of that crew who had the slightest idea that the little car had been aboard! It always pays to have the troops on your side! I always got along fine with the flyboys; it was the chair-borne types that gave me trouble. In fact, I left Travis under somewhat of a cloud. I think part of my trouble in that case was the MATS policy that no one over the rank of Major could act as a crewmember. I had been religiously ignoring that directive, so that the Brass could get their flying time for pay purposes riding in the back, drawing Command Pilot's time. Sometimes you just can't please everybody!

I bought a nice little house over in a new sub-division in St. Paul. When our furniture showed up, I had just enough time to make the home livable before Eleanor and son David arrived. (We had dropped Jimmy off at Knoxville where he would be a sophomore at UT.) I had tried to get a VA loan on the house, but I was not considered a Veteran yet, as there still had been no break in service. You must have either discharge or retirement papers to qualify. That's the way it works.

I quickly learned why I was called an Advisor. Formerly the Regular Officers assigned to the Guard had been called 'Instructors'. Apparently the Guard didn't feel they needed any instructing; so each Monday I would show up and ask if they needed any advice – which they didn't – so I had a lot of time off. We made a few non-military friends in our neighborhood and had some pleasant get-togethers, but the Guardsmen were rather clannish. We did drop in, unannounced, on one family, but after that we stayed pretty much to ourselves. (I couldn't help wondering if cold weather contributes to cold shoulder.) At least we took a nice trip through parts of Canada when my sister Julia and her husband Henry came to visit.

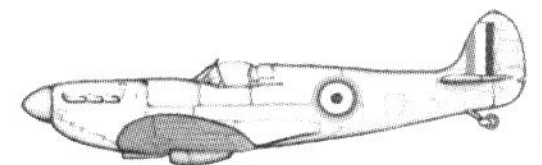

After the crews had been checked out locally, we started making long overseas trips to Tachi, and a few to Europe. The crews performed well. On these trips I acted as Instructor Pilot, but that was about all the flying I got to do.

Air National Guard photo

Tough Duty with the Minnesota Air Guard

That fall during hunting season I went on several deer hunts. On the first hunt, while we were all gathered at some café for supper, I listened in on the recounting of the day's happenings. One fellow said he hadn't seen a deer all day, but had gotten off one 'sound shot'! After that, I always made a practice of finding a big tree to sit up against, where I would listen to the others stomp around in the woods, sounding like a troop of dismounted cavalry. I always got my deer by just sitting still and letting the others stir them up.

I shot one jumping across a railroad track. After gutting it, I hung it up on a telephone pole and sat back against my tree, right out in the open, all dressed in red. Along came a pair of hunters walking beside the tracks. When they were about fifty feet away, I called to them:

"Howdy."

They both jumped. When they finally spotted me, they asked if I had seen a deer.

I said, "Yep."

"Which way did it go?"

"Right up that telephone pole!" The deer was hanging right there in plain sight. Makes you wonder.

That night I was introduced to the Swedish version of a steam bath. The steam room has a charcoal fire, on which someone occasionally pours water. It gets real foggy in there. When you turn a nice pink, this old woman comes in with a bundle of fir switches and whips the dickens out of everybody. Then you slide out into the snow! Most refreshing.

Those guys did a lot of ice fishing. They have a small portable hut they park over a hole they've cut through the ice out on some lake. I understand they have a small kerosene heater with them, but I wouldn't know. I would much rather cuddle up with a nice warm book or something. For some reason a lot of them like to drive their cars around on the frozen lakes, with the obvious results that some of them break through and drown. Fun and games!

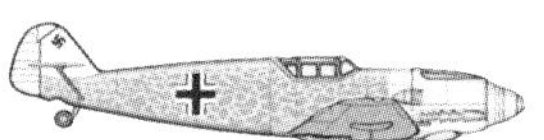

Driving to Memphis for Christmas, we learned a lot en-route about handling a car in ice and snow. On the return trip, with the temperature forty below – way out in the boonies in the middle of the night – the engine stalled out. That was scary. I knew I could survive, but what about Eleanor and little Dave? The gas line was freezing up. We would sit awhile; then the engine would start up again. We would drive for a few minutes, but then have to sit some more. Finally we made it to a little town that happened to have a filling station open where we could buy a can of fuel treatment. After that, we were able to make our way home.

That was a bitterly cold winter…thirty and forty below. The house was so tightly built that no air could get in or out. When I came home at night, the air would be so dry it was stifling. I would turn the water faucets on wide open until there was enough moisture in the house to make it livable. (Like Mobile, for example!) Eleanor – my true Memphis Belle – came down with a bad case of pneumonia and almost died. In the hospital she was given penicillin, which caused her to swell up like a balloon and break out with a bad rash. That was a rough time.

We stayed in Minnesota for two years and were most happy to depart for Nashville. The day we left, the weather was bright and clear – with the thermometer showing 25 below zero. There were guys on our street prancing around in their shirtsleeves yelling, "Spring...Spring!"

Grenley family photo

the Colonel's sister Julia
with husband Henry Grenley and son Henry Walker Grenley

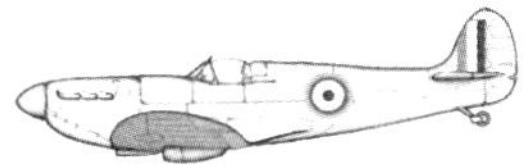

Haun family photo

Haun family photo

by permission: The Nashville Tennessean - *Gerald Holly photo, 1969*

Haun family photo

Haun family photo

chapter twenty nine

NASHVILLE

1961 – '64: "SIDE-STEPPING GOOD 'OL BOYS"

Nashville was an entirely different place. We knew how to get along with these folks – we even spoke the same language. Over the years we had lost some of our thick Southern dialect, but we could still make ourselves understood. So we rented a nice little two-and-a-den house in a good neighborhood and soon made some friends. Later I assumed the loan on that house; we're living in it still. I think I paid the former owner about a hundred dollars for his equity and got a good hunk of cash when it was paid off. The property backs to a heavily wooded bluff that drops off some two hundred feet to farmland bordering the Stones River, just above where it joins the Cumberland. A beautiful, quiet setting. I paved a parking area behind the house and mounted a basketball hoop over the garage door. David and his neighborhood buddies practically lived out there, banging the ball off the garage doors and making a terrific racket. I would welcome that sound again. Lately the Opryland Hotel has built an English-style golf course down on that former farmland. Several times I have seen the floodwaters clear over to our bluff, so I hope they diked it well.

I got the attention of the Guard's personnel right off. One of the duties of the Air Advisor is to certify the payroll for drill periods. In looking over the list of all the people who had attended weekend drills and the money due them, I spotted the name of our esteemed Governor. Now I knew full well that the Governor of the State of Tennessee, in the rank of a Lieutenant Colonel in Supply, had not attended a drill in that, or any other, capacity. If I signed this, I would be certifying a false government document, which I was more than loathe to do. I called in the young Captain who had delivered the document and queried him at length. He insisted that the Governor, as Commander-in-Chief of all the Tennessee Guard, was, *ipso facto*, always on duty! I got the impression that there were probably a rather large number of 'Good-ol-Boys' around. The State Guard was headed by a Major General over at Guard Headquarters, who, I pointed out, outranked any Lieutenant Colonel in the organization a little bit more than somewhat. Finally I told the lad that if he would take the document back to Headquarters and have the General sign a statement to the effect that the above is a true and accurate payroll, then I would also sign it. He took it back, and no one got paid until a revised payroll had been prepared. There was a marked increase in attendance.

Major General Howard Butler showed up at the next drill, in proper uniform and eager to fly. I took him in a C-97, which he thoroughly enjoyed jockeying that day. He was a good pilot, and I flew many hours with him, locally and overseas. He was also a dedicated hunter and fisherman, so we had some fine times together. On top of all this he was the State Prosecuting Attorney – quite proud of how many violent criminals he had sent to the electric chair. Of course Nashville being the State Capitol, I also got to know Governor Clement fairly well; he never berated me for getting him off the payroll.

The Guard is a fine place for a Regular Officer to make the transition to civilian life. In the military, RANK is the be all and end all. Your status among your peers is plainly defined by the insignia on your shoulders, and is universally accepted. Not so in civilian life, where there are numerous different standards by which you are placed on the social ladder – wealth, age,

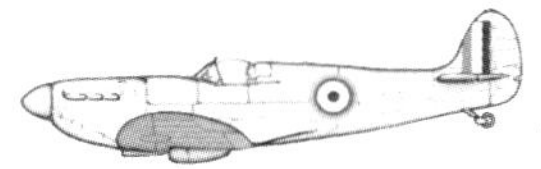

Haun family photo

accomplishments, etc. I have seen many senior officers retire expecting to find the same preferential treatment and courtesies they had been accustomed to on active duty. They are in for a rude awakening. While it is true that the Guard on weekend drill is all military – with 'yes Sir' and 'no Sir' all over the place – after five o'clock, it's, "Hey Buddy, let's stop off for a beer." And that's a good thing. The first week I was there, I listened to a Sergeant give General Butler a royal chewing out over some misuse of the noncom's boat, for which the General apologized profusely – and promised to return the boat in spotless condition the next time.

I learned quickly, and became accustomed to being called 'Jim' in short order, and liked it. From that day I have never introduced myself as 'Colonel', but strangely enough, that's what everybody else calls me. Maybe it's like saying 'Doctor', or 'Judge'. I don't know.

The Minnesota crews had liked to go west to Tachi, but the Tennessee boys seemed to like Madrid better. We made several trips to Tachi, but now the favorite trip was to Europe. Our hi-mileage C-97s gave excellent service, as our maintenance was top notch. It may surprise you, but the 97 had the same 4360 engine as Old Shaky, with the exception that the 97 funneled the exhaust down to or through the turbo-supercharger, which eliminated the cylinder-change problem.

While I don't recall us having any engine trouble to amount to anything, the radio equipment was getting a little tired. There was a huge overnight improvement when we got single-sideband radios, which also eliminated the need for radio operators – with that continual chirping behind our heads. I remember one operator who always plugged a loudspeaker into his set, which nearly drove me up the wall. With the new stuff, even out in the middle of the Ocean, it was like talking to the tower. We listened in on some interesting conversations before the crews learned that the whole world was tuning in!

For instance, one night we were off the Azores, homeward bound, on autopilot and nothing much to do. Butler was in the left seat and I was co-pilot. We heard an Air Force pilot giving his hourly position to Andrews Airways. When that was finished, he came on again:

"Andrews Airways, this is Air Force 1234, can you patch me through to Wright Patterson?"

He could, and the Base operator answered, "How can I help you, Sir?"

"Extension 732 please."

The phone rang and a sweet young thing answered.

"Hi Doll, I'll be there tonight. Everything all right?"

"Yeah."

He called Andrews again: "Andrews Airways, this is Air Force 1234; can you patch me through to Scott Air Force Base?"

He could. The Scott operator rang extension 326.

"Hellooo…"

"Hi Doll, I'll be there tomorrow morning. Everything all right?"

"Yeah, you know 'tis."

And again, the next call was to Barksdale Field; young Lochinvar would be there tomorrow night. Before he could break the connection, I picked up the mike and whispered:

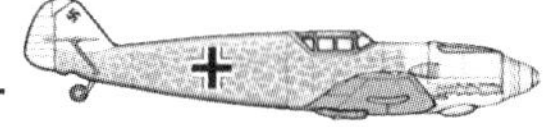

"Doll, I'll be there *tonight*!"

Then from all over the world came calls:

"I'm gonna go where the wild goose goes!"

"Hey Doll, gotta friend for me?" – until Andrews finally told us to clam up. Butler has told that story many, many times.

Butler decided the Guard needed a training flight to Las Vegas, and talked it up around the Courthouse, with the result that at departure time there were three times as many people trying to get aboard as the bird would carry! I asked Butler what he was going to tell those left behind and he just grinned. Somehow we squeezed everybody in. The only Guardsmen aboard were the crew. We had everybody from the Mayor on down, the core of the Tennessee Democratic Party! They had a high old time as guests of one of the Casinos, and I was definitely the designated driver on the trip home!

We had another mob scene on a deer hunt out in Montana. I was worried about all the shenanigans transpiring, and knew full well I could get myself into a lot of trouble if I continued to have any part in such goings-on, so I began to distance myself from these semi-civilian outings. Naturally I was promptly ostracized from the group, but as my retirement date was approaching, I just didn't care, and made no effort to get back in their good graces. The intra-group politics was too much for me to fathom anyway.

Butler died recently from a heart attack.

I read with great pleasure of the good work the Guard did in Desert Storm and elsewhere. Today they have good equipment and fine training, a combination that enables them to fit right in with the Regular forces and perform with distinction. I am proud that I may have had some small part in their development.

with General Butler in Madrid

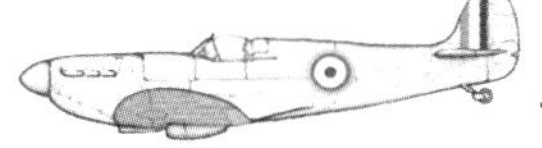

"One each EAA Bi-plane from plans!"

by permission of The Nashville Tennessean - *Gerald Holly photo, 1969*

Proud Nashville Homebuilder

"When it came time to assemble the wings...we didn't have many sit-down guests during that period."

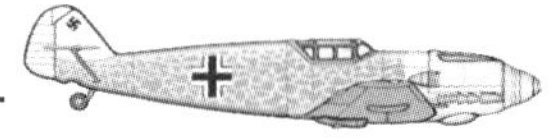

chapter thirty

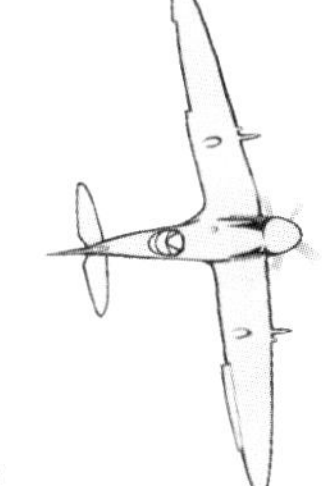

RETIREMENT

1965 – 2001: "HOMEBILTS & FLYING STUDENTS"

The long-expected notice of my retirement arrived. I had somehow avoided the 'up-or-out-after-five-years' policy, having now been a Bird Colonel for fourteen years; so I was long overdue. One thing made me a little mad. In figuring my time-in-service for retired pay, I was just five days short of an additional 'fogey', which would have given me an extra hundred bucks a month! I could have used that money, as I still had to get David through college. We were not rich by any means, but we were comfortable and had no serious debts. I certainly couldn't just sit around doing nothing; I had seen too many retirees do that – and die shortly thereafter.

Back before the War, I had been a pretty good salesman of bottlers' supplies, so I decided to try my hand at Real Estate.

Nashville had a night school that helped prepare an ambitious type for the real estate license, so I enrolled. With my handy-dandy circular slide rule in my shirt pocket, I had no trouble doing the required math and soon had my license. The class instructor, Bob Freeman, offered me a job with his company here in the Donelson suburb, and I went to work. Actually, I was fairly good at the business and made some money. During 1966-67 the country was in quite a slump, so I was able to assume the loans on several houses, rent them for enough to pay the notes, and finally sell them at a nice profit.

I stayed with these efforts for around five years, until I burned out on the game. While in this endeavor I had learned that there are three ways to do business: the right way, the wrong way – and whatever way you can legally get away with. It was the barely legal deals that turned me off. And if a man tells you, "My word is my bond," it's a good idea to hide the family silver!

I missed the flying most. I was too old for the airlines and too spoiled for corporate flying, so that left only instructing – which I wasn't quite ready for.

I had joined the EAA (Experimental Aircraft Association) and learned about the many home-built aircraft under construction in and around Nashville. On the cover of the first issue I received of *Sport Aviation* was a photo of a neat little single-seat open-cockpit biplane that resembled a Fleet I used to fly – and I was sold! I just knew I could build one like it, so I promptly ordered the plans. I had a small workshop in my one-car garage where I made all the bits and pieces. When it came time to assemble the wings, I had to use the combined living-dining rooms to have enough space. Eleanor graciously put up with that, but we didn't have many

Haun's Home-built

Haun family photo

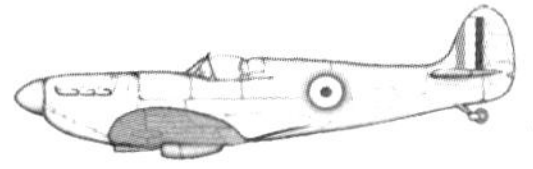

family photo

Curt Franklin

sit-down guests during that period; we just retreated to the den! It took me two years to finish that bird, even with a lot of help on those things I couldn't do, like the welding.

There was another EAA Biplane being built in the neighborhood by Curt Franklin. Curt is a long, tall country boy from Alabama, and a gentleman in the true sense of the word. I have seen him tested. He does fine work and his ship turned out better than mine, both in workmanship and looks. Mine flew well, although it did have some peculiar traits; such as – at the top of a loop, the slightest bit of backpressure would result in the cutest little slow snap roll. Also it had the gliding angle of a streamlined brick. I had a lot of fun with that little thing and flew it for about two years. However, I soon found that I could no longer stand to fly an open cockpit plane in the dead of winter. When I was a kid I reveled in the icy blast, clad in a light jacket, helmet, and goggles – my face almost frozen stiff. I needed something with an enclosed cockpit.

That little airplane has been re-sold at least seven times that I know of. The last I heard about it was from a man out in California who called to say how much he loved it. Worries me sometimes that someone may fly it into the side of a mountain and I get sued for 'Product Liability'! That could actually happen under today's weird legal system. At least nobody will ever pull the wings off – I tried!

The Hump Pilots Association held reunions in Nashville, several of which I attended. There I met Jess Stallings, the owner of Capitol Airlines, with home office here. We talked about old airplanes and how much he wanted to find one to rebuild. I knew where there was a '36 model Cabin Waco that might be for sale. It was the same one I used to fly years ago and was still owned by old Harry Wilson, who had it stored out at his private field, east of Memphis. Jess said if I could talk Harry into selling it, he would put up the money; the work would be done in his shop, by his people, and all I had to do was supervise – after which I would be half owner. Sounds like a good deal!

"I dood it!"

Haun family photo

I drove to Memphis and saw Harry. The old airplane was stored in a badly leaking shed and looked terrible. We dickered awhile. Harry was very old and feeble. He had forty or more cats roaming the place, as emphasized by a stack of empty cat food cans at least ten feet high outside his office. There were old airplanes of many kinds lying about where they had been tied down shortly after WW II – and left to rot. There was a BT-13 with a tree growing right up through the cockpit. There were two Bamboo Bombers with their wings rotted and drooped to the ground. There was

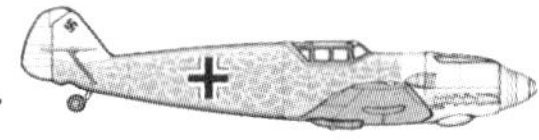

even the faint outline of a WW I Jenny never removed from its original crate. Plus all sorts of little tail draggers – Cubs, Aeroncas, Porterfields and such – all ruined. Harry was always saying he was going to rebuild all those aircraft, but just never got around to it. He told me about the scores of people that had tried to buy that Waco, but he just couldn't stand to see it go. We talked about old times and the people we had known who were long since dead and gone.

Haun family photo

Finally he agreed to let me have it – provided I put it back in exactly the same shape it had been when it was new. I agreed, and went back to see Jess. He gave me a check for two thousand dollars made out to Harry; I rented a big flatbed and went down to pick it up. Eleanor followed me in our car. In the real estate business I had learned a lot about people, money, and property, so I had the Bill of Sale made out to both Jess and me. Then I promptly sent the registration to Oke City! (Turned out I was exactly right, as you'll see.)

"Fini-done!"

Haun family photo

After the Waco was rebuilt, Curt and I took it to Memphis to show it to Harry. He cried like a baby. After Harry died, a developer bulldozed all those relics into a hole and buried them.

It took two years to rebuild the Waco. All that talk about me only having to supervise was just that talk. I had the fuselage stripped and sandblasted. The FAA guys came over, almost daily, and pointed out what tubing must be replaced, etc. On the few occasions when I asked the shop people to give me a hand, 'Miss B' would spot such unauthorized activity from her vantagepoint up on the balcony, and such assistance quickly vanished! About halfway through the project, Jess asked me to become the 'Fixed Base Manager'. The pay would be ten thousand a year. Why not? I would be out there every day anyway.

That was the worst job I ever had in my life! I quickly learned why I was the nineteenth guy to hold the job in four years. I wasn't the manager at all: Miss B was. One of the line boys, Shorty, was Miss B's spy; whatever I told anyone to do, Shorty would run upstairs to see what Miss B thought about that. I could neither hire nor fire any of the line-boys, nor did I have a clue what anyone was paid – although I'm sure it was the absolute minimum. Our line-boys were the dregs – one just out of reform school! Besides, Shorty was stealing them blind. He got caught switching dice in a crap game downtown and spent a month in the hospital recovering from stab wounds. I stood it as long as I could and told Jess to get someone else while I went back to work on the Waco.

Capitol also had a flight school, with Paul Booth as the chief instructor. Paul was a member of the EAA and helped me a lot on the Waco. We became good fishing buddies. Old Paul Booth was

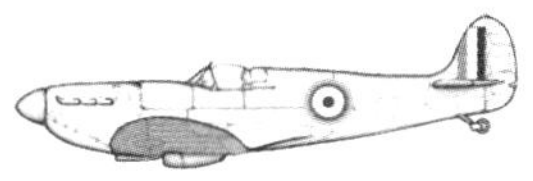

Haun family photo

always immaculate in his dress – the only person I've ever seen work on an airplane and never get the first spot of grease on his clothes!

I decided to get an instructor's rating and wanted Paul to help me prepare for the flight test, as I knew from experience that the FAA had their own ideas of just exactly how they wanted various maneuvers performed. It dawned on me that I now had a piece of paper that said I was a real, sure-enough Veteran, and therefore eligible to have Uncle Sam pay for my training. I applied and was granted twenty hours training in the Cessna 150s the school used. There was to be a written exam, taken from two large manuals from the government press. One had something to do with the actual flying, while the other was all about how to teach. This latter was written by some learned Doctor of Education and required the use of Mr. Webster's Dictionary to determine just what his points were. After memorizing all the big words and phrases, I passed that OK.

The FAA Inspector assigned to give me the flight test turned out to be a helicopter pilot with very little experience in fixed-wing aircraft. He did most of the flying, just sightseeing. I finally insisted on showing him the difference in the way FAA wanted Chandelles performed and the way I liked to do them (like when the railroad track you are following suddenly runs into a tunnel!). On our return to the airport, the Tower happened to put us on the longest runway. To keep from having to taxi an extra mile, I dragged the bird on the prop at about two feet down to the turnoff. This amazed him, as he had been under the impression that when an airplane had once leveled out, that was where it landed, willy-nilly. So I passed that check, more or less by default.

As the Waco was now finished and flying, I decided to hang out at Capitol and teach the kids to fly. Of course you can't make any money at this activity, but it paid for the gasoline driving back and forth from home, and maybe a little for lunch – but mostly I was doing something I thoroughly enjoyed. I get great satisfaction from watching a student as he or she gains confidence and skill. I have known instructors who delight in taking a student on that first intro ride and scaring him or her half to death with wild gyrations. This type of performance has nothing whatsoever to do with teaching and is indulged merely to impress the student with what a hot-rod pilot the instructor considers himself. Besides, it usually ends up being the prospective student's first *and* last ride – which doesn't put money in the till. I may have acted like that when I was 19 or 20, but I don't think so.

"So you want to learn spins..."

Haun family photo

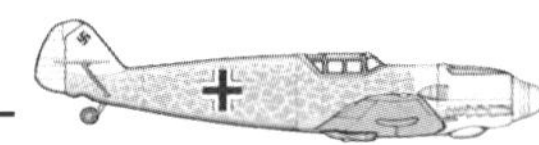

Haun family photo

"I'm not going to let you hurt ME!"

I always take the opposite course. Up high, slow and easy – and look at this beautiful world! Two fingers and the tips of your toes.

"Look," I assure them, "I'm not going to let you hurt ME, so relax."

I usually take a little longer than most to solo a student. First I want to be absolutely sure the fledgling is ready; after that, I just sit there until I can tell the student wants me to get out and let him or her go on their own. Then, always without warning, I will pull off to the side of the runway and climb out. This doesn't give them time to get nervous:

"Take it around twice and pick me up right here."

Back in the 'Good-old Days', before it was fashionable to object to smoking, I used to always just sit meditating in the right seat, puffing on my pipe while they practiced landings. I've had many students tell me how this posture calmed them, and I'm sure it did. (Of course that was before the Woodstock Alumni took over the country.)

I have no idea how many people I have taught to fly, but it must be well into the hundreds. Boys and girls, men and women, many married couples – and one guy with only one eye! Some of the kids I soloed on their sixteenth birthdays are now old Airline Captains. I wish now I had kept up my logbook, but I quit bothering with it twenty years ago. (Yes Joe, I know I'm supposed to keep it up, but after twenty thousand hours, what's it matter? When I go for my annual physical, I look at what I wrote last and add a few hours to that.)

After a minor confrontation, we sold the Waco. Jess had never flown it; he only wanted it as a conversation piece. I had asked him to buy me out, but he wouldn't do that, so I told him I would look around for someone to buy my half. He didn't go for that either, so I showed him the bill of sale and registration. I had put in two hard years of work on that bird – for which I intended to get paid. I found a buyer, had the check made to me, then paid Jess his half. I never saw him again, and he died a few years later.

"Oh very well..." Haun family photo

Capitol closed its fixed base operation at Metro and moved their headquarters out to Smyrna, Tennessee. But Nashville Flying Service, also at Metro, already had a flight school operated as a side line with their other business. I had known its head honcho Ed Jones for many years, as we were both Q.B.s (Quiet Birdmen fraternal outfit). He invited me to come instruct for them, which I did.

Nashville Flying Service was later taken over, on some sort of lease arrangement, by a man named – I think – Allen, who introduced a novel system of financing. He sold a complete Private course for *X* number of dollars with no cash required! The student

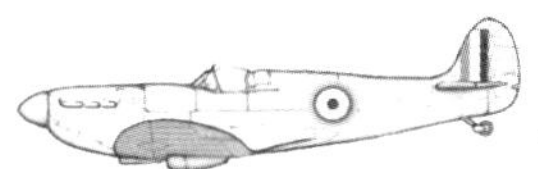

merely signed a note for the entire course, which note Allen then discounted at some bank, or banks. With a fleet of brand new Pipers and masses of students, we kept those airplanes hot; many times I flew eight hours a day instructing. Allen was a fine, high-type, upstanding Born-Again-Christian gentleman! But he seemed a bit confused about finances. In the end several banks found they had all financed the same airplane or airplanes. I recall there was one brand new Piper Navajo (or 'Navi Joe' to us) that several banks claimed belonged to them. Allen retired to the state penitentiary while this mess was being cleared up. I don't think he stayed long, as he was such a nice fellow.

I sold my homebuilt biplane and bought a beautiful little Swift. This was one of the last ones built by Temco in 1951. I wanted it because it flew pretty much like the old fighters of WW II, and in fact had much the lines of the P-40. It was fully aerobatic and fairly fast for its day. I 'hate' to boast, but, believe it or not, I used to lay my lit pipe on the dash of that bird and do a slow roll where the pipe would just sit and rock a bit throughout the maneuver. There was very little corrosion on the polished aluminum. Of course it kept me busy buffing and polishing to keep it shining like a new nickel. I held onto that little bird for seventeen years, until I became physically unable to properly maintain it – plus I'd run out of small boys to do all the polishing required. I sold it to Ted Beckwith, who, in addition to several needed modifications, had the engine completely rebuilt. I am sure he will be the proud owner of the next National Champion at the upcoming Swift Fly-in at Athens, Tennessee.

Temco Swift

Haun family photo

After becoming well acquainted with the Swift, I still needed another project. Some years ago Curt and I had found a basket-case Aeronca up in East Tennessee. We took it home and went to work in his basement. I built a complete set of wing ribs while Curt worked on the fuselage. This is tiresome work and requires frequent pauses to refresh one's self with a beer or two. In Tennessee, a beer – or a little taste of any alcoholic beverage for that matter – is called a 'Splo'. When rebuilding an airplane under these conditions, a number of 'glitches' or other slight imperfections have been known to occur, which become visible under bright sunlight – which is probably why we named it 'The Splo Bird'. Originally built for the Army, when we got it, it had a little desk and swivel chair in the rear cockpit. The FAA would not license it in that configuration, so we mounted a beer cooler in that space that would hold two cases,

Our 'Splo Bird'

Haun family photo

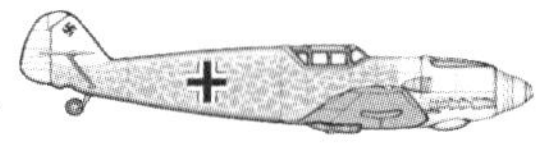

iced down. But at least we restored the 1940's military paint job. A really fun airplane; I taught Curt's son Bobby to fly in it.

We traded that bird to Jerry Kirby for a clipped-wing Cub with a Franklin engine that would barely run. It was a fair trade because when Jerry sat down in his new Splo Bird, the seat collapsed on him! Meanwhile I had to stagger the Cub back to Smyrna with it turning at most 1500 RPM. When we opened the Franklin 135 HP engine, we found one cam lobe worn completely round and two push-rods bent. It had been over-sped trying to do outside loops.

Haun family photo

my good pal Red Lane

When the operation at Metro folded up in 1971 or thereabouts, I took my Swift and moved out to Smyrna Airport. Ed Lowe and his wife Kathleen had opened up the Stones River Flying Service there at Smyrna a year before. They had one hangar over on the northwest side of the Field, with their office in an attached building. Ed had flown Corsairs in the Navy and had been aboard the carrier *Franklin* when it was hit by a Kamikaze. After the War he was with the old CAB, so he has a lot of tales to recount. He's an easygoing, laid-back type, who's an excellent mechanic – when Kathleen can pry him out of his lounge chair! Such an atmosphere naturally attracts an abundance of characters like me. We all delight in the company of other part-time daredevils who love to sit around swapping tales of derring-do – even if stretched a bit in the telling! Hangar flying at its best.

I have many pleasant memories of those days. Of course we flew the students, if they had the cash. In any case, we thoroughly enjoyed ourselves. When the weather was flyable, there was always something interesting going on. For one example, because there was no control tower in operation at that time, aircraft of many different types from several different airports could be using the runways – at the same time – which often became quite sporting! They could use any runway they chose, regardless of wind or other traffic. It was not unusual for two airplanes to be taking off or landing from opposite ends of the same runway – or to be dodging each other at the intersections. We played 'Chicken' a lot.

One day there were four of us shooting landings on 18, when a light twin entered the pattern and started using runway 36. Our radio calls went unheeded, so I stopped on the runway and blocked the guy. I crawled out all full of wrath, but the other guy got out too and he was a great big dude. I cooled down a bit, but had made some bold talk in front of my student, so I had no choice but walk to meet him, prepared for battle. Fortunately he pulled his sunglasses off – and I recognized one of my old Q.B. buddies! So we discussed the advisability of turning your radio on when approaching an uncontrolled airport.

Stearman

Haun family photo

Then there was the time Harry Ringler, American Airlines pilot and another former (Marine) Corsair driver, put his wife in the front cockpit of his Stearman. He got out the hand crank and proceeded to wind up the

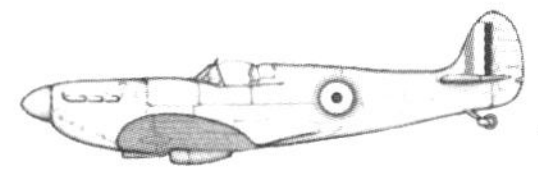

Haun family photo

starter on the potent radial engine. The switch was 'on' and the throttle must have been cracked a bit more than a hair. Anyway, when the starter was up to speed he pulled the handle and all hell broke loose! Maybe his wife had bumped the throttle a bit, as the big engine let out a roar and the airplane started rolling. Harry grabbed at it about mid-wing and then at the tip, which didn't help a bit, as that merely served to turn the bird toward a line of parked aircraft. He made a dash for the cockpit and managed to grab the rim with one hand, but the biplane pulled away from him. Harry is a bit hyperactive anyway, and now he was in high gear, yelling unheard instructions at his poor wife, who, in terror, accidentally stomped on the left brake, which fortunately stood the airplane on its wingtip with the nose pointing at the ground. I don't remember if the prop hit the concrete or not, but the engine stopped. I felt constrained to gently rebuke Harry for the ungentlemanly remarks made to his poor wife. I think my comment was something about who was the 'Pilot-in-Command'.

Such incidents can be the spice of life – once they're over. I almost scuttled my beautiful Swift out there. I was rebushing the gear retracting mechanism, with Paul Booth helping. There is a right way and – I now know – definitely a wrong way to replace the long bolt in the scissors! After we were finished, I figured we should put the bird on jacks and run a retraction check. But Paul was in a hurry and there was no one else to help, so I put it off to another day. Besides, it looked OK. The next day there was still no help, so I flew it anyway. When I had tired of practicing slow-rolls and was headed back toward the Field, I put the gear handle 'down' – but only the right gear came down and locked!

I fiddled with that thing for forty minutes, but the right stayed down and the left stayed up. There is an 'emergency down crank', which I tried. It was extremely hard to crank, so I bulged my muscles and pulled until I broke the pull-down cable and the crank spun in my hand – with the left gear still retracted. I called Ed and asked him to alert the Smyrna Fire Department. I had never used my shoulder harness, but this time managed to get it on. I asked what I was offered for this pretty bird, and Red Lane came back with a bid of a dollar-ninety-eight! I don't recall if I said 'Sold' or not. Anyway, Red didn't hold me to the deal.

Haun family photo

I had plenty of time to figure out how I was going to land on that right wheel. With the right wing low and touching down on our grass strip, then, when it slowed down, maybe I could ground-loop violently to the right and keep the left wing off the ground as long as possible – just maybe I could get away with minimal damage. The fire trucks arrived, and I lined up for the grass strip. On final I put down full flaps – *and felt the gear come down!* Sure enough, the gear showed 'down and locked'! I slid over and landed on the runway, waving "Thank you" to the firemen as I rolled by.

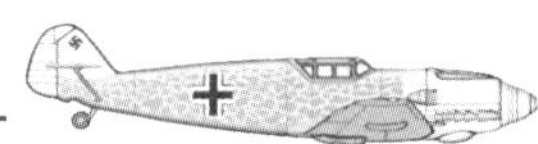

Haun family photo

I had time to light my pipe as I taxied to the hangar – so I could arrive looking unperturbed! What had happened was, the pulldown cable had hung up on the head of that bolt I put in backwards. The cable must have been almost rusted out so I could break it. Since the hydraulic system has an electric pump, when I put the flaps down, that also put power on the gear – and down it popped! The moral of this tale is quite obvious.

We had a big storm come through. We were watching it from the large picture window and hoping the glass wouldn't blow out. There were some ten airplanes tied down in a straight line on the ramp, when some sort of little twister came through. The strangest thing happened. Every other airplane in that line stood up on its nose and flopped over on its back! None of the others were damaged. Imagine! Every other airplane, tied down wing to wing.

Several years later Ed moved across the Field to the large hangar where the operation is now. The City had modified the building into what they thought a Flight Operations should look like, so most of that had to be torn out and rebuilt. Also they had opted for electric baseboard heaters, which nearly froze us to death that first winter. Then when spring came, for some reason the blackbirds swarmed in, building nests and making a mess all over the airplanes. Ed put up a dummy owl to scare them, but that didn't work, so I brought out my little twenty gauge, with light loads, to go to work on them.

In the hangar that day a light twin, owned by a bunch of gangster-looking people, was being worked on. Another bunch from the Mob had also been out claiming that it belonged to them. Ed, who didn't care who owned the airplane as long as someone paid the bill, had called the Sheriff to see if he would come visit with us. At this juncture, I walked through the lobby with my 20-gauge and told Ed I was going bird hunting in the hangar. I fired one shot…now a 20-gauge makes a lot of noise inside a hangar. From across the hangar one of the Mafia-types came crawling on his hands and knees, his face as white as this sheet of paper. Maybe he thought the argument had been settled! I forget how that all turned out.

We had a large number of students over the years, of all makes, models, brands, and breeds. We drew most of our line-boys from MTSU out at Murfreesboro; they were an exceptionally fine lot: most of them got their licenses; some became instructors; some are flying for the airlines, the Air Force or Navy. During our most recent Smyrna Air Show, a young kid I taught to fly came in to visit me. I asked him what he was flying these days; he pointed to an F-18 parked on the ramp. Makes you feel good. We had a large number of black students from TSU. There are two of whom I am particularly proud: Rueben Flowers and his brother, Sailor. They had to work extra hard to make the grade, but they are now both flying for an airline.

Haun family photo

Age 84 - Last year instructing

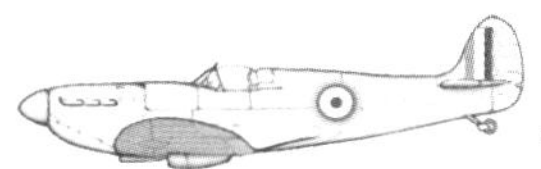

Ed sold out to Johnny Boatman, and I stayed on with him. While I still owned my Swift, Curt and I traded our clipped-wing Cub in on one of the school's old Cessna 150s. Ed had used it for many years as a trainer, and it was a sad looking bucket of bolts – but after a completely rebuilt engine, a fresh paint job, new upholstery, and some good radio equipment, it is now a fine little playtoy. With it I could crawl back into Smyrna when the birds are walking. Ed has a grass strip and a hangar on his farm nearby. It is only 1300 feet long and has telephone lines across the middle and one end, so I don't go in there with my little 150 unless the weather is cool and the wind is right. We visit a lot, since I'm still only 83. Now I get around to the not too distant airshows in the 150. As I don't walk much anymore, I carry a folding chair in the back seat that I set up in the shade under the wing and enjoy the show. Invariably someone will approach me with:

"I hear you were President Truman's pilot."

Then I have to explain, "No I was not. Frenchy Williams was Truman's pilot."

Always happens. I wonder how many times I have had to go through that bit.

For the purists among you, should you find any discrepancies in names, dates, and places – please remember this book has been dredged up from almost eighty years of memories. All of the people I have written about from the old days are either dead or going extra innings like me. The flight surgeon asked me, some time back, when I was going to stop flying.

I told him, "When they pat me in the face with a shovel." Who says there are no 'old, bold, pilots'?

Haun family photo

I could go on with stories about O'Neil and Gerald and Jim and Clyde and Tommy and Tim and dozens of others. And those lovely young ladies. Someone once wrote an article about the different ways female students view their instructor. Depending on the student, there are Sir Galahad, Prince Charming, A Father Figure, Hagar the Horrible, or a Dirty Old Man! I have never inquired just where I might fit into that list.

But without a doubt, there is a special bond between pilot instructor and student that's hard for me to explain. Perhaps it comes with the change from being earthbound to experiencing the joyous freedom of flight, coupled with a wholly new perspective on this beautiful world. I know I never tire of being up there marveling at what I see – the mountains, the plains, the rivers, the lakes, the oceans. I even love the storms, and though I well know their destructive might, I am drawn to them by a terrifying desire to test their strength. I wish I could express all I feel, but the best I can say is that – to me – flying is like being in church.

Haun family photo

Now, said the Polar Bear, my tale is told.

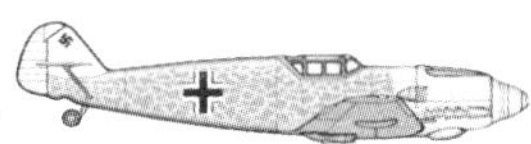

Epilogue

"To Whom Honor is Due"

from son, Jimmy

My Dad, the Colonel, finished his book in 1994. He lived seven more years, dying peacefully, of no specific ailment, in his own bed at home, attended by me and my brother David.

Our mother had gotten her wish of being the first to depart two years earlier. On his Christmas cards for 1998 the Colonel included this message:

Haun family photo

"Eleanor, my wife for sixty three years, passed away on September 25. She was a wonderful woman; quiet, reserved and deeply religious. She had a deep and fervent love for all her family. Everyone that really knew her loved her. Her passing leaves a void in my life that will never be filled…My old dog, BUD, moved into my room at night and sleeps on the floor near me. I wonder how he knows."

Haun family photo

Curt's Hot Rod

His flying adventures didn't cease during those last years – like the time he and flying buddy, Robert O'Neil, made a forced landing up near Kentucky when the exhaust manifold on his 150 burned through, putting a nice scorch around the cowl and firewall. He loved that chance to dig up replacement parts and oversee repairs. Through most of the '90s he would still fly down to visit Ed Lowe or to the other grass strip near Columbia, Tennessee where his friend Curt Franklin was souping-up a biplane. Meanwhile he had

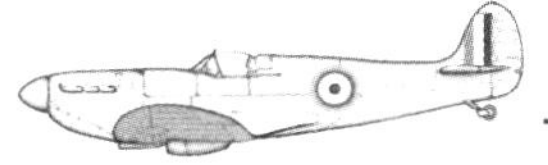

Daughter-in-law Peggy meets the Swift

reluctantly abandoned his cubbyhole at the flying service where for so many years itinerant pilots had looked in on him engrossed in Tom Clancy or Winston Churchill. (After he quit instructing, he swore he wasn't going to become "another pitiful old airport bum.") At age 84, his last flying student turned out to be my cousin, his sister Evelyn's son, Tom Taylor, who soloed in April of '95 and quoted Dad saying as he turned him loose:

"I think you'll like the way she climbs, so watch your altitude...and don't make me walk back!"

His legs had been giving out for twenty years, especially that left knee which tormented him ever since his famous Monocoupe crash of 1934. But midway through his last decade he determined he was simply going to have that knee replaced and a fancy custom brace rigged up so he could 'play golf again'. He wrote to his model, General Lee, in 1997: ***"I am having a blast. You know the story of Douglas Bader, the RAF pilot with no legs. If he could do it, so can ol' Jim. A man here is making me a similar set. Not perfect yet but definitely workable. I get another fitting tomorrow. Bolted around the waist, hinges at hip and knee, uncomfortable as Hell but they will work...I will hunt ducks among the pin oaks again."***

General Robert M. Lee
by permission of Mary Lee

This plan was carried right on through knee surgery and several agonizing trips downtown to fit the heavy jointed contraption around the bad leg. Sadly, by that time both legs were too weak to support him even with crutches. The necessity of a wheelchair was a major blow to his indomitable spirit, but like every other obstacle throughout life he dealt with it. I built a ramp from the back door to where he parked his rusting diesel Rabbit, right in front of our big heavy doghouse. My wife Peggy and I would ease him down this ramp in the same folding wheelchair Mom had used and help him gingerly swing himself into the driver's side of the VW – being 'damn careful' not to bend that left knee past 90 degrees! Then he'd drive himself out to Smyrna where his 150 was parked, pull up under the wing, and usually find a friend to help dislodge him from one vehicle and semi-hoist him into the other. He was always on the lookout for somebody wanting to 'go fly'.

He loved to point out that all one *physically* had to do in order to operate an airplane was "be able to wiggle your fingers and toes." So by this time he was still thoroughly competent in the air while his car-driving ability was starting to cause alarm. That old Rabbit had a manual transmission with, 'naturally' – as he might say – a clutch pedal. Poor circulation was causing his lower legs and feet to swell badly. With trepidation, Peggy and I could see he had reached the point where he could just barely rotate the right foot from gas pedal to brake pedal – but even more challenging was the

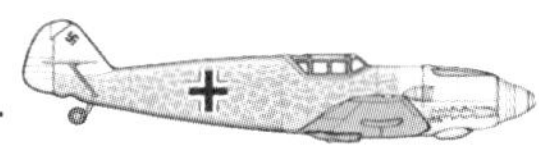

hugely painful effort to raise that left toe to push the clutch. His mind with all its hard-wired aerobatic skills was unquestionably sharp as ever, but we began diplomatically promoting the idea of 'maybe trading' his beloved 300,000 mile Rabbit for an automatic. Without admitting it aloud, he knew he was gambling with shrinking limits and quit driving for several weeks.

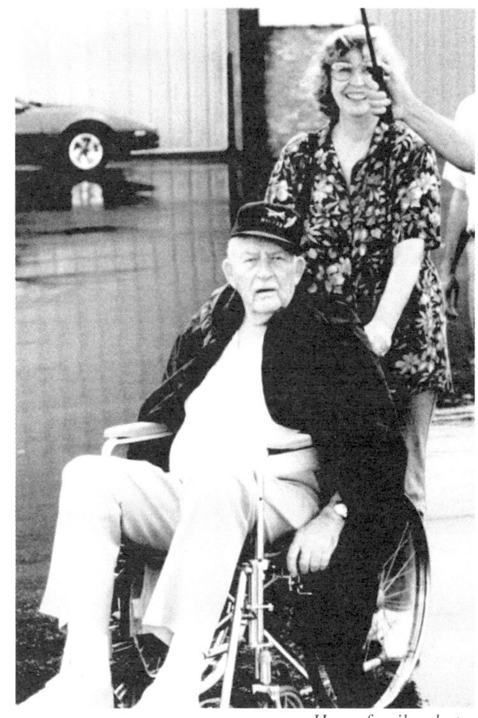

Haun family photo

Then one afternoon he hoisted himself from the rattan chair by his front window into the wheelchair and announced, "I'm just going to go out and smoke my pipe in the Rabbit awhile."

Yeah, right. Anyway, I played along and helped him gingerly shoehorn himself into the car. Back in the house about thirty minutes later we heard the familiar rattle of the four-cylinder diesel starting up. Prediction number one fulfilled. Never one to give the Colonel orders, I prayed and waited to see what would happen next. Sure enough, we soon heard the whine of reverse and saw the car backing in a half circle to point itself out our driveway. ***...Bogies inbound from Dûsseldorf!*** Nearly a minute passed before the mahogany-colored Rabbit succeeded in shifting gears to ease off through the carport and out onto the street. Second prediction accurate and more prayers going up against unintentional Kamikaze events***...as the Rabbit roared into the wild blue yonder toward Europe.*** About a half-hour later we were overjoyed to hear the rattle returning***...but moving much faster this time.*** Luckily our single-lane carport is bounded on the outside by a low but sturdy brick planter. This proved providential – ***as the Major was obviously having to fight his controls on final.*** The Rabbit glanced loudly off the planter, which actually helped him whip the hard ninety left to get around behind the house – but I guess the brakes were just out of reach. Always ready with a backup plan, he managed to centerpunch that heavy doghouse, knocking it a good six feet into the yard but bringing the Rabbit to a safe stop against the metal railing of the back steps. ***...Good show, old chap!***

Haun family photo

Neither he nor we ever said a word about this excitement, but soon thereafter the Rabbit was traded for a used Jetta, with automatic transmission.

The dreaded day finally came in the spring of 2000 when he sold his 150 (at a good price) to a man buying it for his teenage son. Always the Stoic, Dad betrayed no emotion as we watched the blue-trimmed Cessna take off from Curt Franklin's strip, piloted by its new owner. He only allowed himself the pregnant comment, "This is a sad day."

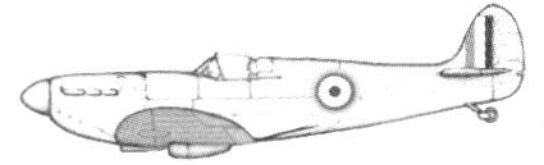

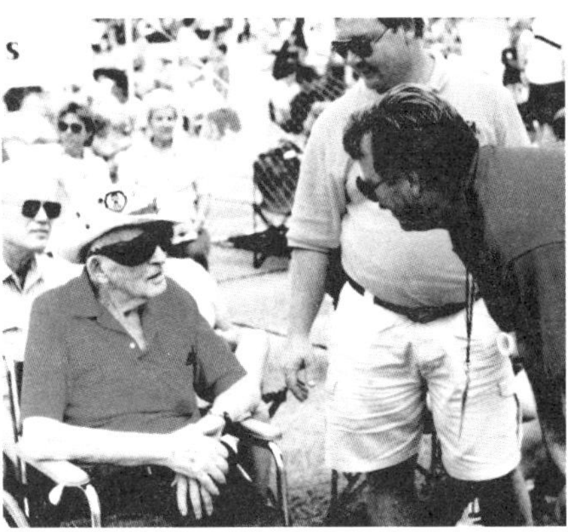
Haun family photo

We drove him out to the Smyrna Air Show that year, where we were ushered through to choice seats on the flight line under the Q.B. tent. I watched several of the featured aerobatic pilots, after their thunderously dramatic routines, come up and warmly shake his hand. He truly had a thousand friends – and no enemies to speak of.

Another big day came when we discovered that one of the original Lockheed Constellations from his old 'VIP Squadron' at Washington National had stopped in Nashville on a national 'flying museum' tour. When we wheeled the Colonel out on the ramp – sure enough, its sleek polished-aluminum length still bore the familiar yellow-and-blue MATS paint scheme.

"Old 609!"

Haun family photo

Even more thrilling, when Dad saw the tail number, 8609, he burst out, "That's my plane! That's the plane I had!"

The crew of this favorite ship he'd flown many times during the Eisenhower era was happy to assist him up the movable stairway and then forward, clear down into the left seat. There he commented on a few noteworthy changes wrought by technology, but figured he could 'still handle her' if given the chance. Another local visitor that day, Durward Willoughby, turned out to be a Crew Chief from the same Squadron who reminisced with his former CO over long-gone events and people.

As you may have gathered from his book, Dad considered his relationship to the Creator an intensely private matter. I can count on one hand the times he spoke of it, but allow me to record what I know about his spiritual journey. Despite his contempt for those who wore their religion like a badge, he reported having had a powerful 'born-again experience' in his late teens, about which he said, "It felt like piano had been lifted off my shoulders." But then he added ruefully,

Haun family photo

"I could still handle her..."

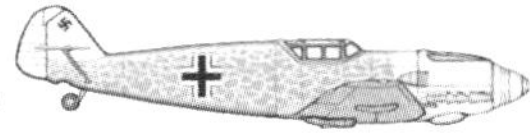

"The very next night I went out and blew it – I lost it." Or such was his thinking.

As an adult he was never a regular churchgoer – just on special occasions. I remember him being highly offended by the hymn *Showers of Blessings*. On the other hand, his favorite hymn throughout life, *How Great Thou Art*, he always requested his sister Evelyn to play for him on her organ. While commanding the C-124 Troop Carrier Wing at Tachikawa he wrote a Christmas message for the Base newspaper in which he referenced the child born in Bethlehem as 'our Savior'.

with sister, Evelyn Taylor

Despite a vital curiosity concerning the afterlife, in his middle years he displayed an independent, skeptical streak, with little confidence concerning his personal ultimate destiny. When we lived in the Washington, D.C. area, for example, he once commented that when he came to stand before God, he was determined to simply give "Name, rank, and serial number." (This of course the military rule for one fallen into the hands of an enemy!)

Also at that time, on a particular evening, he had an unprecedented, and never repeated, episode of intense emotion, involving real weeping, as if 'under conviction', saying that he had lived his life for the wrong values – 'sailboats' and such.

In later years, if the subject of religion came up, he would only say he believed the Bible 'up to a point'. Yet in my 30's, when I was off on a quest into eastern philosophy, he was scornful enough of such shallowness. On the other hand, when later, in the mid-seventies, I made a radical profession of Christian faith, Dad seemed at first put off – as he was to be even more so by the Jimmy Swaggart embarrassment. He couldn't tolerate the idea, however false, that I might start 'talking down' to him in this sensitive area. At the same time, however, I noted he couldn't abide a TV mockery of the Last Supper, saying, "That turns me off."

Gradually, after I married Peggy – whose faith in the God of the Bible no one could deny Dad figured maybe his rapidly graying son had actually done a 180 after all. And truth be told, when once a year the Colonel asked the blessing over Thanksgiving turkey, he always addressed the Lord humbly as "Father." (Once also my wife and I think we caught him praying for our safety while we made last minute preparations to depart on a 5000-mile motorcycle trip.) Then as we cared for both my mother and him through their dying process – seeing the genuineness of love in action – he came truly to trust us. It was at that point, maybe a year before his death, that Peggy gently confronted the dear crustacean about 'how he stood with Jesus'.

Haun family photo

September 21st, 2000

89th birthday

"That's none of your business!" was the instant retort.

"Maybe not – but you owe it to your son to set *his* mind at ease."

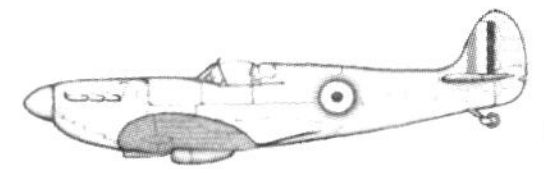

There followed an exchange with his daughter-in-law in which he alluded to old infidelities that he knew God couldn't overlook. Peggy asked him if he remembered the Old Testament verse about the Lord being able to separate us from our sins *'as far as the east is from the west'*.

The navigational analogy apparently hit home. "Does it say that?"

"Not only that – it says God can cast our transgressions into *'the sea of forgetfulness, never to be remembered'* against us. The blood of Jesus on the cross made that provision. Do you believe in your heart God declared him to be the only begotten Son by raising him from the dead?"

"Of course."

"Then let's pray and tell Him so."

The self-reliant old warhorse whose mother had died five days before his ninth birthday then raised his right hand to the God who sees all and conducted ultimate business. Thereafter a new peace, patience, and sweetness permeated the Colonel's remaining months.

U.S. Army Air Corps photo

FINAL FLIGHT

Col. James R. Haun
U.S. Air Force, Retired

April 2, 2001

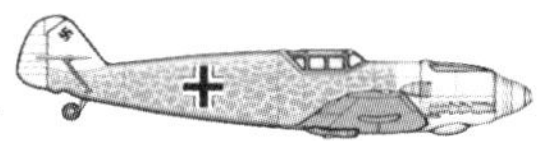

His 'final flight' from this world occurred at age 89 on April 2, 2001.

Nashville's Channel 4 News came to our home the next day to tape a segment interviewing former students, friends, and family. His funeral played to a packed house.

His one specific funeral request was that the famous poem ***High Flight*** be read – an assignment I was honored to fulfill. Most readers know it well, written in England in 1941 by a 19 year old American after testing a Spitfire V above 30,000 feet, just three months before being himself killed in a zero-visibility mid-air collision:

High Flight

by John Gillespie Magee, Jr.

Oh, I have slipped the surly bonds of earth

And danced the skies on laughter-silvered wings;

Sunward I've climbed, and joined the tumbling mirth

Of sun-split clouds...and done a hundred things

You have not dreamed of...wheeled and soared and swung

High in the sunlit silence. Hov'ring there,

I've chased the shouting wind along, and flung

My eager craft through footless halls of air.

Up, up the long, delirious, burning blue

I've topped the windswept heights with easy grace

Where never lark, or even eagle flew.

And, while with silent, lifting mind I've trod

The high untrespassed sanctity of space

Put out my hand, and touched the face of God.

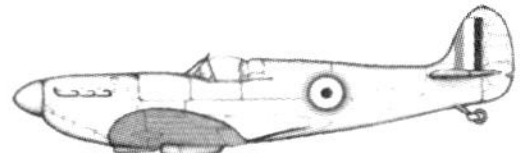

After the funeral, Dad's appointed pallbearers – close friends and pilots all – were on hand for the move to the hearse and out again at graveside. There he was buried with full military honors by an Air Force rifle team, the leader of whom displayed, amazingly, honest tears as he handed over the smartly folded flag from off the coffin.

For what it may be worth, a week later while cleaning house I was struck by a sudden powerful impression, as if in reassurance, that my old man had – literally and in fact – touched That Face.

(Aftermath to one more 'paint job', I'm sure.)

Haun family memorabilia

On March 14, 2002 Colonel James R. Haun was among the first four inductees into the Tennessee Aviation Hall of Fame at the Tennessee Museum of Aviation in Sevierville, Tennessee, where many artifacts from the Colonel's career remain on permanent display.

Appendix

Note on Fred Hook - by Jim Jr.

Despite limited appearances in my father's chronicle, 'Fred Hook' – or simply 'Hook' as the six-year younger pilot was unfailingly tagged by 'Big Jim' – was a huge figure in Dad's life. Until his death from cancer in1989, by then Brigadier General Fred G. Hook, Jr. remained our Colonel's lifelong, and possibly closest, friend. Birds of a feather, their bond was a gift for flight thundering deep in blood and bones.

Less prone to weight around the middle than his buddy Haun, Fred Hook – always hawk-eyed above a pencil-thin mustache – portrayed the quintessential figure of the dashing fighter pilot. I'll never forget as a kid witnessing him wring out a P-51 at a 1949 Memphis air show. Diving out of a moist overcast, he threw that ship across the field like pitching a clipped-wing fast-ball, corkscrewing in continuous rolls at a hundred feet, then continuing to roll gracefully as that beautiful hot-rod droned up and out of sight. I had never seen an airplane move that fast, or that smoothly! Seeing him afterwards, up close, still harnessed in his military parachute and wearing the backslapping grin of a man coasting on leftover adrenaline, I felt the awe of meeting some kind of bigger-than-life hero. This was my Dad's pal!

Born in Oklahoma City in 1917 to Fred Hook, Sr. and Lelia M. Hook, a seamstress, he became a member of the Memphis Police Department in the mid 1930s. He enters my Dad's story in '36 or '37 as the motorcycle cop eager to graduate to barnstorming. Readers will recall Dad's retelling of his future friend's antics during Hook's first flying lesson (upper teeth stuck out, cap backwards, shooting at buzzards!) inspiring instructor Haun's instant recognition of a kindred maverick – definitely 'the sporting type'!

After the pair joined the Army Air Corps because "We want to fly those big airplanes," this two-man threat soon managed, on maneuvers, to earn the ire of General George Patton by clipping his tanks' aerials with their propellers. ("Very realistic," was Patton's terse comment.) As the only pilots at Fort Knox much interested in target practice, they spent their off-hours at the skeet range burning up every one else's ammunition.

In January 1999 General Robert M. Lee, three months before his 90th birthday, wrote to Dad to offer condolences for the recent loss of my Mother, Eleanor, whom he remembered from the Godman Field/Fort Knox days. To which he added:

U.S. Air Force photo

Speaking of Godman Field, about 1939, I was commanding the Base and the 12th Squadron. Being a bachelor at the time, I had a girl in Memphis that I used to fly down to see. On one of these trips, I ran into Bill Tunner whom I knew from 1927 at West Point…In '39, he was in charge of the Air Corps Reserves in the Memphis area. He asked me if I could use a couple of topnotch pilots. General Arnold saw that war was coming and authorized units to 100% over strength in pilots and enlisted, which I was doing. Of course, I said 'sure!' He said one was a motorcycle patrolman and the other was a cotton duster. That's

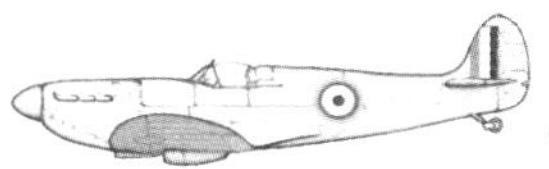

how on or about 1 January 1940 Hook and Haun showed up as my new pilots in the 12th Squadron. Bill Tunner was right as you both proved him to be later in Europe.

During the war Hook received the Legion of Merit, Combat Air Medal, and Purple Heart. Afterwards, in 1946 he organized the 155th Fighter Squadron for the Tennessee Air National Guard P-51 unit based in Memphis. As flight instructor there he was instrumental in the 155th Squadron's receiving national recognition for stunt flying. Then, before Fidel Castro took over in Cuba, Hook served in the early '50s as Chief of the Air Force Mission there. Later, by 1956, already Colonel Hook, having graduated to jets as "supersonic Fred," this pilot's pilot assumed leadership of the 52nd Fighter Group and Commander of Suffolk County Air Force Base on Long Island. Two and a half years later, the 26th Air Division at Syracuse, New York credited Base CO Fred Hook with having contributed outstandingly to giving the Suffolk facility a complete physical transformation.

In 1959 at age 42 Colonel Hook was promoted to head up the Air Guard's Operations Office of the National Guard Bureau in the Pentagon. There, as Director of Operations, he served under the Air Guard chief, Maj. General Winston P. Wilson.

Retiring from that Pentagon Bureau with the rank of Brigadier General, Fred G. Hook, Jr. in the early '70s became one of the original employees of Federal Express Corp., where his piloting skills helped establish the company's flight operations. Launched in 1973, that huge enterprise was conceived and overseen by Hook's stepson, Frederick W. Smith, ongoing president, chairman, and CEO. Fred Smith, himself a commercial pilot from his college days at Yale, said at the time of his stepfather's death at 72, "He was a very well-known, almost a legendary aviator."

As a final conjunction of these histories, Frederick W. Smith and Colonel James R. Haun, along with flight instructors William K. Kershner and Evelyn Bryan Johnson, constituted the original four inductees into the Tennessee Aviation Hall of Fame at a formal ceremony held at the Tennessee Museum of Aviation in Sevierville, September 7, 2002.

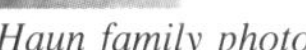

Haun family photo

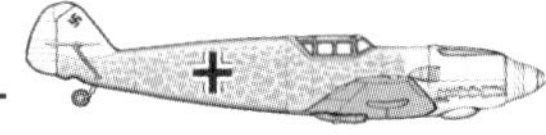